CATTLEMEN
vs.
SHEEPHERDERS

Five Decades of
Violence in the West
1880–1920

By Bill O'Neal

EAKIN PRESS ⋆ Fort Worth, Texas
www.EakinPress.com

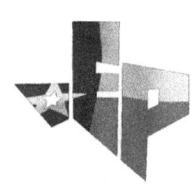

Copyright © 1989, 2005
By Bill O'Neal
Published in the United States of America
By Eakin Press
An Imprint of Wild Horse Media Group
P.O. Box 331779
Fort Worth, Texas 76163
1-817-344-7036
www.EakinPress.com
ALL RIGHTS RESERVED
1 2 3 4 5 6 7 8 9
ISBN-10: 1-57168-856-0
ISBN-13: 978-1-57168-856-9

Library of Congress Cataloging-in-Publication Data

Cattlemen vs. sheepherders : five decades of violence in the West / by Bill O'Neal.
    p.   cm.   Bibliography: p.
Includes index.
ISBN 1-57168-856-0
    1. West (U.S.) — History — 1848–1950. 2. Violence — West (U.S.) — History. 3. Cattle trade — West (U.S.) — History. 4. Sheep industry — West (U.S.) — History. 5. Land settlement — West (U.S.) — History. I. Title. II. Title: Cattlemen versus sheepherders.
F595.O55   1988
978'.02'088636 — dc19
                                                      88-16449
                                                        CIP

*For the Feilds — Uncle Mark, Aunt LaVerne,
Stan, Buddy, Linda, and Andy.*

*My favorite boyhood memories and first love of the West
were nurtured at the Feild ranch.*

Contents

Preface		vii
Acknowledgments		ix
1	Cattlemen, Sheepmen, and the Open Range	1
2	Trouble in Texas	17
3	Colorado Conflicts	33
4	Arizona's Pleasant Valley War	43
5	Miscellaneous Hostilities Across the West	66
6	War in Wyoming	88
7	Tom Horn in Wyoming	100
8	More Wyoming Hostilities	117
9	Turning Point at Ten Sleep	130
10	Final Troubles	149
Endnotes		165
Bibliography		179
Index		187

Preface

After exhaustive research on the cattleman-sheepherder conflict, I really did not have a fine focus on the reasons behind such a conflict until a moment of sudden awareness one day in Wyoming.

I had spent the morning at the courthouse in Sundance, reading trial documents pertaining to the Crook County raids of 1908. That afternoon I drove south, intending to investigate the 1903 raid that occurred forty miles north of Lusk. When a construction project on Highway 85 halted traffic for a considerable time, I got out of my car, walked across to a fence, and photographed sheep and cattle grazing peacefully together in the same pasture.

I stood for a long time, a dry wind blowing in my face and rippling the tall grass in stately waves as far as the eye could see. Suddenly, I understood the deepest cause of the long war between cattle and sheep graziers. There was indeed a mutual enmity between cowboys and sheepherders, and an instinctive hatred of sheep by cattlemen. But the most fundamental reason for the conflict was economic — a conflict over the grass that blanketed the plains of Wyoming and West Texas, that sprouted in the valleys of Arizona, Colorado, and Oregon, that covered the Texas Hill Country and the mountain ranges of Wyoming, New Mexico, and Colorado.

Even though cowboys detested sheepherders and bleating woollies, the primary basis for the half century of struggle between cattle ranchers and sheepmen was grass — grass which could produce wealth in the form of beef and mutton and wool. Men have always been willing to fight for wealth, and this fight was waged in the wide-open spaces of America's last West. Indeed, the brutal fight persisted long past the closing of the frontier, and was the final sustained violence engaged in by westerners. The roster of participants included cattle barons, famous law officers, and notorious gunmen, as well as hundreds of nameless but fiercely resolute small ranchers and cowboys and sheepherders. Their battlefield was the magnificent terrain of America's final frontier, and their adventures form a story of tenacity and cruelty and high courage.

Acknowledgments

During the 1870s my great-grandfather worked as a Texas cowboy in Lampasas County, trailing cattle to the Kansas railheads and fighting under Pink Higgins in the murderous Horrell-Higgins range war. In adjoining Burnet County my uncle's grandfather, a pioneer sheepman, killed a cowboy who hated woollies and men who worked them. As a boy I delighted in riding horseback over my uncle's sheep ranch, and sometimes I was permitted to get in everyone's way at shearing time. My family heritage encompasses both sides of the conflict between cattlemen and sheepmen, and I approached this project with keen personal interest.

From 1983 through 1987 I enjoyed a series of research trips across a great deal of the West's most magnificent terrain. I camped in Brown's Park and southern Idaho and Wyoming and New Mexico and alongside the Canadian River in the Texas Panhandle. I stood before the graves of combatants in Arizona's Pleasant Valley, and I inspected the murder site at remote Ten Sleep, Wyoming. At intervals I shaved and cleaned up to visit libraries and state archives and museums. Along the way I was aided by many people, and always I was treated with traditional western hospitality.

Gwen Rice, head of reference and interlibrary loan at the Wyoming State Supreme Court Library in Cheyenne, was extremely helpful in providing materials. Across the street I was greeted by the cordial and resourceful staff of the Wyoming State Archives; Jean Brainerd, Cindy L. Brown, Paula West Chavoya and Ann Nelson made my visit immensely productive and pleasant.

Dr. Murray Carroll, of Laramie, Wyoming, was an unfailing source of information and encouragement. At the University of Wyoming in Laramie I am indebted to Dr. Gene Gressley and to Emmett Chisum, research historian at the American Heritage Center. I owe a special word of thanks to Paula J. McDougal, photographic archivist at the Center, who took the initiative to inform a stranger of the materials available through her office, and who responded promptly to requests for photos.

In Thermopolis, Wyoming, Linda Zierke, curator of the Hot Springs County Museum, was most helpful, and so was the staff of Lusk's Stagecoach Museum. Arna Montgomery, deputy clerk of courts at the Crook County Courthouse in Sundance, Wyoming, provided me with numerous legal documents. At Ten Sleep I was generously assisted by Margaret Sutherland Cogdill, Ronald Cogdill, Bob Brouh, and Helen Starr.

I was expertly aided in Tucson by Lori Davisson, the highly capable and cooperative research assistant at the Arizona Heritage Center. Barbara Bush, photo librarian, also provided welcome help in acquiring photographs. At the Arizona State Archives in Phoenix I was greatly assisted by Carol Downey, Shirley Macias, and Wilma Smallwood. When I ventured into Pleasant Valley I was welcomed by Wilma Haught. Her husband is C. A. "Tobe" Haught, a lifelong resident of Pleasant Valley whose grandfather was in the area during the 1887 hostilities. The Haughts live in the old Perkins Store, which they have converted into an enviably rustic home, and which I was permitted to tour.

Annette Bartholome, research assistant at the Oregon Historical Society in Portland, came to my aid on several occasions. In Albion and Rogerson, Idaho, several local citizens were most informative, and I received the same kind of help from gracious residents of Colorado's San Luis Valley.

Joyce Chapman, head librarian at Panola Junior College in Carthage, Texas, went to a great deal of trouble during the past few years to provide me with materials through interlibrary loan. Mary Rose Johnson and Barbara Bell, members of the PJC Library staff, also came to my rescue in various ways. Another friend and colleague, Joe Kyle of the mathematics department, once lived and worked near Brown's Park, and he offered considerable information which enriched my visit to that historic area.

On various occasions my uncle, aunt, and two cousins, Mark, LaVerne, Buddy, and Andy Feild, have told me details of the 1889 killing near their Burnet County ranch. I am grateful to Lynda Holder, Burnet County deputy district clerk, for pursuing information about that killing. In San Saba, also located in the Texas Hill Country, I was assisted by Winnie Brown, head librarian of the Rylander Memorial

Library. Dave Richards of the Texas State Archives in Austin expertly assisted me during a visit to that rich storehouse of materials.

I am indebted to my twin daughters, Lynn and Shellie, who detected numerous errors through their able proofreading efforts. Melissa Locke Roberts capably edited the manuscript, providing further corrections and improvements.

My wife, Faye, helped me throughout this project with suggestions on grammar, style, and organization. I am deeply grateful for her encouragement and support as I developed this book.

1

Cattlemen, Sheepmen, and the Open Range

If you meet a sheep-raising so-and-so on the trail with a broken leg, break the other leg and go on.
— Anonymous U.S. forest ranger

Ten Sleep . . . the Pleasant Valley War . . . the Tie Siding Raid . . . the murder of Willie Nickell and the subsequent execution of Tom Horn . . . and scores of other violent incidents marked the furor between cattlemen and sheepmen in nine western states or territories. This bitter conflict took the form of a guerrilla war that lasted for nearly five decades. There were more than 120 raids and skirmishes, producing more than fifty human casualties and the slaughter of at least 53,000 sheep.

Hostilities began in the 1870s, with scattered strife in Texas and Colorado. During the 1880s the clash intensified greatly in Texas, where 2,400 sheep and four men were killed, and a malignant fence-cutting war erupted. In 1887 Arizona's Pleasant Valley War was triggered by the introduction of sheep into cattle country, and more than a score of men were shot. Two years later, in a Mexican sheep camp in Arizona, a fight broke out which resulted in the death of five sheepherders, along with the wounding of a cowboy and the sixth herder.

There were a few more violent incidents in Texas in the early

1890s, but the scene of conflict expanded during the decade to Colorado (where 6,600 sheep were clubbed, rimrocked, and shot in four raids) and to Wyoming, Washington, Oregon, and Idaho. The first decade of the twentieth century witnessed the butchery of 30,000 sheep in Colorado, Montana, Oregon, and Wyoming. More than 10,000 sheep were killed in just five Oregon raids. Over twenty clashes occurred in Wyoming, including the brutal Ten Sleep murders, and more than 13,000 sheep were slain. Hostilities slacked off noticeably during the next decade, but a final outbreak of violence erupted in 1920–21: two fights in Arizona resulted in the killing of three sheepmen, while four clashes in Colorado produced another sheepherder fatality and about 1,500 dead sheep.

More than 16,000 sheep perished in Wyoming, almost 14,000 were slain in Colorado, and over 10,000 were slaughtered in Oregon. On at least seventeen occasions more than 1,000 sheep were killed in a single raid, and during seven raids 3,000 to 4,000 sheep were slain. Five of these mass slaughters took place in Wyoming, five more in Colorado, and four in Oregon. During the Pleasant Valley War, thirteen cattlemen or cowboys (or rustlers) were killed. Only three other cowmen died in conflicts with sheepmen, although several others were wounded. By contrast, at least twenty-eight sheep owners or herders were slain, another half dozen or more suffered wounds, and many others were beaten or whipped with ropes. Eleven sheepmen were killed in Arizona, ten in Wyoming, four in Texas, two in Idaho, and one in New Mexico.

A primary factor in the dispute was the enormous disparity and mutual dislike between the men in the arena of conflict, cowboys and sheepherders. Cowboys were mostly young men, in their twenties or late teens. They were high-spirited, proud, tough. They possessed the majestic feeling of power and height and superiority of mounted men throughout history. Notoriously ill-at-ease out of the saddle, the cowboy held in contempt men who worked on foot — men such as farmers and sheepherders. A cowboy's work was hard and long and dangerous. Cattle were big, ornery beasts, capable of and inclined to inflict harm upon men and horses. Cowboys had to ride, rope, and master other athletic skills to handle these cantankerous creatures. In their daily tasks, cowboys often experienced the exhilaration of the hunt. Their work demanded bravery and physical endurance. Vigorous and aggressive, "if they had to fight they were always ready," said pioneer cattle baron Charles Goodnight. "Timid men were not among them — the

A TIME-HONORED TRADITION

Western cowmen who despised sheep were merely carrying on an ancient tradition. The prophet Ezekiel (34:18, LB) recorded biblical annoyance: "Is it a small thing to you, O evil shepherds, that you not only keep the best of the pastures for yourselves, but trample down the rest?" Virginia politician John Randolph once declared that he would go a mile out of his way any day to kick a sheep.

Emerson Hough, western traveler and writer, described (in The Cowboy, 309) a culinary prejudice in cow country: "A popular contempt was entertained for 'sheep meat' and any one addicted to the habit of eating it was considered of degenerate tendency. The little cow town hotel at times served this meat on its tables, but even the waiter girls had scorn in their voices when they called to the cook through the kitchen window for a 'plate of sheep!'"

When he was fifteen, Charlie Russell was sent west to work on a sheep ranch. Russell fell in love with the West, but loathed sheep. "I'd lose the damn things as fast as they'd put 'em on the ranch," he said, and this intentional carelessness cost him his job. He became a magnificent western artist, but painted a picture of a sheep just once.

R. K. Siddoway, a prominent sheepman who was elected president of the National Wool Growers Association, had once found a sheepherder's disgusted verse on an aspen tree:

> I've summered in the tropics,
> Had the yellow fever chill.
> I've wintered in the Arctic
> Know every ache and ill.
> Been shanghied on a whaler
> And stranded in the deep,
> But I didn't know what misery was
> Till I started herding sheep.

life did not fit them."[1] By the time trouble with sheepmen became widespread, the American press had begun to lionize the cowboy as the most admirable cavalier of a fading frontier. Conscious of their romantic public image, cowboys spent much of their salaries to upgrade their utilitarian but dramatic clothing and gear. Clad in chaps, bandanas, big hats, boots and spurs, cigarettes dangling from their lips, brandishing six-guns, scowling fiercely at the camera, cowboys eagerly lined up in groups to be photographed. In town many cowboys tried to live up to their rakehell image by roistering from one saloon to another.

> ### COWBOYS WHO *HELPED* SHEEPHERDERS
>
> *Not all cowboys automatically persecuted sheepherders. In 1882, for example, several cowboys were trailing 500 head of cattle from Pendleton, Oregon, into Wyoming. As they approached the Green River, they were asked by sheepmen to drive their remuda to the river to force a large flock into the water.*
>
> *The sheepmen had set out from New Mexico the previous year, driving 9,000 woollies toward Oregon. But the anticipated sale did not materialize, and the sheep were pointed toward Cheyenne. In eastern Oregon the two herds had first encountered each other, and the cowboys had helped drive the sheep across a small stream.*
>
> *The sheep again had balked at a crossing, refusing to enter the water for forty-eight hours. Once again the cowboys cooperated, driving their horse herd into the river. The sheep promptly followed the big animals into the water, and the entire band crossed within a few minutes.*
>
> *When two New Mexico cowboys spotted a sheep dog seemingly trying to attract their attention, they followed the dog to his sheep camp and discovered a herder lying on his suggan. The herder was delirious, one leg swollen from a rattlesnake bite.*
>
> *The cowboys cut the wound and sucked out as much of the venom as possible. The herder was placed on a cow pony and one cowboy packed him toward the railroad tracks, intending to ship him by the first passing train for the nearest medical aid. The other cowboy, V. H. Whitlock, stayed behind, voluntarily assuming the disagreeable responsibility for the flock. He cooked supper for himself and the dog, then found it necessary to shoot a coyote and help the dog chase away a wolf. He cleaned the dog's wounds with coal oil from a lantern and applied a coat of bacon grease.*
>
> *Whitlock tended the flock through the next day before being relieved at dusk by the owner and another herder. The owner took Whitlock to his ranch in a buckboard, relaying the news that a doctor felt the herder would live, and that his leg probably had been saved by the efforts of two Good Samaritans wearing big hats and high-heeled boots.*

Cowboys were zealously loyal to their spread, to "their" brand. Riding across the plains like a medieval knight, the cowboy felt a feudalistic bond to his ranch. Cowboys often were armed with revolvers or rifles, and they worked in a land of few peace officers and courts. If rustlers or prairie fires or Indian raiders or predators threatened the ranch, cowboys fought with every weapon to preserve their herds. When the threat to their range was posed by sheep, their response was fueled by a virulent contempt for bleating woollies and the strange men who herded them.

Those strange men often were Mexicans, Basques, or other foreigners, which added racial animosity to the conflict. Racial intolerance was rampant on the frontier, and cowboys readily added ethnic hatreds to their loathing of woollies. Frequently, Utah sheepmen brought their flocks across state lines, and adding to the subsequent antagonisms was the fact that most of these intruders were Mormons.

Sheepherders were solitary men, loners who tended small, timid animals. The sheepherder was accustomed to being his own boss most of the time, and generally he planned his own work. Sheepherders were paid higher wages than cowboys, especially during winter months (in fact, during the open-range era most cowboys were unemployed during the winters). Many sheepherders were avid readers (mail-order catalogs were termed "the sheepherder's Bibles"), but kept a close enough supervision over their flocks to distinguish the personalities of individual sheep. Often sheepherders fashioned their bedrolls with square blankets, and cowboys contemptuously described them as "trying to find the long end of a square quilt."[2]

The cowboys' scorn for sheepherders was reflected clearly in the language of the range. Regarding sheepherders, Ramon Adams pointed out: "The cowman never called him a *shepherd*. Since Christ was a shepherd, that word sounded too pastoral and honored, and the cowman had anything but Christ-like feelings toward the sheepman. As one cowboy said, 'There ain't nothin' dumber than a sheep except the man who herds 'em.' " Cowmen also derisively referred to sheepherders as "mutton punchers," "lamb lickers," and "snoozers" (cowboys felt that sheepherders did little besides sleep). A Mexican sheeptender was disparaged as a "scab herder" (scab, a skin disease, was the scourge of the sheep industry, a dreaded malady against which flocks were "dipped").[3]

Rustlers sneered that a faithful cowboy was a "sheep dipper" — a drover so loyal that he would stay on a ranch even if woollies were brought in and he was forced to dip sheep. Sheep were cursed as "hoofed locusts," "stinkers," "stubble jumpers," "maggots," and "baa-a-ahs" ("If you want to start a fight," declared Adams, "just blat this at a cowboy"). Westerners labeled their liquor everything from "base burner" to "snake poison" to "tonsil varnish," but a cowboy's name for rotgut whiskey was "sheepherder's delight." The term "sheeped out" meant range that had been grazed bare by sheep, or a cattle ranch abandoned because of the influx of woollies. Adams commented that cowman Steve Gates told of one ranch that was "so ag'in sheep I wouldn't ride through it with a wool shirt on."[4]

* * *

The range cattle industry began to develop in Texas prior to the Civil War.[5] Millions of longhorns grew wild in the brushy wilderness below the Nueces River. From hard-riding *vaqueros* Texas "cow boys" acquired the techniques of handling these large, surprisingly agile beasts, and adapted equipment and colorful attire which would exert a lasting appeal: big stock saddles, *lariatas, chapparos,* jangling spurs, broad-brimmed hats, high-heeled boots. Early cattle drives were made from Texas to Louisiana, to gold fields in California and Colorado, to military posts, and to Kansas City and St. Louis as eastern shipping points.

Most of these markets were closed during the Civil War, but spectacular drives were conducted after the war to Kansas railheads and to numerous other points. Successful drives often produced enormous profits, while swaggering cowboys, bucking broncos, roundups, branding, chuck wagons, and other colorful elements of the western version of the cattle industry captured the imagination of the country.

Open-range ranching spread across the Great Plains. The stockman might secure title, perhaps by a 160-acre homestead claim, to a ranch headquarters which enclosed a stream or water hole. Usually there would be a cabin or a dugout, and a stable and corral. The cattle herd ran loose on surrounding range, to be rounded up in the spring for branding and in the fall for shipment to market. During the 1870s two-year-old steers cost more than heifers, because steers could be fattened in one or two years at great profit, while the increase from heifers could not be profitably sold for at least three years and the heifers themselves would not bring as high a price as steers. With such a concentration on male animals, herd increases were not as great as later, and the quality of herds improved slowly, because controlled breeding was impossible on the open range.

By 1880, however, the range was becoming heavily stocked. Cattle prices were climbing, demand exceeded supply, and ranchers were buying more heifers to increase their herds. Under these conditions, cattlemen began to recognize the need to abandon the open-range system, improve the quality of their herds, and acquire control of land through purchase or lease, although federal land policies made it difficult to accumulate adequate amounts of range. Even as the cattle business changed to a land and cattle business, great amounts of investment capital from the East or Europe placed herds throughout the West, and large companies began to squeeze small operators off the range.

Sheep appeared in increasing numbers during the open-range period, but conflict between cattle and sheep graziers was limited because there was ample room in most regions for both kinds of livestock. As the range became overstocked in the 1880s, violence between cattlemen and sheepmen increased correspondingly. The winter of 1885–86 caused considerable loss of cattle. A dry summer in 1886 further damaged overburdened ranges, and cattle went into the next winter in poor shape. The arctic winter of 1886–87 produced the "Big Die-Up," as thin cattle died by the thousands in blizzard conditions. The open-range cattle business ended as ranchers realized it was unprofitable as well as inhumane to leave cattle untended.

Cattlemen who wanted to succeed had to purchase or lease land, fence it in, breed better beef, grow winter feed, and carefully supervise smaller, better herds. Competition for remaining public domain was intense among large cattle ranchers, small stockmen, homesteaders, and sheepmen. The number of sheep increased slowly but steadily across the West. Increases became more rapid after the mid-1880s, as sheepmen filled in numerous voids following the Big Die-Up. Many cattlemen, now on the defensive after long dominance of the range, lashed back savagely, and troubles between sheep and cattle interests became more widespread and violent.

Economic reality lent growing appeal to sheep ranching. One great advantage of raising sheep was that the sheepman had two products to sell, wool and mutton, while the cattleman marketed just beef. Cattle prices fluctuated wildly from season to season, while wool and mutton, even though also subject to great fluctuation, remained dependably profitable throughout the late 1800s and early twentieth century. Furthermore, a sheep raiser could enter business with a much smaller initial investment than that required of a cattle rancher. And while a cattleman had to wait three or four years from the time of his original investment to realize a profit from the increase of his herd, a sheepman might expect a profit of twenty percent the first year, a similar increase the second year, and healthy increases the third and fourth years.[6]

The grazing habits of sheep helped to produce greater profits. Sheep could subsist on range that would not support cattle; sheep

> ### HOW TO GIVE A SHEEPHERDER RHEUMATISM
>
> *The sheep wagon originated in 1884 in Carbon County, Wyoming. Rawlins blacksmith James Candlish built the first one. The idea and basic plan were brought to him either by George Ferris, who did not have the tools to finish the wagon he had begun on his ranch, or by rancher Joe Hurt. Prior to the development of the sheep wagon, herders had to camp in tents or open bedrolls, or they had to drive their flocks in to home corrals each night. The sheep wagon brought far greater mobility and comfort to herders, and was a critical step in the success of the western sheep industry.*
>
> *Suggestive of a modern camper vehicle, the sheepherder's home on wheels featured a bed across the rear, with cabinets and drawers underneath and a table that could be pulled out. There was a bench across each side, and a lid on the top of each bench could be opened for more storage space beneath. At the rear was a window above the bed, while the door was at the other end above the wagon tongue. Just inside and to the right of the doorway was a "go-to-hell" stove for cooking and heating. A cupboard was behind the stove, while the stovepipe extended through the roof covering.*
>
> *The covering consisted of several layers of canvas, rendering winter temperatures more bearable. But according to one sheepherder, rainwater dripping through a bullet hole would cause rheumatism, an irresistible temptation to any cowboy aware of this diabolical possibility.*

could manage on sagebrush and could thrive on sparse upland grasses. Sheep required far less water than cattle, and could even lick the morning dew from grasses on waterless range. Therefore, considerably more land was available for sheep than for cattle. Sheepmen also supervised their animals more closely than did cattlemen. While cattle were left to shift for themselves on the open range, sheepherders stayed with their flocks twenty-four hours a day, or penned their animals securely every night. Sheepmen also learned early the wisdom of having hay on hand for winter feed. Because sheep usually were more carefully tended, sheepmen suffered fewer losses than did cattlemen, even in disastrous winters.

Bryant B. Brooks, a pioneer Wyoming cattle rancher who served as governor from 1905 to 1911, was initially appalled at the invasion of transient sheepmen. "Their migratory flocks would graze off my pastures, preventing my cattle from getting fat, and destroying most of the winter range," he wrote. "I concluded the only way to meet this new menace was to go into the sheep business myself, fighting fire with fire."[7] In 1892 Brooks bought his first sheep, a band of 3,000, in Denver. The band had not been shorn nor lambed, and Brooks quickly realized a handsome profit, which encouraged him to invest more heavily in sheep.

Brooks observed that sheep brought year-round jobs to Wyoming, and a steadier measure of prosperity than any other agricultural enterprise could offer in the state. He also realized that sheep were less injurious to the range than cattle or horses. "Cattle graze over the same range all the year and feed differently from sheep, invariably eating the coarser, taller grasses first, thereby destroying the seed stalks so the ranges do not re-seed. Sheep eat the flowers, weeds, and fine grass first, and let the stalks alone. Then, too, sheep rarely graze long in one place, and the balance of the year the range rests up."[8]

On the open range it was preferable to place sheep in high country during the summers and to use sheltered valleys for winter grazing. Range lambing occurred in April and May (ranchers who had constructed sheds supervised shed lambing earlier, in February and March). After dark, lambing areas often were encircled by lanterns to discourage predators. Shearing was conducted as weather permitted following lambing. A band, consisting of perhaps 1,200 ewes and 1,500 lambs, would be slowly trailed to mountain ranges in late May. Each band normally was tended by a sheepherder, although this was not always a solitary arrangement. Sometimes two or even three herders accompanied a band. More often, however, a lone sheepherder was assigned to a band, with only a sheep dog or two to keep him company. Favorite breeds of sheep dogs included the border collie and the Kelpie.

Sheepherders slept in tents or, after they were developed in Wyoming in 1884, sheep wagons. Conscientious herders, like cowboys, arose in the darkness to be with their animals before daybreak, and most sheepherders worked on foot, feeling that they could detect few problems among their flocks from atop a horse. (Of course, cowboys held pedestrians in contempt, and found lone sheepherders easy to attack.)

Many of the techniques of sheepherding had been worked out by the Spanish, who introduced flocks to the Southwest on their missions and *ranchos*. On a large operation a *pastor* and a couple of sheep dogs would tend a flock of 1,500 or more sheep. A *vaquero* was in charge of two or three *pastores*, designating the grazing areas and watering holes for each day. A *caporal* supervised several *vaqueros*, while a *mayordomo* commanded the *caporales* and the entire operation. The most common animals were Chaurros, lean creatures immune to many diseases and capable of subsisting on marginal ranges. But Chaurro flesh was tough and stringy, and each animal produced only about two pounds of wool per year. By the post-Civil War period, however, breeding had improved the texture and flavor of the meat, while the annual wool clip per animal had more than doubled.[9]

There was a strong demand for choice lambs in the East, the textile industry provided a ready market for wool, and the spread of railroads across the West greatly facilitated the shipment of mutton and wool. Also, a sheep operation required less investment capital than cattle ranching would. Sheep husbandry expanded across the West and triggered an increased conflict with cattlemen, who often had arrived first on the public domain of the frontier. But the boom in sheep ranching was suddenly checked in 1894, when President Grover Cleveland eliminated the tariff on wool. Western sheepmen were staggered until the Dingley Tariff of 1897 again afforded protection from foreign competition.

Profit-minded cattlemen began to rear sheep on their land, discovering, as did Bryant B. Brooks, that sheep and cattle mixed efficiently on the range. Some ranchers abandoned cattle to raise sheep exclusively. However, many cattlemen obstinately refused to have anything to do with the detested woollies, and certain of these men, backed readily by diehard cowboys, continued to wage war against the encroachments of sheepmen.

Cattlemen frequently were termed the aggressors in these clashes. They would warn sheepmen to take their flocks out of a certain area, and often they would announce deadlines prohibiting sheep from various regions. When sheep came in anyway (at which point cattlemen accused sheepmen of being the aggressors), cattlemen frequently launched attacks (for which they were considered the aggressors by sheepmen).

Usually these attacks were aimed at isolated sheep camps, although occasionally a sheep ranch might be assaulted. The attackers were mounted cattle ranchers and cowboys who often wore masks, sometimes made of gunnysacks. A favorite tactic was to rimrock a flock, driving the sheep over a cliff or the steep bank of a stream, thus killing or crippling a maximum number of animals with a minimum of effort. Raiders most often shot sheep, which was especially effective if the animals were penned. Frequently the animals were clubbed with

> **BRINGING IN THE SHEAVES . . . OR SHEEP?**
>
> In Cow People (257–258), J. Frank Dobie told of a hard-bitten but greatly respected cattleman named Jim Callan who hosted a circuit-riding preacher overnight. The preacher asked Callan to help him arrange a worship service.
>
> "Before we settle on anything," stated Callan, "I want to know straight out whether you are a cowman's preacher or a sheepman's preacher."
>
> The preacher answered for cowmen, and Callan announced that he would send three riders through the district proclaiming a preaching service on Sunday morning at Pecan Crossing on the San Saba River. A large crowd gathered on Sunday, prepared for a brush-arbor service and dinner on the grounds afterward. The preacher had readied a sermon suitable for people whose livelihood depended upon grass and water, and he selected the Bible's best-known pastoral passage as his text.
>
> Callan arrived late, just as the preacher read: "The Lord is my shepherd. . . ." The cattleman wheeled and left, but confronted the preacher after the noon meal.
>
> "When you got here Friday I asked you fair and square if you were a cowman's preacher or a sheepman's preacher," seethed Callan, "and you said you were a cowman's preacher. I did what I said I'd do, and you found a good crowd waiting to hear you preach. As I walked up to the arbor, the first words I heard you utter were about some damned sheepherder. The next time you want to preach in this country, you can go somewhere else."

ax handles or spokes from the wheels of just-destroyed sheep wagons. Many clubbed sheep were not killed outright, but their backs were broken or they were otherwise so badly maimed that they would have to be destroyed, often after a considerable period of pitiful suffering. Over 11,000 sheep (more than one-fifth of the total slaughtered in raids) were clubbed to death, while at least 7,100 (fourteen percent of the total) were rimrocked. Raiders also sometimes cut the throats of sheep or poisoned water holes or pastures used by flocks. Occasionally, sheep were dynamited or even set afire, and in 1875 Texas raiders destroyed about 500 sheep by driving them into quicksand. Sometimes a herd of horses would be stampeded through a flock, cruelly trampling sheep underfoot.

Raids on sheep camps often were launched at night, although daylight attacks frequently occurred. Commonly, just one or two herders would be present, and often they would be captured while asleep. Herders were usually bound, but some were beaten or shot. Sometimes herders were forced to help club their own sheep. Customarily, tents and sheep wagons, or even corrals and ranch buildings and haystacks, were burned during a raid.

At times sheepherders or, more frequently, the owner of a flock would shoot back, despite being outnumbered. Sheepmen also launched ambushes against their antagonists, or sniped from concealment at cowboys or grazing cattle and horses. Cattlemen might employ quick-triggered "stock detectives" to back up their deadlines, but sheepmen also resorted on occasion to hired gunmen. Sheepherders and cowboys sometimes engaged in saloon brawls. Cattlemen formed associations to present a united front against their adversaries, but sheepmen also formed associations. In Oregon there would even be two "Sheep Shooters" associations.

Just as different tribes of Indians fought against settlers and the army throughout the West, just as gunfights erupted in saloons and dusty streets throughout the West, just as peace officers clashed with lawbreakers throughout the West, so did combat break out between cattlemen and sheepmen in a great variety of western locations during half a century of conflict. Warfare between cattle and sheep interests, stamped out for the time being in one area, would then break out somewhere else, like a prairie fire that could not be extinguished for good. Long after warlike Indians had suffered their final defeat, after gunfighters and outlaw gangs had disappeared, cattlemen and sheepherders ignored the pressures of civilization and continued to battle for the range. As the years passed, sheepmen and cattlemen resorted to legal or legislative action, but through the second decade of the twentieth century there continued to be vicious outbreaks of hostilities on the range.

* * *

In many western regions, federal policies regulating forest grazing areas were instrumental in halting warfare between cattle and sheep graziers. In 1896 a forestry commission recommended to President Grover Cleveland the creation of thirteen forest reserves (later called national forests) totaling twenty-one million acres. Western newspapers registered reams of protest, but lumbermen were far more agitated than ranchers, and in any event no provisions were made to manage the reserves. When the first forest rangers began to instruct stockmen to report the number of cattle or sheep they grazed in the federal reserves, individualistic ranchers ignored such requests, often "with ill-concealed disrespect for the ranger's authority." Equally ignored, at first, were 1897 instructions that stockmen must obtain a permit covering every head of stock to be grazed in the reserves.[10]

But many stockmen recognized the benefits of government allotment of grazing rights in federal timber reserves. During the late 1880s, when the disastrous effects of overstocking the range changed the cattle business to a land and cattle business, cattlemen filed on as much land as possible, purchased as many tracts as they could afford, and fenced in the public domain. The Wyoming Stock Growers Association steadily lobbied for any kind of federal policy that would make possible legal tenure of forest ranges. Sheepmen also favored such policies, since timber reserves afforded the best summer ranges for their flocks. When the National Live Stock Association met in Denver in 1899, the sixteen-man delegation from Wyoming was instrumental in the passage of a resolution urging the government to allow sheep to graze on the forest reserves. Congressman Frank W. Mondell, an important Wyoming sheep rancher, campaigned energetically to obtain grazing privileges for sheep, securing permission in 1899 from Secretary of the Interior Ethan A. Hitchcock for the use of Wyoming reserves at a minimal fee.[11]

In 1898 Gifford Pinchot, a highly capable and imaginative person, accepted appointment as chief of the Division of Forestry at the Department of Agriculture (by an act of Congress in 1905, the agency was elevated in status to the United States Forest Service). Under Pinchot's aggressive leadership, the agency became highly active in administering the forest reserves. The western rancher's resentment of government interference in their ranging patterns was tempered by the fact that most of the early forest rangers were usually cowboys, lumberjacks, sheepherders — men who "understood the West and the people" and who were known locally. "They had very little practical knowledge of forestry or the effects of overgrazing on watersheds," testified Will C. Barnes, a key figure during this period of the service, "but were admirably suited in every way" to handle a critical new assignment.[12]

Pinchot insisted that each federal reserve rangeland be subject to a field examination and that grazing suitability should never be based on generalized instructions. An Arizona stockman, Albert Potter, was enlisted by Pinchot to supervise grazing policies in the forest reserves. Potter went to the ranchers themselves, sending out a questionnaire to which 1,400 stockmen responded regarding range conditions. Wyoming ranchers returned 218 responses, more than from any other state.

Seventy-six Wyoming respondents raised cattle and horses, fifty were cattle raisers, thirty-three were sheepmen, and eighteen raised both cattle and sheep. Wyoming ranchers stated overwhelmingly, 175 to 23, that they favored federal control and management of forest reserves. And while a majority stated their opinions that the carrying capacity of the ranges was declining, only twenty-eight blamed excessive sheep grazing (overstocking the range was the chief cause of blame).[13] After assessing the ranchers' response, Potter informed Pinchot of his certainty that western ranchers would embrace an allotment system based on flexible regulations and careful reconnaissance of the carrying capacity of individual ranges.[14]

During the early years of the twentieth century, the size of the Forest Service staff and budget increased rapidly, as well as areas designated as forest reserves. As larger and larger grazing regions came to be administered by the Forest Service, conflict between cattle and sheep graziers declined dramatically, often permanently. In 1905 the government began to charge grazing fees, but by controlling use of desirable ranges, causes for disputes swiftly diminished. Of course, there was inevitable resentment of grazing fees, particularly when increases were announced. In 1910, for example, annual fees ranged from thirty-five to sixty cents for cattle and ten to eighteen cents for sheep. Fees were raised in 1915 to forty cents minimum and $1.50 maximum for cattle, while sheep were charged at twenty-five percent of cattle rates. In 1917 the Forest Service announced that fees would be doubled over the next three years.[15]

Cattlemen predictably protested each increase, while sheepmen maintained that their fees were always too high in proportion to those charged for cattle. The National Wool Growers Association regularly campaigned against Forest Service fees. (When the Forest Service initiated a program in 1914 to provide wire and staples to stockmen who would supply fence posts, the association issued its first-ever endorsement of a Forest Service policy.) Sheepmen felt that many forest rangers who had been cowboys sympathized with cattlemen, and early in his tenure Gifford Pinchot learned of an agent who apparently had been offered a $10,000 bribe by cattlemen to report that sheep grazing had a negative effect on forest reserves.[16]

But in 1907 Forest Service experiments included sheep grazing within coyote-proof fencing. Furthermore, the substitution of regulated grazing proved visibly restorative to ranges that long had been overgrazed by uncontrolled numbers of cattle and sheep. Forest Service grazing policies and the persistent, tactful efforts of forest rangers were instrumental in bringing order — and thereby lessening conflict — to ranges previously disputed by cattlemen and sheepherders.[17]

CHRONOLOGY OF HOSTILITIES

Year   Place (number of incidents) and fatalities

1873   Colo.; 20 sheep killed.
1874   Colo. (2); 254 sheep killed.
1875   Texas; 500 sheep killed.
1877   Texas.
1879   Texas (3); Mont.
1880   Texas (3); 240 sheep killed.
1881   Ariz.; 20 sheep killed.
1882   Ariz.; 200 sheep killed.
1883   Texas (12); Wyo.; 460 sheep killed.
1884   Ariz. (2); Colo.; New Mex.; Texas; 5,500 sheep killed, 1 sheepman killed.
1885   New Mex.; 1 sheepman killed.
1887   Ariz. (12); Texas; 2,000 sheep killed, 5 sheepmen and 12 cowmen killed.
1889   Ariz.; Texas; 5 sheepherders and 1 cowboy killed.
1890   Texas (3); 15 sheep killed, 1 sheepherder and 1 cowboy killed.
1891   Texas (2).
1892   Ariz.; Idaho; 1 cattleman killed.
1893   Wash. (5); Wyo. (4); 330 sheep killed, 1 sheepherder and 1 cowman killed.
1894   Wyo. (3); Colo. (2); 5,300 sheep killed.
1895   Wyo. (2); Idaho; 2,000 sheep killed.
1896   Ore. (5); Idaho (2); Colo.; 300 sheep killed, 2 sheepherders killed.
1897   Idaho.
1899   Wyo.; Colo.; 150 sheep killed.
1900   Ore. (2); Mont.; Texas; 8,400 sheep clubbed.
1901   Wyo. (3); 20 sheep killed, 2 sheepherders killed.
1902   Wyo. (3); 3,040 sheep killed, 1 sheepman killed.
1903   Wyo. (3); Ariz.; 925 sheep killed, 3 sheepmen killed.
1904   Ore. (2); Wyo. (2); Mont.; 3,364 sheep killed, one sheepman killed.
1905   Wyo. (3); Ore.; 5,000 sheep killed, 1 sheepman killed.
1906   Ore.; Wyo.; 2,100 sheep killed.
1907   Wyo. (2); 4,400 sheep killed.
1908   Wyo. (5); 350 sheep killed.
1909   Wyo.; Colo.; 3,030 sheep killed.
1911   Colo.; 90 sheep killed.

1912 Wyo.; 60 sheep killed.
1916 New Mexico.
1917 Ariz.; 700 sheep poisoned.
1918 Colo.; 2,000 sheep rimrocked.
1919 Arizona.
1920 Colo. (3); Ariz. (2); 1,186 sheep killed, 4 sheepmen killed.
1921 Colo.; 300 sheep poisoned.

CATTLEMEN-SHEEPMEN WAR STATISTICS				
	Violent Incidents	Sheep Killed	Killed	
			Sheepmen	Cattlemen
Wyoming	35	16,305	10	1
Texas	29	3,215	4	2
Arizona	23	5,420	11	13
Colorado	15	13,750		
Oregon	10	10,064		
Idaho	5		2	
Washington	5	300		
Montana	3	3,500		
New Mexico	3	700	1	—
Totals	128	53,254	28	16

2

Trouble in Texas

"Ba-a-a."
— Concho County cowboys to
any passing sheepherder

When cattlemen squared off against sheepherders in Texas, flockmasters faced few dangers they had not grappled with in the past. Since Spanish *pastores* first drove sheep into Texas in the seventeenth century, Indians had attacked exposed flocks, and Mexican desperadoes long had crossed the Rio Grande to raid Texas livestock. Herders were slain and sheep were stolen, scattered, butchered, drowned, or shot by Comanches, Kiowas, Apaches, Tonkawas, Wacos, Mexicans, and occasionally even the French.

In one attack, Indians on foot drove 1,500 sheep over a precipice, fatally injuring almost the entire flock. George W. Kendall, a notable early Anglo sheepman, was hounded by Comanches until he posted heavily armed sentries. Along the border Juan Nepomuceno Cortinas, the legendary Cheno, led raids which ran off or destroyed thousands of head of livestock. In 1878 a combined band of hostile Indians, Mexican outlaws, and at least one American desperado launched a predatory, devastating raid into Texas which lasted for six days. Texas Rangers and the United States Army battled such incursions, but by the time raids from Indians and Mexicans were controlled, sheepmen found themselves similarly engaged against Texas cattle ranchers.[1]

The pioneer cattleman from Texas, Charles Goodnight, experienced occasional difficulties with sheep. In 1875, when Goodnight was headquartering in southern Colorado, he sent a cattle herd into vast, unfenced eastern New Mexico for the winter. He established a camp on Rano Creek and another ten miles to the west, and defined the limits of "his" range. It had been customary for as many as 100,000 sheep from the west to be wintered in the vicinity of Goodnight's new camps, but he ordered his cowboys not to harm the sheepherders as long as they stayed outside the range he had designated for his own use.

Goodnight returned to Colorado for the winter, but among those he left behind in the new camps were Dave McCormick, a *vaquero* called Panchito, and Scotsman J. C. Johnston, who owned a part interest in the cattle and who later would become a director of the Matador Land and Cattle Company. Panchito, riding line out of the western camp, discovered a large flock of sheep inside Goodnight's claim on the Canadian River. Panchito reported to McCormick, who rode out and ordered the *mayordomo* to move. McCormick and Panchito rode back to the sheep camp the next day, only to discover the herders building a winter dwelling. McCormick's temper flared, and he and Panchito rounded up the sheep. Shouting and chunking rocks at the *guias*, the two cowboys forced the lead goats into the Canadian, and as the flock followed, four or five hundred drowned or died in the quicksand. Before the winter ended, a deputy sheriff came out from Las Animas and arrested Johnston, but Goodnight paid damages, and there were no further repercussions.[2]

In 1876 Goodnight moved his operation to the Texas Panhandle, summering on the Alamocitos, a tributary of the Canadian. Sheepmen again crowded his herd, but he had determined to establish a ranch in the magnificent Palo Duro Canyon, only recently cleared of hostile Indians by an army campaign. Goodnight pledged to the *mayordomos* that he would vacate the Canadian Valley (which he intended to do anyway) if they would stay out of the Palo Duro. When a Mexican brought his flock into Palo Duro Canyon, Leigh Dyer, Goodnight's brother-in-law, doubled his lariat and whipped him out of the country.[3]

But many sheepmen from New Mexico abided by the agreement, settling in the Texas Panhandle north and west of Palo Duro Canyon. In the fall of 1876, Casimero Romero moved his sheep operation to the

Panhandle from a ranch in New Mexico's Sangre de Cristo Mountains. Romero's relatives and herders piled their belongings into fourteen covered wagons, each painted blue and drawn by four oxen. This caravan and Romero's flocks proceeded along an old *comanchero* trail to the north bank of the Canadian River, where the town of Tascosa soon would take shape.

Romero and his people built a *plaza* — a cluster of stone and adobe dwellings and sheep pens consisting of low rock walls. During the next couple of years, other flocks streamed in from New Mexico, and approximately a dozen *plazas* were formed along the tributary streams and rich grasslands of the Canadian River Valley. A couple of *plazas* had as many as two dozen dwellings, some boasted a store or saloon, and by 1880 the Mexican-American population of the Canadian Valley had reached 300 persons.[4]

By 1880 cattlemen also had moved into the Canadian Valley, but sheepmen had first established their operations, a reversal of the usual order. Cowboys delighted in the company of *señoritas* and happily attended dances at the *plazas*, but conflict could be expected when cattlemen tried to expand their "Beef Bonanza." An ambitious cattle rancher named W. M. D. Lee, however, provided a remarkable and courageous alternative to the potential range dispute. Lee and Albert Reynolds had made a fortune freighting army supplies and buffalo hides, but Lee persuaded his partner to help him form the LE Ranch. Headquartered a few miles east of the New Mexico line in Oldham County, the LE branded 20,000 longhorns within a year. But the partners quarreled bitterly over Lee's plans to improve the herd, and Reynolds bought out Lee. Lee found a new partner, Lucien Scott, and the Lee-Scott Cattle Company would form the LS Ranch. Lee and Scott perceived that the days of free grass were numbered, and they began to purchase land, soon acquiring title to more than 220,000 acres in Oldham, Potter, and Hartley counties.[5]

Among those who sold out to the LS were the Green and the Austin-Campbell sheep ranches. However, several *pastores* continued to operate out of the old *plazas*, grazing their sheep on land they did not own. Lee shared the typical cattleman's loathing of sheep, but he did not use typical methods to remove the flocks from his range. In 1884 he packed $35,000 in currency in a valise, hitched a team to a buggy, placed the valise at his feet, and drove off to buy *plazas* along the Canadian River. Starting at the Trujillo *plaza*, he made his way alone through rugged but beautiful country, unconcerned that outlaws

> **A SHEEPMAN'S GLOSSARY**
>
> *Chaurro* — Sheep which is immune to many diseases and hardy on marginal ranges.
> *Ewe* — A female sheep.
> *Ram* — A male sheep.
> *Wether* — A castrated ("marked") male sheep.
> *Bummer* — A motherless lamb nursed by a cooperative ewe.
> *Clip* — The amount of wool sheared from one sheep.
> *Black sheep* — Many flockmasters would place one black sheep for every 100 in his flock, to facilitate counting.

would have murdered him in an instant for the fortune in cash that he carried. At each *plaza* that still was inhabited, Lee usually encountered people whose command of English was no better than his Spanish usage. But he would brandish a fistful of *dinero* and state, *"Vamoose pronto,"* and everyone got the idea. Soon flocks of sheep were grazing their way toward New Mexico, followed by wagons loaded with women, children, and household goods. The LS used some of the vacated *plazas* for line camps and razed the others to remove clutter from the range. Sheep vanished from the Canadian Valley, but the removal was amicable, thanks to the legendary buggy ride of W. M. D. Lee.[6]

Outside the Panhandle, conflict was more serious. As in the Panhandle, flockmasters were the first stockmen into Nolan County. Sheep were driven into the area about 1876, and when cattle followed during the next few years, there was "considerable dispute" between the factions. During the ranching boom of the late 1870s and early 1880s, in many locations sheepmen, not cattlemen, were the first to begin purchase of the open range, and the Gonzales correspondent of *Texas Wool* said that cattle ranchers were "indignant."[7]

During a two-month period beginning in December 1879, there were half a dozen raids against sheep camps in San Saba County. The cattlemen developed a pattern, waiting until they could locate a solitary unarmed sheepherder before striking his flock. Peter Bertrand was ordered out of the country and a dog was released to attack his sheep. When he tried to stay, night raiders shot his sheep in their pen. The worst depredation occurred on Monday, January 12, 1880. The Ramsay brothers owned 7,000 head of sheep, which they grazed in southern San Saba County and just across the line in adjacent Llano County. One flock of 1,300 sheep was located at Fall Creek Prairie in lower San

Saba County, where a herder named Colvin kept his animals confined at night inside two pens. The raiders struck after the flock was penned, shooting a number of sheep while Colvin, camped a short distance away, offered no resistance. The raiders dismounted, entered the pens, and began cutting the throats of the bleating sheep. Finally tiring of this bloody work, the raiders opened the gates and scattered the surviving sheep. Two hundred and forty sheep lay dead and "a large number" were wounded. The San Saba *News* railed against "these cowardly outrages."[8]

A Coleman County sheepherder was chased into his tent one night by "cougars," which stayed outside for hours making blood-curdling howls. Two nights later these same animals (which were two-legged critters wearing boots and big hats) returned, again making fearsome noises and tearing the tent. The next morning the sheepherder drove his flock out of the area. In Hamilton County one band of sheep was destroyed by raiders, other flocks were scattered, and sheepmen were forced out of the region. Reacting to such incidents, the editor of *Texas Wool* grumbled: "In almost every case the aggressors have been the cattlemen. As a class, the sheepmen of Texas are quiet, law abiding, and industrious, while in very many instances cattlemen are notorious for their turbulent disposition, and inclined to take by might what is not theirs by right."[9]

When sheep ranchers stood their ground, the results, gratifyingly, were not always violent. In 1877 Billy Green drove a flock of sheep onto rangeland in the northern part of Coleman County. Although cattlemen got together and ordered him out of the county, Green simply ignored them, and soon managed to win their friendship. That same year Joseph Tweedy drove a flock from the Rio Grande to Dove Creek onto land he had leased at one cent per acre. Cattleman R. F. Tankersley rode over and asked what he was doing there with sheep. Tweedy replied that he would keep his sheep off any land that Tankersley owned or was leasing. Like most cattlemen of the day, Tankersley grazed his stock on open range. "Well," Tankersley admitted reluctantly, "I suppose that's right but it's sure hard on us cowmen. When my cattle smell those sheep they'll run clear to the Pecos." But the cattle and sheep got along amicably and so did their owners, who soon became close friends.[10]

In 1879 twenty-one-year-old Christopher Columbus Doty left his Missouri home for Texas. The next year he acquired a flock of sheep in the San Angelo vicinity, intending to graze his animals along the Concho River in what is now Schleicher County. Sheep had not been introduced to this range, and Doty was warned of a possessive cattleman who arbitrarily claimed the entire area and who detested sheep. Shortly after Doty established a camp on the Concho, the cattleman rode up and ordered him to leave within three days or risk being hanged. Three days later the cattleman and two cowboys rode to the camp, but Doty calmly announced: "I've decided to stay here if it makes no difference to you." Doty's show of backbone worked — the cattleman led his men away with no trouble. Doty then solidified his position by sending a map of the disputed area to the state land commissioner in Austin, who replied that the cattleman held title to just 400 acres. Soon an old sheepman came into the region with a half-starved band, and within a few days the cattleman rode to his camp. The old herder was out with his flock, so the cattleman shot his barrels full of holes and left word to move out within three days. Worried, the old herder sought out Doty and asked his advice. Doty told him to move his camp nearby and stay close. On the third night the cattleman rode to the old herder's camp, then lost his temper when he spotted Doty's adjacent camp. The cattleman stormed over to confront Doty, but the plucky sheepman immediately revealed his discovery that the abusive rancher held just 400 deeded acres. Doty then told the rancher if he caused any more problems that within three months there would be 50,000 sheep in the area. His bluff called, the rancher promptly changed his attitude. He befriended Doty, had his cowboys brand mavericks for the sheepman, and surely enjoyed a measure of satisfaction when Doty eventually began to run cattle.[11]

Feeling pressured by sheepmen moving onto numerous Texas ranges, cattlemen lobbied for legislative relief (in Texas, public lands were owned by the state, not the federal government). In 1881 the Texas legislature appointed state sheep inspectors with the power to quarantine diseased sheep, and, of far greater concern to sheepmen, made it illegal to graze *sheep* (cattle were not mentioned) on land belonging to someone else without consent from the owner. The editor of *Texas Wool* branded this law as a disgrace in a state that had eight million sheep on its tax rolls. Sheep ranchers thereby were obliged to buy or lease land, and spend money fencing their property, whereas cattlemen remained free to graze their stock on open range — or on unfenced land owned by sheepmen — and their capital could go toward enlarging their herds. In April 1883 another law was passed, requiring that, before sheep could be moved across a county line, a certificate of inspection had to be obtained proving that the animals were free of scab.[12]

Despite such legal harassment, the tidal wave of sheep swept inexorably across Texas grasslands. In January 1882, for example, an article from the Lampasas *Dispatch* that was reprinted in *Texas Wool* reported that sheepmen were purchasing land and improving it, while cattlemen were pulling up stakes and moving west out of the county. To the west of Lampasas, conditions boded little better for cattlemen. One cowboy groused that "the town of Brady was full of sheepmen and the county was full of sheepmen, and pretty soon if a man did not . . . talk sheep in Brady, he would have no more attention paid him than a common justice of the peace." In January 1881 a sheepman from Colorado City generously testified: "The cowman, or 'boy' is not as bad by a large majority as he is painted. In fact when you come to know him you will find him a good fellow, . . . [who] means no harm. Sheepmen coming to a country where cattlemen are more numerous . . . are not generally met by a brass band, but deep and apparently ominous growls greet him, which will perhaps make each individual hair on his head stand on end like the fretful bristles of a mad Mexican hog; but if he will attend to his business and keep a stiff upper lip, all bluster will soon subside."[13]

Not all Texas cowboys were as easily tamed as the drover from Brady, however, and many cattlemen did not bluff or bluster. Cattleman C. F. Adams and two partners drove a herd of longhorns to the mouth of the Pecos River, where a Southern Pacific Railroad construction camp was located. The senior partner soon clashed with sheepmen in the area. Adams, founder of the town of Sonora, later reminisced: "At that time no cattleman had any reputation who had not punctured one or two sheepmen." Hoping to establish a proper reputation, the senior partner opened fire on a German sheepman, plugging him in the calf of the leg. The cattleman promptly left the country, leaving Adams and the third partner to be thrown into jail, "charged by their enemies with shooting a Dutchman and by their friends with bad marksmanship." Cowboys who would grumble that a leg wound in a sheepman signified bad marksmanship were the same type who, in the San Angelo country, contemptuously bleated "Ba-a-a" whenever they saw a sheepherder. In 1884, near Laredo, a Mexican herder was murdered when he ignored an order to leave the country. Charles Hanna, who had introduced sheep to Brown County, found an entire flock of 300 lying in his rock corral one morning, their throats slit. Other

Brown County sheep raisers had their flocks shot at and their houses and pens burned, and one sheepman who moved had his flock attacked by night raiders in his new location. E. K. Fawcett, who helped to drive a flock of sheep into the Del Rio area in 1883, received a hostile reaction from locals: "Young men in Del Rio never heard of a sheepman, since the customary title for them was damn sheepman. Sheepmen were little better than a pelon dog."[14]

The sheepherder-cattleman conflict in Texas reached its peak in the drouth year of 1883. In August of that year eight raiders struck the Hamilton County sheep ranch of a man named Plinton, twelve miles from Hico. Plinton's sheepherder was blindfolded and more than 100 sheep clubbed to death. A sheepman named Reilly, who ran a flock in Hamilton County near Carlton, was roughed up and a number of his sheep were clubbed. When George McCall of Llano County drove a flock of sheep to Taylor County, he attempted to water his animals at the well of cattleman Bart Stevens. Stevens ordered McCall off his property, but McCall, whose sheep had been without water for three days, refused to move. McCall stated that there were no cattle in the area and that his sheep would cause no harm. Stevens then rode off, gathered up two of his cowboys, and returned to the well to beat up McCall and kill a number of the sheep. Six miles from Dublin, ten raiders began killing sheep belonging to J. H. Langston, and when the sheepman tried to defend his flock he was badly wounded.[15]

* * *

Considerable violence was associated with the Texas fence-cutting wars, which climaxed in 1883. As barbed wire restricted open range throughout the West, fences were cut in many states, and often the violence was between homesteaders and cattlemen, or even between open-range cattlemen and cattle ranchers who had fenced their range. Half of the counties in Texas reported fence-cutting, and there were many instances which did not involve sheepmen. Nevertheless, in Texas, barbed wire seemed to bring to a head the bitter antagonisms between sheepmen and cattle ranchers.

The first primitive wire fences were put up in Texas in the 1860s, and by the 1880s fencing bees had helped to close off open range across the state. By 1883 the "Knights of the Knippers" had cut fence in half of the state's counties.[16] A Central Texas sheep rancher wrote to the editor of *Texas Wool* that if sheep ranchers in his area used any fencing material other than rock, the fence would be cut or burned within the year. Indeed, in Brown County, thirty-four pasture fences were destroyed in 1883 — and five of them had been constructed of rock. In 1883, in Tom Green County, sheepman C. B. Metcalfe had completed four miles of a fence around his 10,000-acre Arden Ranch when riders from a cattle spread north of the ranch cut the wire between every post of Metcalfe's fence. Metcalfe stubbornly rebuilt the fence, then armed himself with a shotgun and rode into San Angelo. He found his inhospitable neighbor and, underscoring his arguments by use of a shotgun, convinced the cattleman not to touch his fence again.[17]

Horace Starkweather and G. W. Mahoney purchased 9,000 head of sheep from Santos and Carlos Benevides of Laredo in 1881 and drove them to their Coleman County ranches. During the turmoil of 1883, miles of Mahoney's fence were cut, the wire snipped twice between each post. After he began repairing his fence, Mahoney found that a coffin had been dumped on his gallery one night, with a warning note tacked to it: "This will be your end if you keep fencing." Mahoney ignored the warning and converted the coffin to a horse trough. But his fences continued to be cut, and for decades the spliced wire was visible near Santa Anna. Late in the year, Starkweather's fences were cut, and his sheepfolds, sheepherders' houses, and 2,000 cedar fence posts were burned. Within a few weeks he had repaired the fences and was in the process of placing rock under the bottom wire when thirty miles of fencing was cut. Scabby sheep then drifted onto his range, and Starkweather had to dip his 8,000 sheep. He later traveled to Chicago to arrange a business loan and had almost concluded the negotiations when newspapers appeared on the streets of Chicago headlining a fence-cutting rampage in Texas. Five hundred miles of fencing had been cut, and among the listed victims was Horace Starkweather, whose repaired fences once again had been struck. Starkweather's loan request was denied, and the following year he sold half of his land to a cattle rancher, while Mahoney soon subdivided his spread into small farms.[18]

In response to the fence-cutting wars (which reduced tax valuations in Texas by as much as $30 million), Governor John Ireland called a special session of the Texas legislature to meet in Austin on January 8, 1884. The legislators were deluged with petitions and letters protesting the lawless depredations. Because "fences are being continuously destroyed in many parts of the state by Lawless persons," lawmakers suspended the usual legislative process and hurried to make fence-cutting a felony punishable by one to five years in prison. Furthermore, it was made a misdemeanor knowingly to fence public lands or lands belonging to others without the owner's consent. Anyone who had built such fences was given six months to take them down, and any rancher who built fences across public roads was required to place a gate every three miles. As these laws were enforced, the fence-cutting wars in Texas came to a halt. Although during the next few years there were occasional flare-ups of wire-cutting, usually caused by drouth conditions, fence troubles ceased to be the focal point of violence between cattlemen and sheep ranchers in Texas.[19]

* * *

In the remainder of the decade there was an appreciable decline in troubles between sheepmen and cattlemen, but tensions still existed.

In May 1884 a sheep rancher was taken to court for grazing his flock on land he did not own. He was convicted and fined twenty dollars, and his appeal to a higher court was turned down. Another sheepman, driving his flock through the Big Spring region, could find little water or grass in that thoroughly fenced area. At a particularly appealing pasture his sheep left the road and slipped under the fence, then scattered out to enjoy the grass. Soon an angry cattleman rode up, balancing a Winchester across his saddle horn. "What in hell do you mean driving them damn sheep in my horse pasture?" he exploded. With disarming forthrightness the sheepman blurted out, "Why, because the grass looked so much better here!" The astonished cattleman sat back wordlessly in his saddle while the trespasser gathered his flock and returned to the road.

Jeff Moore, ranging his sheep south of the Concho River, was confronted by cowboys from the Door Key Ranch. The Door Key foreman and his well-armed men rode to Moore's chuck wagon and ordered the sheepman to move on. Moore flatly refused, stating that he had as much right as anyone to any open range in the region. The foreman cursed, then grudgingly allowed, "Well, I guess there's room for us both." The cowboys rode away peacefully, and Moore eventually became a prominent rancher.[20]

About 1887, sheepman M. H. Kilgore obtained a lease in the Big Bend country, locating his flock at Rosillo Springs. But an area cattleman had sworn to kill any man who brought sheep onto the range, and within a few days three of his cowboys rode into Kilgore's camp. Although outnumbered too badly to fight it out, Kilgore decided to play upon a cowboys' assumption that sheepmen were *loco* — "crazy as a sheepherder" already was a cliché on the open range. Kilgore had been reading Jules Verne's *From the Earth to the Moon,* and he began to rattle off a paraphrased version to the astounded cowboys.

Kilgore told the cowboys that he and his partner had built a machine to take a trip to the moon. After loading their spaceship with water and food — and a faithful sheepdog — they soared up to 5,000 feet. At midnight, however, they began to lose altitude. Forced to throw everything overboard, including the poor sheepdog, they finally stabilized — and spotted their faithful dog treading right beside them in the air! As Kilgore narrated this fantastic story, the leader of the cowboys finally concluded: "This damned fool is crazy. Let's get out of here."[21]

Even though many ranchers were no longer inclined to resort to violence, sheepmen still could encounter mortal danger. In Tom Green County, cattlemen arbitrarily established a deadline against sheep at the North Concho River. They notified sheepmen that cattle would be ranged north of the river and that all sheep should be kept south of the stream. When a sheep rancher and two herders approached the river driving 9,000 sheep northward, a delegation of cattlemen rode up to remind them of the deadline. Defiantly, the sheepmen crossed the boundary, inviting retaliation. Cattlemen responded by donning gunnysack masks with eyeholes cut out (this incident may have initiated the term "gunnysacker"), then swooping down on the sheep camp. The owner of the sheep and one of his herders were killed, but the other herder escaped back to the river. The gunnysackers then leisurely slaughtered 2,000 sheep before finally breaking off the raid.[22]

Mortal danger could extend in two directions. At the end of the decade animosity against woollies still festered in the psyche of many Texas cowboys. One such drover needed a job badly enough to hire on at a Burnet County sheep ranch owned by Andy Feild. Andy's father, Dr. Marcus A. Feild, had come to Burnet County in 1856 and opened a medical practice at Strickling, a community forty miles northwest of Austin. After the Civil War Andy married, established a spread near Strickling at a crossroads hamlet called Sage, and began raising children and sheep.[23]

In 1889 he needed a herder. The country remained largely unfenced, making it necessary for a herder to police the flock during the daytime, then pen the defenseless animals for the night. The rider who asked Feild for a job wore the garb of a cowboy. There was a six-gun strapped to his waist, and he was reticent about his past, but the man voiced a willingness to tend sheep.

Feild showed the newcomer where he wanted the flock to graze during the next few days, carefully indicating the boundary of his neighbor Taylor's range. But soon Taylor came to Feild complaining that the sheep were grazing on his land. Assuming that the new man had misunderstood the boundary markings, Feild rode out with his hired hand to indicate the range limits again. A day or two later, Taylor returned with the same complaint. It was obvious that the cowboy was not supervising the flock. That evening, after the sheep were penned, Feild described Taylor's second visit, then told the cowboy he was fired. Feild added that he could stay the night in his shed room off the kitchen, but must leave the ranch following breakfast. The discharged hand took the news with ominous silence.

The next morning Feild was dressing when his wife came to tell him of sounds, like the clicking of a revolver, that she had heard from the shed room while she was preparing the morning meal. Feild pulled out a .41-caliber revolver he rarely wore, stuck it into his waistband, then went to the pen to mend harness before breakfast. His nine-year-old son, Albert, tagged along.

The disgruntled cowboy wolfed down his food, then rode his horse to the pen. He dismounted and tossed his reins over the low fence.

"You son-of-a-bitch," he spat out, "you've fired your last man!"

He jerked out his handgun and snapped off a shot. The slug missed, and Feild whirled around, gun in hand. Feild charged, firing rapidly, and hit the cowboy in the elbow and chest. The man fled on foot, already in shock from his wounds and surprised that Feild was armed. As he looked back over his shoulder to see if his pursuer was gaining, Feild triggered another bullet which caught him between the eyes and hurled him to the ground.

After Feild calmed his family, he saddled a horse and rode into Burnet, the county seat, to tell the sheriff. His sheepdog went to the fallen figure and began to lick at the wounds. Suddenly, the "corpse" moaned and began to move.

Mrs. Feild and Andy loaded the cowboy into a wagon and took him to the house of a neighbor named Murphy. Dr. Feild was summoned and the wounded man lingered through the day and night, but he died just before dawn. The cowboy was buried in a plot beside current Farm to Market Road 963. Authorities promptly exonerated Andy Feild, whose brief and unwanted career as a gunfighter was ended.

The killing on the Feild ranch seemed to usher in a new era of violent incidents. The West's premier assassin, Killin' Jim Miller, was reputed to have murdered "a dozen" sheepherders. According to his biographer, he was hired by Texas cattlemen at $150 per killing. With typical disdain for sheepmen, he confided to a Fort Worth acquaintance: "I have killed eleven men that I know about; I have lost my notch stick on sheepherders I've killed out on the border." [24]

In 1890, at Big Spring, a herder watering sheep owned by W. E. Havens was jumped by three cowboys. While one cowboy held his gun on the sheepherder, the other two killed a dozen of the sheep. And as they rode away, each cowboy roped a woolly and brutally dragged it to death. That same year, cowboys thundered into a sheep camp at night after the herder had gone to sleep. The cowboys took target practice on the herder's pots and pans, then scattered his sheep and galloped away.[25]

In the lower Pecos Valley, cattlemen and farmers were incensed by New Mexico sheepherders who began to drive their flocks into the valley each fall. The sheepmen would move slowly, grazing their flocks all the way to the Rio Grande, then gradually moving back through the Pecos country to New Mexico in time for spring grazing. Although the sheepmen claimed they were moving their flocks from one of their ranches to another in order to take advantage of seasonal grazing, cattlemen did not believe them, and in any event resented the presence of sheep. Injunctions were filed in Pecos County to keep sheep away from water holes, but the flocks kept coming.[26]

A spunky ranch wife, a Mrs. Williams, took more direct action against the encroachments of New Mexico sheepherders. Her husband worked at Fort Stockton, twenty-eight miles away. The flocks would pasture on grass needed by Williams livestock, and on occasion the sheep would crawl beneath Williams's barbed wire fences into crop fields. When yet another New Mexico flock was spotted heading toward her spread, Mrs. Williams had a team of horses hitched to her buggy and, cradling a shotgun across her lap, she drove out to the approaching sheep. "I'll not shoot you," she grimly told the herder, "but I'll start shooting the first sheep that go under that fence." Taking the lady at her word, the herder carefully kept his animals on the move and safely away from Williams property.[27]

The strain between cattlemen and sheepmen around Fort Stockton became so strong that the two factions traded at separate stores. Cattlemen took their business to the Fort Stockton establishment owned by Herman Kochler, while sheepmen traded at Billy Young's store. When a French sheepherder named Brutelle was shot to death in

Fort Stockton by a cattleman, the killer entered a plea of self-defense. He was cleared of charges by a jury of his peers.[28]

John Caruthers obtained permission to winter his sheep on 7D range north of Fort Stockton. Aided by his two brothers and a few Mexican herders, Caruthers passed the winter without incident. In the spring he led a drive back to his Terrell County ranch, but after he crossed the Pecos River his sheep piled up against a fence around a water hole near Centralia Draw. Caruthers noticed a house about 300 yards away, and so he turned his horse in that direction. Suddenly, a bullet whizzed near him. Caruthers sighted a man with a Winchester at his shoulder, and he yelled at the gunman. But two more rounds were fired at Caruthers. Unarmed, he could merely shout curses, but his men got their guns from the chuck wagon, and the sheepmen approached the house. The cattleman, brandishing his Winchester, and a cowboy walked out to meet them. "What the hell are ye doin' here?" blustered the cattleman. "Get them damn sheep away from my water!" He leveled his Winchester at Caruthers and the sheepmen brought up their guns. The antagonists were able to talk over the situation, and the moment for shooting passed. Caruthers and his men drove the sheep away with no further problems.[29]

A drifting sheepman stirred up more trouble in the Fort Stockton area about 1891. When he stopped his large flock on range north of town, several cattlemen rode out to order him to keep moving. The sheepman flatly refused, then produced a gun and ran the cattlemen off. Soon they posted the water holes he was using, but the obstinate sheepman ignored the notices. A cowboy at Fort Stockton's Stag Saloon then made a ten-dollar bet that he could ride out and drive the sheep off. The bet was enthusiastically covered, of course, and he rode north, locating two Mexican sheepherders. While the cowboy pummeled one of the herders, the other *pastor* ran off to find his boss. The sheepman hurried to the rescue, opening fire on the belligerent cowboy. He succeeded in killing the cowboy's horse and disarming the dumbfounded drover. The sheepman tied up the cowboy, administered a beating with a doubled rope, then untied him and fired several shots to hurry him along. Reportedly, this incident triggered a series of killings and the sheepman finally left the region.[30]

Another killing with an incongruous twist occurred in Terrell County, when a Mexican cowboy warned an Anglo sheepman to drive his flock away from Beaver Lake. The sheepman had no intention of accepting threats from a Mexican, and in the resulting gunfight the cowboy was shot to death. Gunplay somehow was avoided in another incident, when two sheepmen herding a flock were confronted by two cattlemen. All four men pulled out their Winchesters, but after talking over the problem the two sheepmen moved their flock away from the area.

During the early 1890s, the Tippett brothers herded sheep on open range in Fisher, Kent, and Stonewall counties. But when area cattlemen sternly hinted that they remove their sheep from the region, the Tippetts decided to avoid conflict and leave the country. John Caruthers took a bolder course in Scurry County during the 1890s. Cattlemen were riding into sheep camps at night and shooting two or three hundred head, then scattering the flock. But Caruthers told one cattleman that he "would kill every .... who rode into his sheep day or night," and his flocks were not molested.[31]

During a severe drouth in Coleman County in 1893, all the cattle were removed from one stricken ranch. A single cowboy was left behind with orders not to allow any sheep onto the damaged range. One morning, inevitably, he sighted a flock of sheep heading for a receding water hole. The cowboy rode out and confronted two Mexican herders, who did not understand English. He spoke no Spanish, but rounded up the sheep and shoved them through the nearest gate and outside the ranch boundary. It was one of the final abrasive incidents in Texas between cattlemen and sheepmen, and the war long since had been decided in favor of sheep ranchers: in time there were eleven million sheep grazing in Texas.[32]

Even though wool growers had prevailed, and even though sheep raising would remain a vital part of ranching in the Lone Star State, cattlemen did not have to like it. At the turn of the century, Arthur G. Anderson and two Mexican herders drove a large band of sheep into Fort Davis. When Anderson, who once had trailed sheep through the area, inquired about the availability of pasturage, Fort Davis cattlemen deposited him in the "bat cave," a dry cistern beneath the courthouse. The sheepman was dropped through a trap door into the rock-walled room with iron rings set into the stone. A pile of straw provided the dungeon's only furnishing. While Anderson endured medieval incarceration, the Mexican herders kept the flock moving. The sheep owner finally agreed to post a $500 bond and was hauled up through the trap door. Forfeiting his bond, Anderson prudently caught up with his flock and did not return.[33]

Tensions between cattlemen and sheep ranchers existed in Texas from the mid-1870s through the early 1890s, and sporadic violence occurred throughout the period. The fence-cutting war of 1883 produced several violent incidents, and there was another flare-up of violence around 1890. More than 3,200 sheep were killed and one was wounded, while two cowboys were slain in separate incidents (it was also rumored that several other sheepmen were killed).

Before the turn of the century, cattlemen ceased offering resistance to the inexorable spread of sheep ranching across Texas. Although the range cattle industry had originated in Texas, and the Lone Star State would remain a renowned home of the cowboy and of cattle herds, sheep ranching became a prominent part of the Texas economy. Sheep had come to Texas before longhorns had evolved, and after sometimes violent but more often half-hearted resistance by cattlemen, sheep ranchers found ample space on the vast rangelands of Texas.

3

Colorado Conflicts

We'll hang you from your own wagon tongue if you won't leave the country.
— Spokesman for 100 raiders

Problems between sheepmen and cattlemen took place over a longer period of time in Colorado than in any other western commonwealth. The majority of Colorado's troubles occurred in the northwestern quarter of the state, beginning in the mid-1890s. But sheep first were raised in the southern part of Colorado, and inevitably conflicts would arise there with pioneer cattle ranchers.

In 1873, for example, cattlemen of Pueblo County organized and announced that sheep would have to be confined to certain ranges. Sheepmen responded with pluck, holding a meeting on July 20 in Walsenburg, in Huerfano County, located immediately south of Pueblo County. The sheep ranchers issued a strong protest against any arbitrary deadlines and against the cattlemen's organization itself: "If you have not already learned you are now made to understand that wool and mutton are as necessary as 'beef and broad brimmed hats and revolvers.' "[1]

But Colorado cattlemen would do more than simply announce deadlines, as they demonstrated to A. D. Robinson soon after he brought 2,400 head of sheep into Las Animas County, adjacent to both Pueblo and Huerfano counties. One night, after Robinson had penned up his flock, the corral was struck "by eight or ten desperadoes acting in the interest of cattlemen of this county." The raiders stepped into the corral and opened fire point-blank, killing or wounding "quite a number" before opening the gate and scattering the balance of the flock across the countryside.[2]

In 1874 in Bent County, 234 graded Cotswald sheep belonging to Jeremiah Booth were poisoned, and Booth was ordered to leave the country within ten days. That same year, raiders entered the corral of John T. Collier at night and killed all of his imported Merino rams, which were valued at $1,000 apiece.[3]

Cattlemen usually tried to ban sheepmen from public rangelands by claiming prior use, but their hatred of woollies was so virulent that they would resort to violence even when sheep ranchers arrived first. Teofilo Trujillo of Taos, New Mexico, for example, pioneered the San Luis Valley in 1864, bringing in sheep and building a home which included stained glass windows. For two decades, Trujillo stood off Indians and grazed his flocks on the lush grasses of the well-watered valley. Other Mexican-Americans brought in sheep, while a number of Anglos established cattle ranches. With racial lines drawn and the range becoming increasingly crowded, the San Luis Valley was ripe for a classic clash.

In the summer of 1884, when the Trujillo family was away from home, raiders struck the ranch. The Trujillo home was wrecked, the stained glass windows were shattered, and several outbuildings were burned. Then the raiders shot and clubbed Trujillo's sheep, killing or crippling half of his livestock. When Trujillo returned he abandoned his home, taking his surviving sheep and moving his family into the village of San Luis. But his son Pedro made a fresh start on range near Monte Vista, and today Trujillo descendants still live in the lovely valley, where sheep and cattle graze side by side.[4]

While sheepmen of Mexican descent moved flocks into southern Colorado, Anglo cattlemen long had the northern ranges of the state to themselves. Throughout the 1880s, the lower ranges of northwestern Colorado were covered with thick bluestem grass. Every year, thousands of tons of hay were cut without cultivation, while the uncut grass cured under an arid sun and provided winter pasturage. Fat cattle could be rounded up for market during any month of the year without feeding, and herds were trailed into the area from as far away as Texas.

Then a succession of dry years reduced the feed, and the increased numbers of cattle cropped the remaining grass so close that the range was severely damaged. By this time nesters had homesteaded choice sites and fenced off valuable water supplies. "It is hardly to be wondered at, then," commented the Denver *Republican,* "that cattlemen are aroused almost to the fighting point by what they consider the determination of the sheepmen to take what little is left."[5]

When sheep finally appeared, reaction from cattle ranchers would be all the more hostile. On September 10, 1894, raiders struck a sheep camp in Garfield County, wounding herder Carl Brown, then killing 3,800 woollies by driving the flock over a 1,000-foot bluff of Parachute Creek. Another Garfield County raid resulted in the destruction of all but one of a flock of 1,500 sheep.[6]

The worst violence occurred along the Colorado-Wyoming border. As sheep husbandry spread across Wyoming, it was inevitable that flocks would descend into Colorado. Among the first and most persistent sheepmen were Jack, Griff, and George Edwards. Griff had first grazed several hundred head of beeves near Brown's Park, but trouble with his partner caused him to leave the cattle business. For a time the Edwards brothers engaged in wool growing in Australia, but after the winter of 1886–87 they joined the sudden expansion of sheep ranching in southwestern Wyoming, establishing their headquarters at Rock Springs. Cattlemen were sufficiently concerned to call a meeting at the Battle Creek school in Routt County, Colorado, in March 1894, expressing their intention "to give the sheepmen a rub."[7]

By May 1895, the Edwards brothers and other Wyoming sheepmen had banded together 60,000 head of sheep just north of the Colorado-Wyoming line. The plan was to drive these sheep south into Colorado, trailing the animals slowly through Routt County to Wolcott, a station in Eagle County on the Denver and Rio Grande Railroad.

Area cattlemen, aghast at the prospect of tens of thousands of woollies ruining this traditional range, began to assemble in large numbers to offer resistance. On the night of May 19, in a scene reminiscent of Paul Revere, Samuel Prescott, and William Dawes warning colonials that the British were coming, cattlemen rode through the countryside raising the alarm that sheepmen "were contemplating an invasion of the Yampa River cattle ranges." Within a few days 350 cattlemen and cowboys had gathered, and it was estimated that "a force of eight hundred to a thousand men, are holding themselves in readiness."[8]

Sheepmen devised a ruse to test the determination of Colorado cattle ranchers. Early in June an old man in his seventies was sent across the Colorado line, herding 800 of his own ewes. When word reached Hayden in the Yampa River Valley that the expected invasion was beginning, ranchers and cowboys from far and near hurried to the trouble spot. By June 4, about 200 armed riders had congregated in Hayden, with well-stocked chuck wagons from the Two Bar and Sevens ranches providing commissary. Setting out for the headwaters of Fortification Creek, in the Elkhead Mountains about thirty miles northeast of Craig, the cattlemen expected to do battle with a large force of sheepmen. Instead, this formidable expedition encountered merely one septuagenarian sheepherder. Terrified at the approach of an army, the old man fervently vowed to take his flock back into Wyoming as soon as his ewes finished lambing.[9]

Deflated by this anticlimactic event, many of the cowboys tossed their guns into the chuck wagons and meandered back to Hayden. But soon word came that a sheepman named Massey had trailed his flock to public range around Cedar Mountain, near Craig, establishing a base camp with a wagon and a tent. More than 100 riders rode out to confront him, but Massey boldly emphasized that he was on public land and had no intention to leave. Then one cowboy dismounted and pointed Massey's wagon tongue straight into the air.

"Do you see that?" asked the cowboy menacingly. "We'll hang you from your own wagon tongue if you won't leave the country."

Visibly trembling at his obvious danger, Massey agreed to go. Under the glowering eyes of 100 determined cowmen, Massey packed up his camp equipment and drove his flock toward the north.[10]

There were no more incidents during the summer, but Colorado cattlemen kept a line rider patrolling the border country. Although the line rider reported no encounters with sheepmen, two citizens from Craig named Montgomery and Sullivan sighted multitudes of woollies while on a hunting trip. Montgomery and Sullivan went back to Craig empty-handed, claiming that they could find no elk because of all the sheep. It was reported that Jack Edwards had massed 40,000 sheep in ten bands in California Park, just below the Colorado-Wyoming line. Edwards's men told inquiring cattlemen that their boss wanted only "the benefit of the ranges" — he did not intend to drive his sheep through Routt County to Wolcott but would "ship as usual from Rawlins this fall."[11]

Despite the disclaimers of his men, Edwards soon moved large numbers of his sheep across the line to Colorado ranges in upper Routt County. By the spring of 1896 Edwards began constructing shearing pens on Four Mile Creek, thirty miles north of Craig and just below the Colorado-Wyoming border. Edwards also pointedly suggested that he might try to have the state militia called in to protect his range rights. A month later, members of the Snake River Stock Growers' Association, in conjunction with other Routt County cattlemen's organizations, announced that they were "unanimous in their opinion that in all fairness the cattlemen should be left the use of the range within said county." The association resolved that "the sheepmen who have entered sheep, or have threatened to enter them, into Routt County, be requested to withdraw them."[12]

The following month Edwards responded to the cattlemen's "request" by pledging that he would restrict his sheep to the ranges he had used the previous year, and that he would "do all in my power" to prevent "any foreign sheep" from encroaching upon Routt County cattle pastures. Perhaps already planning a move to the Pacific Northwest, Edwards promised to close out his interest in the sheep he held in Routt County before the end of 1899. But the Craig *Courier* editorialized that if Edwards were permitted to run sheep in Routt County for three years, other sheepmen could be expected to bring their flocks. Then the newspaper reported with undisguised outrage: "The Four Mile district presents a sight which will sicken the average stockman. J. G. Edwards has an even thirty thousand head of sheep running in that section. Inactivity of the cattlemen around Slater [is] inexcusable."[13]

Rumors abounded that 125,000 sheep were heading for Slater and California parks. Prodded by this ghastly image — and by the Craig *Courier* — the cattlemen once again moved in force. In mid-June a large band of armed men rode into Slater Park, posted sentries, then descended upon Edwards's sheep camp. Two Mexican herders were cut down by gunfire, then the raiders dismounted and clubbed 300 sheep to death. The sentries intercepted a third herder who had been out of camp when the raiders struck. The terrified herder was directed to bury his dead *compañeros*, then was permitted to leave the camp on horseback. The cattlemen and cowboys pitched their own camp two or three miles away.[14]

The following afternoon Jack Edwards, notified of the attack on his camp, courageously rode alone into Slater Park. He was dragged from his horse and forced to sit on the ground while an ultimatum to remove his sheep was delivered at gunpoint. Edwards agreed to move his ewes out of Colorado. Then, displaying audacious persuasiveness, he extracted a concession permitting him to leave 8,000 wethers in California Park until shipping season in October.

Edwards was allowed to leave without personal harm. But when he failed to move his ewes into Wyoming, three dozen angry cattlemen confronted him a few days later on the banks of Four Mile Creek. Despite his obvious danger, Edwards insisted upon his right to use public range. Although the area is a sagebrush plain, the cattlemen dragged Edwards to a stand of alders beside the creek. The sheepman was blindfolded with a bandana, then his feet and hands were bound. The noose of a lariat was placed around his neck and he was hoisted off his feet. Finally lowered to the ground, Edwards defiantly cursed the mob. He was pulled up again, and as he struggled his features became mottled and a bloody froth came to his lips. When Edwards lost consciousness he again was dropped to the ground. Revived with creek water, he was told that unless he agreed to move the sheep and tear down his shearing pens, he would be hanged again and left to die. Edwards at last promised to remove his sheep and destroy the pens.

But Edwards had no intention of keeping his promise. The sheep stayed and so did his pens, although he did not let himself again fall into the hands of the cattlemen, and issued guns to fifty of his men in case of an armed showdown. By this time Griff Edwards was running sheep in Brown's Park, and Frank Goodman and Charley Sparks were among other sheepmen who brought flocks to the park. Brown's Park is surrounded by towering mountains, but at the bottom a vast, marshy range provided ideal grazing for livestock. Horse and cattle rustlers found Brown's Park an isolated haven from the law, and many small ranchers in the park had built their herds with long loops.

Matt Rash was suspected of rustling by big cattlemen, and in 1900 he would be assassinated by hired gun Tom Horn. But in 1896 Rash was elected president of the newly organized Brown's Park Cattle Association. This association was formed to rid Brown's Park of sheep, and in late December cowboys and cattle ranchers congregated in large numbers at a camp on the Snake River. The men were divided into small companies, each with a captain, and a commander was selected.

When this impressive force broke camp on Christmas Day, seven wagons were necessary to carry supplies and bedrolls.

After pitching camp on the Green River, a detachment of riders was dispatched to order Goodman out of Brown's Park. Although well armed, the riders did not mask themselves, and Goodman refused to be intimidated, stating that he would not vacate the range with his sheep. Taking no action, the riders returned to camp. At the same time, another delegation encountered A. J. Seger, who worked for Griff Edwards, but Seger also stated his intention to stay.

On Sunday, December 27, 1896, the cattlemen's army dispersed to their homes. But their demonstration of unity impressed the sheepmen with the futility of defying such an overwhelming force. One sheep outfit soon moved out and others talked about leaving. Griff Edwards had been through it all before, once being tied to a tree while his flock was slaughtered before his eyes. "In one season he is said to have lost over fourteen thousand sheep," wrote William MacLeod Raine, and apparently Edwards was unwilling to continue running such risks. On January 16, 1897, Edwards published a notice that he was moving his sheep out of Colorado "to stay." Three months later, the pioneer rancher died of a heart attack in Hooper, Nebraska. Frank Goodman disposed of his sheep, and in the fall of 1897 he sold his ranch to Matt Rash.[15]

But Charley Sparks, whose range was north of Brown's Park on the Colorado-Wyoming line, continued to run sheep. And Jack Edwards, despite the recent death of his older brother and his own near-fatal hanging, stubbornly kept his flocks in Routt County. Finally, on his own schedule and terms, Edwards sold out to the Geddes Sheep Company and moved to Oregon. There he bought an interest in a ranch with C. M. Cartwright and J. P. Van Houten. He acquired full ownership of the ranch in 1905, became one of the leading woolgrowers in the Pacific Northwest, and died peacefully in 1945.[16]

Carrying on in the tradition of Jack Edwards, the Geddes Sheep Company promptly placed 2,500 woollies near the winter headquarters of the Sevens cattle ranch. Establishing a base camp on the Little Snake River, the Geddes herders moved their sheep onto previously sacrosanct cattle range.

Routt County cattlemen wasted little time in responding to the challenge. Posting sentries, forty masked riders surrounded the sheep camp at dawn on Wednesday, November 15, 1899. Inside the sheep wagon, foreman Victor Lunis was awakened. He pulled on his trousers and boots, then went outside to investigate. The masked men ordered Lunis to finish dressing and remove his personal belongings, and the Mexican foreman was whipped with a lariat to emphasize the need for haste.

The masked men jerked spokes from the wagon wheels, then set the vehicle on fire. Brandishing wagon spokes, the raiders began clubbing the sheep to death. Lunis was handed a spoke, but when he was observed just tapping the sheep, he was told that if he did not start killing woollies he would himself be killed. As Lunis began clubbing sheep with increased vigor, a sixteen-year-old herder named Candy Sandoval was sent out to round up the Geddes horses. Sandoval wisely did not return to camp, and when the grisly work was completed, Lunis was released unharmed. Nearly 1,000 sheep were destroyed, and the raiders scattered the flock's survivors into the mountains.[17]

The persistent and destructive resistance of Routt County cattlemen subdued area sheepmen, and the next few years passed with little conflict. However, another invasion was inevitable as increasing numbers of sheepmen placed flocks in southern Wyoming and longingly contemplated the cool summer ranges of Colorado only a short drive away.

These ranges proved too attractive for John K. Hart to resist. Hart, who once had worked as a horse wrangler on Ora Haley's Two Bar cattle ranch, first ran sheep with the Cosgriff brothers under a partnership arrangement in the Cow Creek district above Baggs and Savery, Wyoming, about eighty miles north of Craig. But Hart bought the operation for himself, and in 1903 he moved his flocks into Colorado to take advantage of summer pasturage in Big Red and Whiskey parks. Resorting to the successful strategy of the 1890s, Routt County cattlemen and cowboys rode 300 strong and quickly drove Hart's sheep back into Wyoming.

The following summer, however, Hart slipped several bands across the Colorado line, and other sheepmen in southern Wyoming prepared to follow his example. In June, Hart's herders began to distribute their sheep across the heavily timbered area north of Hahn's Park and east of the Little Snake River. The isolated herders were fully aware of the raids of recent years. When two armed riders were sighted by a nervous herder, he immediately pointed his flock north and set his dogs to work. As the fleeing sheep ran through the forest, they hit other bands heading for the cool Colorado ranges. A general stampede ensued, causing many sheep to be crippled as the mixed flocks crashed through fallen timber. More than 25,000 sheep were involved in the wild race for Wyoming. Those animals not killed, crippled, or lost had to be sorted by their owners over a period of several days at the pens located on Savery Creek.

Angry sheepmen blamed Colorado cattlemen for their recent fiasco, although the two riders were never identified (they may have just been hunters) and did not, after all, do anything to precipitate the flight of the flocks. But the Wyoming sheepmen quickly hit upon a means of retaliation for the most recent presumed aggression by Colorado cattle ranchers.

Large numbers of cattle were regularly trailed from ranges in northwestern Colorado to shipping pens in Rawlins, about fifty miles north of the Colorado-Wyoming line, or to the railhead in Wamsutter, forty miles west of Rawlins. Cattle also were unloaded at Rawlins and Wamsutter, then driven to be fattened on Colorado grasslands. This traffic, highly profitable for the Union Pacific Railroad, proceeded to Wamsutter along the so-called Muddy Trail, and to Rawlins by way of the Savery Creek Trail.

But Wyoming sheepmen held vast tracts of land along forty or fifty miles of these trails, having leased alternate railroad sections, which gave them effective control over the public sections in between. The sheepmen decided to turn the tables on the cattlemen, establishing a deadline which would specifically include the Savery Creek and Muddy trails.

The first outfit denied passage was a Two Bar crew which had unloaded 3,500 head of Mexican yearling steers in Rawlins. Passing along the Savery Creek Trail, the thirsty cattle were headed into a meadow of twenty or thirty acres which had numerous springs. The cattle had just started watering when about fifteen heavily armed sheepmen rode up, reinforced by their dogs.

The sheepmen demanded that the cattle be moved out immediately. When the Two Bar men protested that they needed time to water the herd, the spokesman for the sheepmen insisted that his party would move the cattle out if the cowboys would not. "Well," reminisced James Harl Sizer, in charge of the Two Bar outfit, "those yearlings had been chased on the trail and on the train from Chihuahua, Mexico . . . and had had all the 'scare' scared out of them before they reached Rawlins, so now when anything unusual came up, they simply stopped and looked at it, and refused to move, and we knew the devil himself with all his imps couldn't stampede them."[18]

Sizer innocently invited the sheepmen to go ahead and move the herd, whereupon the sheep dogs were loosed on the cattle. But the yearlings merely turned and stared at the dogs. "After several minutes of wasted efforts," recalled Sizer, "they were right where they started, and the sheepmen gave up the idea, but told us to get that stuff out of there as soon as we could, and stay out." The sheepmen warned Sizer not to pass through the area again, and the cowboys perversely let the yearlings water for two hours before finally starting down the trail.

When other Colorado outfits were notified that the Muddy and Savery Creek trails were closed to cattle, ranchers approached Union Pacific officials. The cattlemen demanded that the trails and water holes be made available from Colorado to Rawlins to Wamsutter, or else all cattle shipments would be halted. The railroad had no intention of losing such a profitable business, and quickly facilitated an agreement of passage which headed off a threatening situation.

Many Utah sheepmen regularly wintered in the southern deserts of their state, then trailed their flocks to the forest reserves of western Colorado's high mountains each summer. Colorado cattlemen were increasingly successful at thwarting or at least delaying the intrusions of Utah sheep graziers, but early storms and high water in the fall of 1908 made sheep owners desperate to reach the mountain reserves. Utah sheep owners united to hire a hundred gunmen, then armed their herders and camp tenders. Bunching their bands, they organized their men into advance, flank and rear guards. This forbidding mass marched unchallenged across cattle country into Colorado's forest reserves.[19]

Cattlemen resorted to violence a few years later when sheepmen ignored a deadline in Mesa County, near the Utah border. On May 20, 1909, raiders slaughtered 3,000 sheep near the hamlet of Atchee. Angry sheepmen gathered the next day at Atchee and rode in force to find the raiders, but the county sheriff and several deputies set out from Mack to intercept the sheepmen's posse and a clash was avoided.[20]

Difficulties between cattlemen and sheepmen in Colorado first erupted in the 1870s in the lower part of the state. The most sustained trouble, however, occurred in northwestern Colorado, where cattlemen repeatedly turned out in large numbers to expel sheepmen from Wyoming or Utah. Although the long conflict subsided after 1904, the truce was uneasy, and the final chapter of violence involving Colorado ranchers had not yet been written.

4

Arizona's Pleasant Valley War

The cowboys and sheepmen has [sic] started a quarrel over in Tonto Basin...

— Joseph Fish

Sheep were introduced to Arizona by Coronado in 1540. By the 1600s, Navajo Indians had demonstrated a special affinity for sheep husbandry. Sheep ranching among Anglos began to spread substantially during the 1870s. Drought brought large flocks from California into western Arizona, while migratory bands from New Mexico entered eastern Arizona in search of seasonal forage. The introduction of railroads further stimulated the sheep industry, and wool mills appeared in Arizona. Sheepmen organized the Arizona Sheep Breeders and Wool Growers Association at Flagstaff on October 1, 1886. Flagstaff emerged as a headquarters for sheepmen, including the Daggs brothers, who eventually ran 50,000 head of sheep on Arizona ranges.[1]

Cattlemen inevitably resented the intrusion of sheep, and old-time Arizonans vociferously deplored "the devastation that always results upon the range that is grazed by sheep." In 1881 D. A. Stanford, who owned a large cattle ranch in southern Arizona, foreclosed a mortgage he held on 13,000 head of sheep owned by Tully, Ochoa, and DeLong of Tucson. At that early time, sheep were far scarcer than cattle and, therefore, brought excellent prices. Stanford directed his foreman, John Cady, to sell off his cattle and turn the 13,000 sheep onto his range. Neighboring cattle ranchers immediately sent Cady an ultimatum to remove the sheep, but Cady replied that he took orders only from Stanford. Soon Stanford's sheep began to be killed or driven off, and his herders were shot at from concealment. Although Cady had been close friends with most of the area ranchers, he reported that "several times I myself narrowly escaped death." Three years later, Stanford finally sold the sheep. "I am glad to say," reminisced Cady, "that most of these cattlemen and cowboys, who, when I ran sheep, would cheerfully have been responsible for my funeral, are very good friends at the present time."[2]

Riders on the immense Hash Knife cattle ranch pressured sheepherders in northeastern Arizona. On one occasion, Hash Knife cowboys rode into a sheep camp just as the herders were sitting down to breakfast. At Winchester point, the cowboys forced the sheepherders to break camp immediately, laughing "with glee at their futile attempts to pack a red-hot sheet-iron stove on the back of an unwilling broncho."[3]

In 1884 cattlemen raided a sheep camp on the Little Colorado River. The herders were tied to trees, then the raiders drove 4,000 sheep into the river. Next the cattlemen wrecked the camp, killed the pack animals, and hazed the sheepherders out of the country. That same year, north of Flagstaff, ten bands, totaling 25,000 sheep, had been placed on range near the San Francisco peaks. More than 100 wild horses were stampeded into the sheep; long rawhides had been attached to the horses' tails, and about twenty animals were spooked by large cowbells hung around their necks. Although the herders tried to turn the galloping horses with rifle fire, hundreds of sheep were crippled or killed, and it took several days to separate the bands.[4]

Will C. Barnes was a Californian who enlisted in the army in 1879 and was stationed at Fort Apache, Arizona. He received the Medal of Honor and earned promotion to sergeant, but he took a medical discharge in 1883 to become a cattle rancher near Holbrook. Already "these woolly pests were overrunning the ranges up the [Little Colorado] River to the East." Four bands on each side of the river "were advancing like an invading army" on a front ten miles wide.[5]

Barnes was told of several clashes between sheepmen and cattlemen that already had occurred; of hundreds of sheep killed and injured; of sheep camps shot up and herders beaten. But the sheepmen fought back. Cattle were shot and men were killed on both sides. "To run onto a sheep camp in the cedars meant a volley from the sheepmen's rifles," recalled Barnes.[6]

Barnes knew of a sheepherder who had been caught butchering a steer in a cedar thicket. The cattlemen started to hang him, but the herder begged so piteously for his life that they merely administered "a fearful whipping with their ropes." Not satisfied with such leniency, the cattlemen decided to earmark their victim as an example to other sheepherders. With a sharp knife they notched each ear with an overbit, then told the sheepman to leave the country. Two years later he came back, with long hair covering his mutilated ears. He showed his ears to a lawyer, who notified the cattlemen of his intention to file suit. The cattlemen were advised by counsel to settle out of court to avoid criminal charges, and the sheepherder received a settlement of $10,000.[7]

"Of course I took a lively part in the struggle," admitted Barnes, "and did my full share to stop the onward advance of the herds. But all in vain . . . nothing turned them from their course."[8] Before the sheepmen prevailed, however, Barnes would witness Arizona's bloodiest range war — a vicious feud triggered when sheep were introduced to isolated Pleasant Valley.

* * *

Even today Pleasant Valley is difficult to reach, accessible only by two rough, precipitous dirt roads. A century ago Pleasant Valley was even more remote: the nearest settlement was 100 miles away, and to the south the Sierra Anchas long provided a stronghold for hostile Apaches. To the north, the Mogollon Rim looms spectacularly over the valley. Indeed, in every direction Pleasant Valley, also known as the Tonto Basin, is surrounded by mountains and peaks. The rugged terrain boasts luxuriant grasslands, though, and water is abundantly supplied by Cherry Creek, Tonto Creek, and other bubbling streams. By the 1870s, cattlemen had found their way into Pleasant Valley, establishing an arbitrary deadline at the Mogollon River. Some of the early settlers were rustlers, and other wanted men gravitated to the wild, isolated Tonto Basin.[9]

In 1882 John D. Tewksbury brought his family into Pleasant Valley. Born in Massachusetts, Tewksbury had ventured to California during the gold rush. He took an Indian wife who bore him three sons, John, James, and Edwin. When Tewksbury turned up in Globe about 1880, attracted by a silver and copper boom, his boys were grown but his wife had died. In Globe he married a widow, Englishwoman Lydia Crigler Shutes, by whom he sired two more sons. A lifelong pioneer who always sought wide-open frontiers, Tewksbury and his three grown sons built a cabin on the east side of Cherry Creek. They hunted, tended a small herd of cattle, and occasionally butchered one of the half-wild hogs they had brought with them.

At about the same time, the Graham brothers established a cattle ranch on the west side of Cherry Creek, about ten miles northwest of the Tewksbury cabin. Tom and John Graham had left the family's Iowa farm in the 1870s, spending a few years in California before moving on to Arizona. Like the Tewksburys, the Grahams were in Globe briefly before landing at Pleasant Valley, where they were joined by their younger half brother, Bill Graham.

One of the first cattlemen to take advantage of Pleasant Valley grasslands was Jim Stinson, who built his headquarters in 1880. Two years later the Graham cabin and corrals went up not far to the north, and the Graham boys soon were riding for Stinson. Stinson also employed the Tewksburys to help tend his growing herd.

The Grahams and Tewksburys, utilizing long ropes and branding irons in creative fashion, soon began to add Stinson cattle to their little herds. William and perhaps Tom Graham[10] were indicted for larceny in 1882 and 1883, but they were acquitted when witnesses failed to appear. In 1884 the Grahams charged the Tewksburys and three of their associates with stealing ten head of cattle. The territorial court in Prescott returned two indictments of grand larceny against Edwin, James, and John Tewksbury, George Blaine, William Richards, and W. H. Bishop. These same men also were charged with stealing 100 head of cattle from Jim Stinson. The defendants were cleared of all charges, but a deep enmity had developed between the Grahams and Tewksburys.

Persistent rumors further contended that trouble over a woman aggravated the growing bitterness. Dane Coolidge was told that one of the Graham men began openly sharing affections with a Tewksbury wife. Coolidge also heard that the Grahams "had a color prejudice against the Tewksburys, some of whom were very dark."[11]

Hard feelings increased, and the threat of violence grew between strong-minded men nursing grudges in a remote and lawless locale. In 1886 Jim Stinson's foreman, John Gilliland, encountered Ed Tewksbury while searching for missing livestock. Gilliland, of course, suspected the Tewksburys of stealing Stinson stock, and said as much.

Tewksbury snapped out a harsh denial. There was another exchange of words, then an exchange of shots. Gilliland caught a slug through the leg but managed to flee to safety.

Not long after this skirmish, the Tewksburys were approached by the Daggs brothers with a proposition that would provide the spark which would detonate the Pleasant Valley War. The Daggs brothers, hard-pressed by the Hash Knife and stymied by the lack of suitable winter grazing for their vast flocks, hoped to move past the deadline of the Mogollon River onto the protected grasslands of the Tonto Basin.

The hard-bitten Tewksburys were asked to introduce a flock of sheep into Pleasant Valley. The Daggs brothers felt that if anyone could protect sheep in Pleasant Valley it would be the Tewksburys. The Tewksbury brothers were offered shares of all sheep brought into the valley, and plans were discussed to place great numbers of woollies throughout the Tonto Basin. The Tewksburys realized that sufficient numbers of sheep could crowd cattle out of the valley, thus producing immense profits and providing a delicious measure of revenge against Stinson and the Grahams. Hard feelings had been present for years in Pleasant Valley, but not until sheep were introduced would the tensions explode into one of the West's most notorious range wars.

The Tewksburys hired a Basque herder to tend the first flock.[12] In February 1887 the sheepherder was riddled by gunfire, and the murderers' trail led to the Graham ranch. Soon after the killing, the sheep were driven out of Pleasant Valley. The Tewksburys, already prevented from rustling Stinson stock, now would lose anticipated profits from Daggs sheep. Resentment must have turned into blood lust for the Tewksburys.

"Old Man" Mart Blevins evidently became the second casualty in the burgeoning range war. His ranch on Canyon Creek was an acknowledged haunt for rustlers. During the past year or two, a horse-stealing ring had developed with Andy "Cooper," the son of Mart Blevins, as a key leader. (Will Barnes and others stated that Cooper was a half brother to the Blevins boys, but solid evidence exists that in earlier years he killed a man in Texas and "changed his name to avoid detection."[13]) Operating from northern Mexico to Colorado, the gang especially liked to hit Mormon freighting trains, because the Mormons had "unusually fine teams." The Canyon Creek ranch was a central rendezvous point, where brands were altered, manes docked, tails thinned out, and tracks obliterated. Will C. Barnes, who once trailed stolen horses to the Blevins ranch, stated that others who had looked for missing animals had been beaten with ropes, turned back with warnings, or ambushed and killed.[14]

Andy Cooper not only was the ringleader at Canyon Creek, he also was a major force in opposing sheep in the Tonto Basin.[15] Old Man Blevins, however, undoubtedly was involved in the illegal activities at Canyon Creek and was identified with Cooper's anti-sheep stance. In the summer of 1887, while searching for missing stock, Old Man Blevins disappeared. Presumably he was waylaid and killed in the wilds of the Tonto Basin, and it was natural to assume that the Tewksburys were responsible.[16]

In early August, Hamp Blevins rounded up a crew of combative riders to search for his father. Texan John Paine was eager to go; he lived with his family at Four Mile Spring in Navajo County, and he had been assigned by the Hash Knife to keep sheep away from the area. Tom Tucker, a big, affable Hash Knife cowboy, also joined Blevins. Five other men who rode for the Hash Knife or the Grahams agreed to go.

On August 3, Hamp Blevins finished gathering his search party at a summer roundup camp at Big Dry Lake, about thirty miles south of Holbrook. They borrowed all of the surplus ammunition in camp, engaged in "medicine talks" all night, and stated their intention to "start a little war of our own." Will C. Barnes and Hash Knife foreman Ed Rogers tried to talk them out of looking for trouble, but the party rode out at dawn.[17]

A week later, on Wednesday afternoon, August 10, Blevins and his seven companions rode up to a loop-holed cabin on what was known as Middleton Creek. A rancher named Middleton had brought one of the first cattle herds into the Tonto Basin in the mid-1870s, but on August 10, 1887, Jim and Ed Tewksbury were the occupants of the old Middleton cabin, along with Jim Roberts and other cohorts. Roberts raised horses on a little spread under the Rim at the head of Tonto Creek. He had lost several horses, including a prized stallion, and he assumed that the Grahams or the Cooper gang had been responsible. Roberts would prove to be an expert gunman and a determined fighting man.

Blevins and the seven cowboys approached the cabin late in the afternoon. Jim Tewksbury appeared in the doorway and there was a tense exchange of words. Tucker swung his horse to lead the others away.

Suddenly, a volley of gunfire exploded from the cabin. Hamp

Blevins pitched out of the saddle, a bullet in his brain. John Paine snapped off a shot at Jim Tewksbury, then tumbled to the ground as his horse collapsed from a gunshot. Jim Roberts triggered a rifle bullet that clipped off Paine's ear. The Texan scrambled to his feet and tried to sprint away, but Jim Tewksbury felled him with another rifle slug.[18]

Bob Gillespie was wounded in the buttocks as he spurred away from the cabin, while Bob Carrington was struck in the right arm and right leg. Tom Tucker caught a bullet under the left arm which tore out through his other armpit. Five of the eight riders had been hit by the fusillade, and two were dead. The survivors galloped away.

Tucker soon toppled off his horse and passed out. During the night he was roused by a chilling rain and hailstorm, and he crawled for a couple of hours while blowflies and maggots worked on his wound. Finally he reached the cabin of Bob Sigsby, who soaked the wound with creosote dip. Tucker stayed with Sigsby until his wound healed, then he rode out of Pleasant Valley under the cover of darkness. Tucker and Bob Gillespie returned to the roundup camp at Big Dry Lake, Gillespie sitting his saddle sideways in deference to his hip wound. The two wounded warriors stayed with their old outfit just one night, heading out at dawn for New Mexico. "When I crossed the line into New Mexico . . .," related Tucker to Will C. Barnes, "I headed straight for the old Rio Grande and never again had any hankering to see Arizona."[19]

Back in Pleasant Valley the Tewksburys, with only a handful of fighting men to counter large numbers of cowboys and rustlers, took to the wilderness. Moving from one mountain camp to another, they eluded Graham riders led by a bloodthirsty Andy Cooper and a posse brought down from Prescott by Sheriff William Mulvenon. Mulvenon entered Pleasant Valley with ten warrants for the Tewksburys "and others of their gang." The elusive Tewksburys were nowhere to be found, but the posse encountered the Grahams and Andy Cooper. The sheriff was told that if the posse did not arrest the Tewksburys, the Grahams "intended to take matters into their own hands and make war upon them until they were exterminated or driven from the country."[20]

But the Tewksburys, half-Indians who had spent their lives on the frontier, were at their best at guerrilla warfare. One moonlit night several cowboys crept toward the Tewksbury camp, but one of their number was spotted by Ed Tewksbury. Jim whirled and fired, breaking the man's leg. The other would-be attackers could not move for fear of discovery, and reportedly their wounded comrade bled to death.[21]

Bill Graham, twenty-two-year-old half brother of Tom and John, was the next man to fall in Pleasant Valley. Riding the trail from the Graham ranch to the hamlet of Payson, he encountered Deputy Sheriff Jim Houck, a Tewksbury partisan. There was an exchange of shots, and Graham was badly wounded. He managed to stay in the saddle as his horse carried him three and a half miles back to the ranch. Although nursed by his family, Bill Graham died, and the range war triggered by the presence of sheep became a family vendetta between the Grahams and Tewksburys.[22]

Tom and John Graham, accompanied by Andy Cooper and several other vengeance-seeking riders, went in search of the Tewksburys. The Tewksbury men had returned to the family cabin on Cherry Creek. On Friday morning, September 2, the Graham party crept toward the Tewksbury home. Breakfast already had been served and Ed Tewksbury was repairing his cartridge belt. Outside, John Tewksbury and Bill Jacobs, while going for their horses, were caught in the open about a mile from the cabin.

Jacobs was the sheepherder thought to have led the Daggs brothers' first flock into Pleasant Valley. As soon as the unsuspecting Jacobs and Tewksbury came close to the concealed gunmen, a deadly fusillade hurled both men to the ground. John Tewksbury and Bill Jacobs died within sight of the cabin. Two days later, Andy Cooper would boast that he had shot both men.[23]

The gunmen closed in on the ranch but were driven back by return fire. Ed and Jim were inside the cabin, along with their father, now infirm, and the newly widowed Mrs. John Tewksbury, and, perhaps, the redoubtable Jim Roberts. The cabin's defenders promptly forted up, while the attackers dug in within sniping range.

During the ensuing siege a drove of hogs wandered to the bodies. Within full view of the cabin, the grunting hogs began to root at the corpses. The attackers did not train their gunfire on the hogs but kept the defenders pinned inside the cabin as the bodies were torn apart. A persistent story has a distraught Mrs. Tewksbury dashing out to the bodies with shovel in hand, digging graves while the besiegers chivalrously ceased firing. However, a contemporary newspaper account and Will C. Barnes both related that the Tewksburys slipped away and the Graham party pulled out with the mangled bodies still in the open.

Later, Justice of the Peace John Meadows and other citizens rode from Payson to the scene of battle to hold an inquest. "All we did," reminisced Meadows, "was dig two very shallow graves and roll the swollen, mutilated bodies into them with our shovels."[24]

After the fight, Andy Cooper rode to his mother's home in Holbrook. The three-room frame house still stands (altered and enlarged) north of the railroad tracks which bisected Holbrook's broad main street in 1887. Just east of the little house was Armbruster's blacksmith shop. West of the house was a dwelling with thick stone walls, and further to the west stood Brown and Kinder's livery stable. Also to the west and adjacent to the tracks on the south stood the railroad depot. South of the tracks was a line of structures which made up Holbrook's modest commercial block: Frank Wattron's drug store, two or three mercantiles, a post office, and a few saloons.

Mrs. Mary Blevins had two surviving sons with her in Holbrook: John Blevins, who was in his early twenties, and young Sam Houston Blevins, who has been variously described as twelve to sixteen years of age. A brother-in-law, Mose Roberts, was present, and so were daughter-in-law Eva Blevins, Mrs. Amanda Gladden, and her nine-year-old daughter Beatrice.

Andy Cooper rode into Holbrook on Sunday morning, September 4, 1887. He turned in his horse at the livery stable, visited the Blevins house, then sauntered across the street to talk to several men standing in front of the post office. Cooper crowed that he had killed two men in a fight down in the valley on Friday, and he told Frank Wattron that he would never surrender to a law officer.

On March 26, 1886, a warrant had been issued for the arrest of Cooper for stealing thirty or forty horses belonging to Navajo Indians. But Cooper was widely regarded as a dangerous man, and no effort had been made to serve the warrant — until Commodore Perry Owens became county sheriff.

Born in Tennessee in 1852 and named after a naval hero of the War of 1812, Owens left home as a teenager to become a cowboy. After spending a decade chasing cows in Texas, he drifted into Arizona as a stage station employee, then started a horse ranch at Navajo Springs. Hired by a railroad contractor to guard a horse herd, Owens was rushed by a band of renegade Indians who intended to start a stampede. But Owens, who usually carried a brace of .45s and two rifles, drove them off by fatally wounding two of the would-be rustlers. The fame he garnered from this incident enabled him to win election as sheriff of Apache County in the fall of 1886. Sheepman Sam Brown, who served as chairman of the county's Democratic committee, and Holbrook druggist Frank Wattron successfully pushed Owens as the man to lead a campaign against rustlers and other troublemakers.

Sheriff Owens cut a colorful figure. He wore his hair very long, in the fashion of old-time plainsmen. Armed to the teeth, he holstered his long-barreled revolvers butts forward, for a readier draw while in the saddle. Owens could produce a gun with either hand "with wonderful speed," and he could keep a tin can rolling on the ground by shooting alternately from both hands at a distance of twenty feet.[25]

The new sheriff took to his saddle and soon hounded one band of rustlers out of the county. On several occasions he stopped after dark — and rode out before dawn — at the ranch of W. J. Flake, and they understood that Owens now had taken aim at the "Cooper-Graham bunch."[26]

But the Apache County Board of Commissioners impatiently pressed Owens to serve the longstanding warrant on Andy Cooper. The sheriff was summoned before the board and asked why the warrant had not been served. When Owens stated that he had been unable to locate Cooper, board member Will C. Barnes, an old range acquaintance of Owens, said that he had seen the rustler ride into Holbrook just two days earlier. A "rather lively session" ensued, during which there was the threat of gunplay. The board instructed Owens that if he failed to arrest Cooper within ten days, proceedings would be initiated to oust him from office for failure to perform his official duties.[27]

A few days later, on Sunday, September 4, Barnes was working out of a roundup camp about ten miles north of Holbrook. Sheriff Owens rode up to the chuck wagon, had a cup of coffee and talked with roundup boss Albert Potter, then headed on toward Holbrook. Potter rode out to Barnes and told him that the sheriff was going to Holbrook to arrest Andy Cooper. Expecting an exciting showdown, Barnes immediately threw his saddle on a fresh horse from the remuda and galloped cross-country into town. He unsaddled at his little house in Holbrook at midafternoon, then hurried uptown just as Owens rode in. Barnes went to the depot and took a ringside seat, settling on a bench on the platform with a clear view of the Blevins house.[28]

Owens went to Brown and Kinder's livery stable, put up his horse, then crossed the street to Wattron's drug store. In the meantime, Cooper spotted Owens and asked John Blevins to bring his horse to the house. Blevins tied the bay to a tree in front of the house. Owens returned to the livery stable to pull his Winchester from its saddle scabbard. He checked his guns and left instructions for his horse to be ready. Frank Wattron and several other men emerged from the drug store and hurried over to join Will Barnes on the depot platform.

Cooper, busy saddling his horse, ducked back into the house when Owens came out of the livery stable. Owens approached the house with his Winchester cradled in his arms. He stepped up on the porch and knocked on the door to his right.

Gripping a revolver, Cooper opened the door a few inches. Owens announced that he held an arrest warrant, and Cooper asked for a few minutes to get ready. But when Cooper tried to shut the door he found that the sheriff had slipped his boot into the opening. Owens then swung his rifle up and fired a shot which plowed through the door and ripped into Cooper's stomach.

Owens leaped back off the porch, levering another cartridge into the chamber of his Winchester. John Blevins opened the other door and snapped off a revolver bullet which missed Owens but struck Cooper's horse between the eyes. The stricken animal pulled his reins from the tree, bolted up the street about a hundred feet, then dropped dead.

Blevins slammed the door shut, but Owens quickly fired from the hip. The Winchester bullet crashed through the door and caught Blevins in the shoulder. Spotting movement through the front window to his right, Owens threw another cartridge into the chamber and peered inside. Still clutching his revolver, Cooper was looking for Owens, but the sheriff fired a third round. Struck again, this time in the hip, the mortally wounded Cooper collapsed into his mother's arms.

Young Sam Houston Blevins snatched up Andy's revolver and bolted onto the porch. Cursing Owens, the boy cocked the sixgun. Owens's Winchester cracked once more, driving a bullet through the boy's body at the hips.

Mose Roberts crawled through a window on the east side of the house. He intended to hit Owens from the flank, but the sheriff heard the noise, darted to his right, and drilled Roberts through the chest with his fifth round. Roberts staggered to the rear of the house and stumbled through the kitchen door.

When no one else came after him, Owens turned toward the livery stable to retrieve his horse. Led by Justice of the Peace A. F. Banta, several spectators ran across the tracks to Owens. "Have you finished the job?" asked Banta.[29]

"I think I have," said Owens understatedly. The sheriff led his horse out of the stable, mounted up, and left town.

The Blevins house was a shambles. Blood was everywhere, and crying women frantically worked to patch up the wounded. Sam Houston Blevins died within half an hour, and Cooper would die that night. Roberts would last several days before dying, while John Blevins managed to recover from his wound.

Two days after the battle, Sheriff Owens returned to Holbrook to testify at Cooper's inquest. John Blevins and Mrs. Mary Blevins were among the other witnesses, but after the coroner's jury decided to "fully exhonerate {sic}" Owens, John was taken under arrest to the county jail at Saint Johns. Charged with assault with intent to murder, his trial was delayed a year; although convicted and sentenced to serve five years at Yuma Territorial Penitentiary, he apparently was pardoned by the governor.[30]

Citizens were relieved and pleased to see drastic action taken against outlawry and anarchy in the region. The Saint Johns *Herald* reported that when Frank Reed of Holbrook "raised a cry against Owens" on the day of the shooting, the populace told him "to 'cheese' his racket."

"Too much credit cannot be given to Sheriff Owens in this lamentable affair," praised the *Herald,* which stated that the lawman was supported by virtually "every man, woman, and child in town." The only other newspaper then published in northern Arizona, the Coconino *Sun,* also lauded Owens, pointing out that his victims "were all desperate characters who made a practice of killing anyone who stood in the pathway of their crimes, and openly boasted of their murderous deeds afterwards."[31]

Owens had provided one of the most sensational displays of marksmanship under fire in the history of the Old West. Within a single action-packed moment he fired five rounds, felling four adversaries and earning a special niche in the gunfighters' hall of fame. An admiring Will C. Barnes reported that when Owens returned the warrant to the Apache County clerk, he had written simply: "Party against whom this warrant was issued was killed while resisting arrest."[32]

The scene of hostilities soon shifted back to Pleasant Valley. On Friday, September 16, a fight took place on the Tewksbury ranch. The Tewksbury brothers and Jim Roberts drove a party of Graham riders away, wounding Harry Middleton and Joe Underwood. The cowboys rode back to the Graham ranch, where Middleton died. Shot below the knee, Underwood later found medical care at the San Carlos Indian Reservation and recovered.[33]

In Prescott, Territorial Governor C. Meyer Zulick met with Sheriff William Mulvenon and District Attorney John C. Herndon on September 7. Mulvenon was instructed to sweep the feud district with a large posse, arresting any members of either faction who could be found. The sheriff wired a deputy in Flagstaff to meet him in Payson with as many men as he could deputize, then Mulvenon departed for the Tonto Basin with several deputies.[34]

On September 20 about twenty officers congregated at Payson. That night Sheriff Mulvenon and his posse took possession of the Perkins store, a low stone structure built during the Apache threats of the early 1880s (the building stones came from ancient Indian structures). Perkins was in the process of adding a residence to his store; the incomplete stone walls were five or six feet high. Today the building serves as a dwelling, and the loopholes are still visible. In 1887 the store was in sight of the Graham ranch house.

The following morning, John Graham and Charley Blevins rode over to the store. Sheriff Mulvenon stepped from behind a corner of the building, cradling a double-barreled shotgun. He informed Graham and Blevins that they were under arrest, but the two men wheeled their mounts and reached for their revolvers.

Mulvenon triggered the shotgun, killing Graham's horse. An instant later a volley from posse members stationed behind the stone walls felled both Graham and Blevins. Blevins was dead when he hit the ground, joining his father and brothers as casualties of the Pleasant Valley War. Graham, shot through the body, asked for water but breathed his last within two hours.[35]

The sheriff led his men toward the Graham house. Two riders galloped off to the northeast, and a terrified woman emerged from the house, holding an infant while a child clutched her skirt. The woman stated that only a Mexican named Miguel Apocada and her husband, the wounded Joe Underwood, were inside the house. Mulvenon arrested Apocada, then proceeded to the nearby cabin of Al Rose, a Graham partisan.

After taking Rose into custody, Mulvenon led his posse south to the Tewksbury ranch. Ed and Jim Tewksbury were present, along with Jim Roberts and four other men, and the entire group surrendered peacefully to Mulvenon. As Mulvenon headed toward Prescott with his prisoners, Sheriff C. P. Owens descended into the valley with an even larger posse.³⁶ Owens divided thirty deputies into two patrols, but this sweep turned up no new prisoners, and Mulvenon's captives either were discharged or released on bond.

The surviving faction members had soon returned to Pleasant Valley. Al Rose was killed from ambush, but his murder did not cause a new outbreak of violence. The unprecedented presence of big posses and the interruption of combat served to bring the combatants to their senses. Tom Graham, who had eluded arrest, turned up in Tempe in October to marry Anne Melton, seventeen-year-old daughter of a Baptist preacher. After the wedding the thirty-three-year-old feud leader turned himself in to authorities in Prescott, but he was released on bond and took his wife into Pleasant Valley.

When the grand jury convened in Prescott in December 1887, the principal members of both factions came to town armed to the teeth. Sheriff Mulvenon stationed a platoon of deputies around town, and many townspeople armed themselves as a precaution. But there was no violence as the grand jury indicted Ed and Jim Tewksbury, Jim Roberts, and four other men for the murder of Hamp Blevins on August 10. When the case came to trial in June 1888, however, witnesses — fearful for their safety — were reluctant to testify, and charges were dismissed. Legal action against the Grahams in Saint Johns, seat of Apache County, proved similarly indecisive.

On August 12, 1888, Jim Stott, Billy Wilson, and Jim Scott were lynched on the Verde trail. Although Stott had a horse ranch on the rim of the Mogollons, Will C. Barnes stated flatly that the triple murder "had absolutely no connection with the Pleasant Valley troubles of the year before."³⁷ But Jim Houck, an Apache County deputy sheriff who ran a band of sheep around a water hole called Houck's Tank, had been heard to boast that he "intended to run his sheep on Stott's ranch."³⁸

Houck claimed that Stott, Wilson, and Scott were guilty of two sniping incidents, and he arrested them. Near Stott's ranch, Houck and his small posse were confronted by a large band of masked men who seized the prisoners and hanged them. Although no legal action was taken in the wake of the lynching, considerable blame was placed on Houck, and Earle Forrest speculated that he may have grazed his sheep on Stott's now-deserted ranch.³⁹

By 1888 Jim Tewksbury was seriously ill from a long struggle with consumption. Hard hit by an attack of measles, he died late in the year at his sister's home in Globe. Ed Tewksbury and Tom Graham

> **CASUALTY LIST: THE PLEASANT VALLEY WAR**
>
> *Basque sheepherder (first fatality, February 1887)*
> *Andy {Cooper} Blevins (September 4, 1887)*
> *Charley Blevins (September 21, 1887)*
> *Hamp Blevins (August 10, 1887)*
> *John Blevins (wounded, September 4, 1887)*
> *Mart Blevins (July 1887)*
> *Sam Houston Blevins (September 4, 1887)*
> *Bob Carrington (wounded, August 10, 1887)*
> *John Gilliland (wounded, 1886)*
> *Bob Gillespie (wounded, August 10, 1887)*
> *Bill Graham (August 17, 1887)*
> *John Graham (September 21, 1887)*
> *Tom Graham (August 2, 1892)*
> *Graham rider (August 1887)*
> *Bill Jacobs (September 2, 1887)*
> *Harry Middleton (September 16, 1887)*
> *John Paine (August 10, 1887)*
> *Mose Roberts (September 4, 1887)*
> *Al Rose (October 1887)*
> *John Tewksbury (September 2, 1887)*
> *Tom Tucker (wounded, August 10, 1887)*
> *Joe Underwood (wounded, September 16, 1887)*
> *Jim Scott (August 12, 1888)*
> *Jim Stott (August 12, 1888)*
> *Billy Wilson (August 12, 1888)*
>
> Widespread rumors contended that several men were shot from ambush during the range war or as a result of lingering enmities. The most likely candidates were Tewksbury partisan Jacob Laufler (wounded from ambush on August 4, 1888) and George A. Newton (disappeared in September 1891), as well as a man named Elliott (killed in Pleasant Valley in 1887 or 1888) and Horace Philly (slain shortly after the murder of Tom Graham in 1892).

now were the only fighting members of the feuding families still in Pleasant Valley. Although there was no further violence, Tewksbury and Graham remained in the valley, each stubbornly reluctant to abandon the range that had cost so many lives. But in 1889, Graham's wife became pregnant. Tom arranged with S. W. Young to work his cattle on shares, and he moved his wife to a farm near Tempe, where a daughter soon was born.

Ed Tewksbury made no further attempt to bring sheep into the

Tonto Basin. The Pleasant Valley War had been too vicious, and Tewksbury did not risk again arousing the wrath of cattlemen. A prominent citizen stated that sheep bands passed through Pleasant Valley along Cherry Creek after the range war ended, although transient flocks were "turned back from the upper Salt River Valley and from the lower Tonto Creek ranges by determined cattlemen."[40] In 1892 Tom Graham returned to his old Pleasant Valley ranch to join a roundup which would divide his growing herd with Young. Graham drove his share of the herd to Tempe.

On August 2, 1892, an unarmed Tom Graham was shot in the back from ambush while hauling a wagonload of grain from his farm to Tempe. Graham died a few hours later, after telling his wife and several friends that the bushwhackers were Ed Tewksbury and John Rhodes. Twelve-year-old Ed Cummings witnessed the shooting, and also identified Tewksbury and Rhodes, stating that Rhodes fired the fatal shot.

Pursuers overtook Rhodes after a chase of ten miles, but Tewksbury galloped to safety, only to be arrested on August 5. Rhodes was arraigned before Justice of the Peace W. O. Huson and an angry crowd. On the day when Ed Cummings and two other children testified that they had seen Tewksbury and Rhodes hiding in the brush, Anne Graham was sitting behind Rhodes in the courtroom. The young widow suddenly produced her husband's .44-caliber revolver from her umbrella, pointed the muzzle at Rhodes's back, and pulled the trigger. The gun misfired, however, and Anne was seized. (Earle Forrest was told that Ed Cummings's mother had removed the cartridges before Anne Graham went to court.)[41]

"Let me shoot him, for God's sake, let me shoot him," Anne had screamed. Taken out of the room, she shouted, "Let me kill him, let me kill him; they will turn him loose."[42]

Her prediction proved accurate. Defense lawyers presented a convincing alibi, and charges against Rhodes were dismissed on August 19. Disgusted onlookers called for the recall of Huson, but Rhodes became a free man.

Tewksbury was tried in Tucson and, despite his claims that he was in the Tonto Basin on the day of the murder, he was convicted of homicide. But his lawyers obtained a new trial on a technicality, and when the second jury could not reach agreement, he was released on bail in February 1895. All charges were dismissed in March 1896.

Ed Tewksbury (who was the model for the Last Man of Zane

Grey's famous novel about the range war) returned to Pleasant Valley and a ranch that had been neglected for years. Tewksbury sold his holdings and moved to Globe, where he served as town constable and Gila County deputy sheriff. Having contracted tuberculosis during his incarceration, he died in 1904.

Commodore Perry Owens found that he had intimidated voters when he gunned down four men in Holbrook. Failing to win reelection, he found employment as a railroad detective and as an express messenger for Wells Fargo. In 1900 he became a merchant in Seligman, married two years later, and died in 1918. John Blevins was bothered throughout the rest of his life by the wound he had received from Sheriff Owens. He dropped out of sight after the Pleasant Valley War but surprised old acquaintances by turning up at a celebration in Flagstaff on July 4, 1926. Later he was fatally injured while riding in an automobile driven by his granddaughter; the vehicle tumbled over an embankment near Phoenix.

Jim Roberts came out of the range war widely respected as a fighting man. Sheriff Buckey O'Neill appointed Roberts a deputy sheriff of Yavapai County in 1889. Three years later he was elected constable of the Jerome precinct, and following eleven years on the job he won election as Jerome's town marshal. After cleaning up the mining town, he was employed in nearby Clarkdale as a special officer for the United Verde Copper Company. Working under a deputy sheriff's commission and carrying his old Colt .45 on his hip, he presided over the peaceful community for the rest of his life.

In June 1928, Willard Forrester and Earl Nelson wheeled up in an automobile to Clarkdale's branch of the Bank of Arizona. Inside the thieves held fifteen citizens at bay, scooped up $50,000, and dashed out to their car. As they sped away the bank manager fired two shots at the car. Jim Roberts, then seventy years of age, stepped off the sidewalk, thumbed back the hammer of his single-action Colt, and drilled the driver — Forrester — through the brain. The getaway automobile careened into a school and Nelson jumped out, firing wildly at Roberts. The old gunfighter gave chase and threw down on the would-be bank robber, who meekly surrendered. The last of the Pleasant Valley warriors died of a heart attack while still patrolling the streets of Clarkdale in 1934.[43]

During the 1880s in Arizona, a growing number of violent incidents had occurred between cattlemen and sheepmen. The conflict crested with the explosion of warfare in the Tonto Basin. The Pleasant

Valley War proved so bloody, so bitterly murderous, that ranchers across Arizona apparently restrained themselves from violent confrontations with rival stockmen. A contemporary Arizona frontiersman observed: "This war and the killing off of so many thieves and desperate characters caused several others to leave the country so that we enjoyed a season of peace . . ., in fact this lawless element never got so bad again. This war where they killed each other was a death blow to the bad men in this country which was a great blessing, and civilization was enabled to take another step onward."[44]

* * *

But civilization took a step backward in January 1889, when seven cowboys who rode for Arizona's Chiricahua Cattle Company encountered a sheep camp on Bonita Creek in Graham County. Six Mexican sheepherders, employees of Don Pedro Montana, were hunkered around a breakfast fire. The cowboys had split up to hunt strays when Walter Birchfield, John Roper, and Billy Woods rode into the sheep camp. The cowboy trio dismounted, ate breakfast, then sat around the campfire talking. Finally, herder Jose Padilla got up to saddle his horse.[45]

At this point Birchfield grappled with Padilla, trying to seize his rifle. The other two cowboys jumped Nestor Sanchez and his brother, attempting to snatch their weapons. As this deadly wrestling match took place, the remaining four cowboys rode up the creek into the camp. The reinforcements jumped out of their saddles, drew their revolvers, and sprinted into the fray. Later the cowboys claimed that Padilla triggered the first shot at Birchfield, but the young cowboy knocked the barrel down and caught the bullet in his knee. Padilla, the only herder to survive the fight, stated that the newcomers started the firing by running up and shooting the Sanchez brothers in the head.[46]

However it started, there was a flurry of close-range gunfire. It was reported that five Mexicans were killed, with powder burns around nearly every wound. Padilla survived, despite wounds in both legs, while Birchfield was the only cowboy casualty. Padilla was brought into Solomonville. Don Pedro immediately mounted an armed force and rode to protect his flocks and herders, and law officers went to the site of the shooting.[47]

Birchfield and Roper were taken under arrest to Solomonville, and even though the cowboys proclaimed that the Mexicans had fired first and that the sheep were grazing on Chiricahua Cattle Company range, there was considerable criticism of the shooting. The Tombstone *Daily Prospector* granted "that it is exceedingly annoying and vexatious to have sheep run on their ranges; but we do not think the provocation great enough to justify such wholesale murder, even if those parties had been trespassing on the Chiricahua Company. And, when the facts are taken into consideration that the sheep were on the White Mountain Indian Reservation by special permit, it makes the killing in this instance still more atrocious."[48] Although the subsequent trial resulted in the dismissal or acquittal of each of the defendants, the cattle faction had taken an unexpected black eye over the Bonita Creek shooting.

A tragic incident occurred in 1903 in the Tonto Basin, about twenty miles west of now-peaceful Pleasant Valley. In September 1903 a large flock of sheep belonging to William W. Berry of St. Johns was sent toward the southwest to find winter pasturage in the Tonto Basin. In charge of the flock was Wiley Berry, son of the owner. Berry was aided by a veteran herder, Juan Rafael, and by Rafael's seventeen-year-old son Vigil. Not long after Wiley left with the sheep, the rest of the Berry family moved to a new home at a ranch near Thatcher, where the winters were not so bitter.[49]

The Berry sheep were driven in leisurely fashion, grazing and advancing no more than four miles per day. By December, the flock was trail-weary and about thirty head had been lost. On December 18, Wiley Berry moved his sheep into Brushy Basin, a sheltered, grassy enclosure in the Sierra Anchas about five miles north of the hamlet of Gisela and eight miles southeast of Payson. On the night of December 21, Wiley told the Rafaels that he planned to take the pack mules into Gisela the next day and bring back provisions and stock salt. Then he intended to catch a stagecoach in Gisela to Globe and take a train to Thatcher so that he could spend Christmas with his parents and three sisters.

But the next morning, Tuesday, December 22, the sheep camp was approached by two riders. Juan was with the flock in a bedground in the timber, but Wiley and young Vigil were preparing breakfast in camp. The armed riders dismounted and talked with Wiley, then produced weapons and shot him at close range. Wiley collapsed face down and died within moments. Vigil Rafael desperately sprinted for his life, but was cut down by .38-caliber revolver slugs before he could reach the timber.

Juan Rafael ran toward the camp as the murderers galloped away, but he had taken a good look at them when they rode up. Wiley Berry's red sweater was smoldering from the point-blank explosions, and Juan splashed water from a bucket onto the burning garment. Horrified, he found his son lying fifty yards away. Assuming that both youths were dead, Juan mounted Wiley's horse, already saddled, and headed toward Payson.

After Juan rode out of sight, the murderers returned to the camp. They fired several more rounds into Wiley's body with his own carbine, but placed the weapon beneath him and fired another shot that cut saddle leather to indicate that there had been a fight. Then the killers discovered that Vigil had regained consciousness and had managed to crawl a few feet. Four .30-.30 bullets in the back extinguished Vigil's life.

In Payson, Juan found deputies John Chilson and Ben Pyeatt. Sheriff C. R. Rogers was telephoned in distant Globe, then Chilson and Pyeatt galloped out to the sheep camp with Juan, soon to be followed by a coroner's jury. An investigation of the site clearly indicated most of the tragic occurrence, and Juan added a description of the riders and their mounts.

Sheriff Rogers and his deputies soon determined that cattle ranchers in the vicinity had become angered at the presence of sheep, and that indignation meetings had been held. Although no leader had emerged, suspicion quickly focused on Zack and John Booth. Zack, the older of the two Booth brothers, was an eccentric bachelor who was noted as a marksman and who sometimes stirred his coffee with a revolver muzzle. On Sundays he frequently donned a tuxedo and a high silk hat, then preached hell-fire and damnation to a backwoods congregation. Although John was a family man, both Booth brothers had been accused of various crimes, and they had beaten charges of rustling cattle and robbing a country store. At one of the indignation meetings, Zack had announced to other ranchers that he would personally run the sheepherders out of the neighborhood.

Deputies Chilson and Pyeatt visited Zack's ranch and found that he was not present, but in the corral there were two horses that had been precisely described by Juan. The lawmen roped the horses, checked their tracks in soft dirt, and measured their strides at the walk and at the gallop. A saddle with a bullet crease was found, along with a holstered rifle and a .38 revolver. Both weapons had been recently fired but not cleaned. John Booth's ranch was nearby, but the Booth brothers were working on a road gang. Chilson and Pyeatt found and arrested them, and Sheriff Rogers took them to a party at Globe's 16 to

1 saloon, where they were identified in a crowded room by Juan. A grand jury indicted the brothers for murder.

Rogers had sent a message to Wiley Berry's family at St. Johns, but the tragic news did not reach them in Thatcher until December 31. Grief-stricken, William Berry and a friend, Dave Lee, went to claim the bodies, which had been exhumed for a belated autopsy after initial burial at Gisela. En route, Berry and Lee encountered a posse which was transferring the Booths to the jail in Globe. "Are these the beasts who murdered my son?" asked Berry. But he restrained himself, and the two parties went their separate ways. Wiley Berry's final resting place was at Thatcher, while Vigil was reburied in the same grave at the pioneer cemetery in Gisela.

The Booth brothers went to trial for the murder of Vigil Rafael on June 13, 1904. Zack admitted his guilt, flatly stating that when he returned to the camp and found Vigil still breathing, he finished the murder. His depiction of grisly details apparently was an effort to shift blame away from John, who was a family man, to himself. He insisted that John had not been present, but he would not identify the other rider. John was declared not guilty, but Zack was convicted and, on June 18, sentenced to hang. Legal appeals were unsuccessful, and Zack Booth was executed on a temporary gallows at Globe on August 16, 1905.

In the meantime, John Booth was tried in June 1905 for the murder of Wiley Berry, but the evidence was inconclusive and all charges were dismissed. Indeed, Zack Booth's conviction — although clearly justified — was deeply resented by cattlemen, who helped to defeat Sheriff Rogers by a landslide vote when he stood for reelection. The murder site became known as Dead Boy Point.

In ensuing years, hostilities ceased between cattlemen and sheepmen in Arizona. In 1903 and 1904 writer-photographer Dane Coolidge visited central Arizona, gathering material that would comprise *Arizona Cowboys,* published in 1938. Coolidge admired and sympathized with cowboys, and he shared the cattleman's disdain for "predator sheep." But in Arizona in 1903–04, Coolidge "saw a new kind of sheepman." He discovered sheepmen who were aggressive and determined, and who had gained the upper hand. "The sheepmen were organized in a powerful association," he said, adding that they had accumulated a substantial war chest for legal action, and "if a cowman killed a herder even in self-defense, they would have him hung for it, anyway." Furthermore, "sheepmen seemed to try to hire herders who had killed people, mostly Mexicans from Chihuahua and Durango who would get their heads blowed off as long as they got the other fellow." Coolidge was impressed by these gun-toting herders: "The sheep-owners hired these Old Mexico *pelados*, fed them well and went with them, and they would cross any deadline in the world. Some of them were like small boys who had been given their first gun. The height of their ambition was to kill somebody."[50]

Coolidge was somewhat dismayed to find that cattlemen "were on their good behavior," intimidated by the presence of tens of thousands of sheep on the open range, by the expanding prosperity of the sheep industry, and by the contentious stance of the sheepmen. He stated: "The modern, fighting sheepman is as different from the old-time sheepherder as a wolf is from a rabbit. He is a big businessman, playing a game for big stakes against every adverse condition. He goes armed, and his herders go armed; and he used to make a hundred per cent on his money, every year he brought his sheep through alive." Drouth intensified the battle for the range, but Coolidge discerned that the sheepman always won. "I know of only one cowman who ever beat the sheep and he had to turn sheepman to do it."[51]

A minor complaint regarding sheepmen was voiced in 1908 in a letter to Governor Joseph H. Kibbey by Carl Hayden, sheriff of Maricopa County. It seemed that during the first three months of each year, large bands of "transient sheep" were driven into the Cave Creek district, about thirty-five miles north of Phoenix, to be sheared. Among the herders and shearers were certain men "who are inclined to violence or other lawlessness particularly when under the influence of liquor." Of course, the same complaint could have been made about members of almost any other group of Arizonans of the day. But the only officer in Cave Creek was a justice of the peace, and since Hayden had been unable to enlist a deputy sheriff from among the Cave Creek residents, he was requesting that an Arizona Ranger be assigned to the neighborhood during the troubled months.[52]

The next year the *Arizona Republican* boasted that "there are an even dozen wool buyers from eastern cities in Phoenix competing for the annual product of the sheep shearing going on at Beardsley, Martinette, Cave Creek, and Peoria." By that time two million pounds of wool were shipped annually from Phoenix in 125 railroad cars. Prices for 1909 were ranging from eighteen to nineteen cents per pound, up several cents from the previous year. Sheep were praised in the newspaper for performing "excellent work in cleaning up weeds and pasturing waste corners."[53]

The clash between cattle and sheep ranchers in Arizona virtually ended after the Pleasant Valley War of 1887. Although trouble between cattlemen and sheepmen had occurred frequently during the 1880s, violence almost halted (occasional explosive incidents would erupt until the 1920s) soon after the slaughter in the Tonto Basin ran its course. The Pleasant Valley War, one of the West's most notorious and sanguine range wars, was caused by various tensions between two neighboring families, but the introduction of sheep by the Tewksburys into a cattle preserve ignited a bloody vendetta that might otherwise have been avoided.

Rumors circulated that the Daggs brothers had put up the money for Ed Tewksbury's defense. When the secretary of the Arizona Pioneers' Historical Society wrote P. P. Daggs in 1926 for his account of events four decades earlier, the old man did not respond in detail but commented acidly: "I ought to know something about the 'Tonto Basin War.' It cost me ninety thousand dollars. General Sherman once said 'War is hell.' He was right."[54]

5

Miscellaneous Hostilities Across the West

It's not worth getting killed over. Head for the brush.
— Retreating sheepman to his herder

Although Texas, Colorado, Arizona, and Wyoming provided the arenas for the most sustained and murderous violence between cattlemen and sheepmen, other states and territories also suffered tensions and sometimes witnessed lethal, destructive incidents. There was occasional turbulence in New Mexico, Montana, Utah, Washington, and Oregon, while the Idaho murders and trials involving Diamondfield Jack Davis form one of the landmark episodes in the half-century clash between sheep and cattle raisers.

Large numbers of sheep had been raised by the Indian and Mexican population of New Mexico since the 1600s. The California gold rush and the industrialization of the East created a great demand for mutton and wool. Sheep hastened the Anglo settlement of New Mexico and played a vital role in integrating the newly acquired territory into the American economy. New Mexico sheep were trailed great distances to market, and also served as foundation stock when the sheep industry shifted westward. The largest concentration of sheep was in the northern half of New Mexico, and profit-minded Anglos eagerly purchased flocks and hired herders. Although cattle were brought to

New Mexico pastures in large numbers, particularly in the southern counties, in 1884 sheep still outnumbered cattle by approximately four and a half million.[1]

Many New Mexico sheepmen were transients, not having a home ranch but slowly trailing their flocks to the best unoccupied ranges. New Mexico sheep graziers frequently drove flocks into Texas, where Lone Star cattlemen hazed them back into New Mexico (such incidents are discussed in chapter 2). But this situation sometimes was reversed. In one instance a transient sheepman from Texas trailed his flock into New Mexico, moved from one range to another, then parked his wagon in an area used by a large cattle ranch. Cowboys soon rode to his camp and ordered him to leave. The sheepman pointed to his wagon and explained that he was missing a broken wheel. It was more than fifty miles to a place where a wheel could be repaired or replaced, and the cowboys began to relent — until one of the riders noticed the missing wheel hidden in mesquite brush. The sheepman soon was on the move.[2]

As cattle raising increased in importance, the New Mexico Territorial Legislature passed a law requiring transient flocks to move at least six miles per day. James F. Hinkle (who rose to serve as governor of New Mexico from 1923 to 1925) ran the CA Bar cattle ranch which controlled forty miles of running water along the Penasco River. Hinkle was bothered by sheepherders who would drive a large flock to the Penasco, then cross the river after watering and graze the sheep out three miles on the other side. The next day the flock would be grazed back to the river, watered, then moved across three more miles — a total of six miles![3]

When the conflict between sheep and cattle interests was carried into court, juries usually favored the cattleman. But during the 1880s, New Mexico sheepmen had a powerful ally in Democratic Governor E. C. Ross. Ross supported policies favorable to homesteaders, bringing him into conflict with big ranchers. He opposed large landed estates, which he identified with sparse population and oligarchic political power. Ross naturally favored sheep interests in the range clash, even though cattle ranchers comprised an influential segment of New Mexico's Democratic Party.[4]

During the winter of 1885–86, Governor Ross discovered that two cowboys from Durango, Colorado, had shot and killed Ricardo Jacques, a New Mexico sheepherder. The cowboys worked for a rancher named Carlisle, who telegraphed New Mexico's attorney general with a plea to see that his men were exonerated. The trial had proved to be a farce: cowboy friends of the defendants brought guns into the courtroom, a cocked Winchester was pointed at any witness considered to be dangerous to their cause, and the killers were cleared of charges.

Investigating further, Governor Ross learned that for years Carlisle's Colorado-based outfit had caused trouble with Indians in northern New Mexico, usurping ranges traditionally reserved for sheepherders. Ross wrote the cattlemen a scathing letter, fuming that Carlisle riders "have for years constituted the nucleus of an element that has practically terrorized that region of the country. You have permitted them to go armed, contrary to laws of New Mexico, and sustained them in their lawless proceedings, till a reign of public disorder seems imminent."[5]

Governor Ross insisted that Carlisle's men stop causing disorder, or else they would be arrested and punished, or driven out of New Mexico. Indeed, within a few months the Colfax County grand jury indicted William Wilson for murder and two other Carlisle cowboys as accessories, and convictions were obtained against all three men.

But sympathetic New Mexico law officers and juries continued to favor cattle interests over sheepmen. In Lincoln County, for example, the sheriff was vice-president of the area cattlemen's association, and sheepherders found themselves treated roughly. In 1884, Arcadio Sais placed 700 sheep on Lincoln County's Carrizozo range, but he was struck by five raiders who destroyed his flock. The next year a sheepherder who ignored orders to leave Lincoln County was shot at by raiders. In July 1885 Governor Ross delivered a speech at Albuquerque in which he complimented the cattlemen on their contributions to the economy and settlement of New Mexico, then warned them that the conflict between cattle and sheep interests must stop. He explained that an orderly, law-abiding atmosphere was needed to attract people to New Mexico: "People are worth more to a state than steers . . . for with people comes capital and the spirit of commercial adventure, development, prosperity, and greatness." Cattlemen, however, could not be convinced that *sheepherders* were worth more than steers. New Mexico cattle ranchers increasingly opposed Governor Ross, and from time to time continued to treat sheepherders high-handedly.[6]

* * *

Cattle and sheep were introduced to Montana at about the same time, several years prior to the Civil War. A few cattlemen became active in Montana during the 1850s, but it was not until 1869 that the first important sheep operation was established, when John Bishop and Dick Reynolds trailed a flock numbering 1,500 head from Oregon to the Beaverhead Valley. But the presence of vast herds of buffalo and dangerous horse Indians severely limited the expansion of livestock raising: the census of 1880 recorded just 428,279 cattle and 279,277 sheep in all of Montana. Because of the uncrowded ranges, there was little cause for conflict between sheepmen and cattlemen. In the early 1880s, however, the slaughter of buffalo by professional hunters climaxed, hostile Indians had vanished, and there was a railroad boom throughout the West. Texas longhorns were brought in large numbers to Montana, although Montana ranchers disliked the presence of longhorns on the open range, preferring the shorthorn herds they had carefully bred for improved beef quality. Tensions between Montana ranchers and Texas cowboys further defused the situation between cattlemen and sheepmen.[7]

Even though there was little trouble by comparison with Wyoming and other sanguinary states and territories, difficulties between cattle and sheep interests occasionally flared. During the winter of 1869–70, long before Montana ranges were crowded by either cattle or sheep, the instinctive dislike of woollies by cattlemen created an early disagreement. John Bishop and Dick Reynolds wintered their flock in a valley near Bannack, but a nearby settler "who had two or three cows" wrote Bishop threatening to scatter the flock and kill the herder unless the sheep were removed. Bishop relayed the warning to Reynolds and provided him with a revolver, and the incident passed without trouble.[8]

A decade later, although Montana grasslands remained uncrowded, cattle and horse ranchers in the Sun River Valley were appalled at the intrusion of sheepmen. On December 10, 1879, "the pioneers of the Sun River Valley" published a broadside opposing the presence of sheep. The ranchers, "having established ourselves here at an early day and . . . taking our chances with the Indians and all other outlaws . . .," were concerned that "if we quietly submit to graze upon our occupied and long established cattle and horse ranges our occupations will soon be gone." Pointing out that "there are millions upon millions of acres of unoccupied grazing land" for the sheepmen to use, the ranchers declared "it our duty to our God, our families and ourselves to oppose to the bitter end all parties owning sheep . . ., and we do hereby pledge our all, our property and our lives if need be."[9]

Fortunately, no one pushed the situation to the bitter end, and another Montana incident passed without real damage.

When a sheepman named Philbrick brought his flock onto open range in the Tongue River Valley, cattle ranchers objected, then stampeded a horse herd through the woollies. The horses caused little damage, so rancher Tom Horton left his cohorts in concealment and rode out to talk to Philbrick. Horton stayed on his mount, with his Winchester balanced across his saddle, while Philbrick stood on the ground. When Horton turned to go, his horse moved suddenly and the barrel of his rifle struck Philbrick, knocking the herder unconscious. Using a state law that whipping a man with a gun was a felony, Philbrick brought charges. But he named the wrong rancher, Charlie Landis, as the defendant, and the judge tossed the case out of court.[10]

By 1900 the sheep population of Montana had boomed to six million, triggering a far more violent incident in the Tongue River Valley. In December 1900, Robert R. Selway, who headquartered in Sheridan, Wyoming, decided to send a flock of 3,000 sheep north to the grassy rangeland around Montana's Hanging Woman Creek. Although this was open-range country, technically available to any stockman, it long had been regarded as part of Montana's Tongue River cattle range.

John B. Kendrick was one of several area cattlemen who, according to an acquaintance, "had enough manpower and firepower, or just plain bluff, to lay claim to certain public range areas and make the claim stand up, even though such claims were illegal." Kendrick, orphaned as a boy, worked as a Texas cowpuncher and helped drive a herd of longhorns north to Wyoming in 1879. Intensely ambitious, he practiced personal frugality and worked constantly to better himself, expanding his skimpy education by pulling books from his saddlebags while fellow cowboys galloped off to squander their wages in frontier dives. He became foreman of a Wyoming spread, married his boss's daughter, and began establishing his own OW Ranch. He and his wife settled in an isolated ranch home fifty miles from Sheridan, and Kendrick began grazing his cattle along the east slope of the Big Horn Mountains in Wyoming and Montana. He fiercely maintained control over "his" rangelands, once successfully ordering cattle from the Tainter FL Ranch to be removed from the east side of the Tongue River because his herds were there first. Kendrick prospered and grew more powerful, and he was determined to do anything necessary to keep sheep out of the country.[11]

Selway, apparently intending to challenge the cattlemen's domination of this range, openly arranged the movement of his sheep into lower Montana. Kendrick contacted an old friend, George W. Brewster, a Bostonian who had arrived in Montana in 1882. By squatter's rights Brewster began ranging cattle near Birney, Montana, on land he claimed as the Quarter Circle U Ranch. He had met his wife, a friend of Eula Kendrick, on the OW Ranch. Kendrick and Brewster agreed upon elaborate — and ruthless — plans to thwart Selway.

Nine other men were enlisted: OW cowboys Booker Lacy, Frank McKinney, Bill Munson, Walt Snyder, and Tug Wilson; two of Brewster's punchers, Barney Hall and J. H. "Shorty" Caddel, a young drover who had come up the trail from Texas; and two Montana ranchers, Charles Thex, a former Texan whose spread was on Otter Creek, and William Boal, whose cattle ranged near Hanging Woman Creek and who was a son-in-law of Buffalo Bill Cody.[12]

Selway sent only one herder with his flock. The sheep were trailed across Bear Creek, a tributary of Otter Creek. On Thursday, December 27, 1900, the flock was bedded on the northwest bank of Bear Creek, less than sixty miles southeast of the Custer battlefield.

Before dawn on Friday, eleven determined men rolled out of their respective bunks or bedrolls, saddled their mounts, and rode through the frigid morning air toward Bear Creek. They converged by prearrangement on the sheep camp, spurred their horses, and within moments held the herder at gunpoint. A couple of the mounted men kept the sheep herded against the steep bank of the creek, which formed a virtual corral because of a sharp bend.

Not a shot was fired during the ensuing slaughter. Apparently the sheep were lassoed, then clubbed to death by horsemen leaning over from their saddles. Shorty Caddel used a shepherd's weapon, a slingshot, to dispatch some of the animals.

It was sundown before the bloody work was concluded, but all 3,000 sheep finally lay dead. The herder was released and the cowmen then rode off through the snow in different directions. Some of the sheep killers fell in behind herds of wild mustangs so that their trails could not be traced. Two "alibi dances" were being held that Friday night, one at the Gilbertson Ranch on the Tongue River and another at Kendrick's place. Shorty Caddel rode nearly sixty miles that day, killed hundreds of sheep, and finished the night at a dance. Little wonder that fifty-six years later Shorty still remembered "being terribly tired."

Selway's sheepherder turned up at the Three Circle Ranch on the Tongue River, but soon left the area and never returned. Selway and various woolgrowers' associations offered handsome bounties for the identities of the sheep killers; word spread that the rewards totaled $16,000. Despite this monetary temptation, not a single thirty-dollar-a-month cowboy revealed any information. Sheriff O. C. Cato, a longtime cattle rancher, told Selway that he had found the bloodstained clubs, and that he intended to arrest the first man who claimed a club. It was hardly surprising that none of the clubs were claimed. Indeed, visitors to Cato's office regarded the clubs as material for humorous comments: "Well, you can't do anything to me. My club isn't there. Whose club is that? Must belong to [so and so]. He's the only one big enough to handle a club like that."[13]

The perpetrators of the Bear Creek raid were never identified or prosecuted. If anything, leading the raid aided the reputations of Kendrick and Brewster. In 1905, George Brewster took a seat in the Montana House of Representatives, and he returned in 1907 and 1909. Brewster was elected president of the Montana Stockgrowers Association in 1911, heading the organization until his death in 1912. John Kendrick was drafted to run for the Wyoming Senate in 1910, elected governor in 1914, and United States senator in 1916. He was returned to the Senate in 1922 and 1928, serving until he died in 1933 at the age of seventy-six. Kendrick also served a term as president of the National Live Stock Association, and while he was a U.S. senator he cooperated readily with the state's senior senator, Francis E. Warren — a millionaire woolgrower.

On several occasions cattlemen in northern Wyoming had become angered to the point of retaliation against Montana sheepmen who crossed the state line for pasturage. A reversal of this situation occurred in 1904, when Wyoming sheepman George Crosby crossed the state line and guided his flock onto Montana grass in the Pryor Mountain area. There he was raided by Montana cattlemen who rimrocked his flock, killing 500 sheep.[14]

The crossing of boundary lines was the primary source of trouble for Utah sheepmen. There were few internal conflicts in Utah, but when Mormon flockmasters drove sheep into Wyoming, Colorado, and Arizona, protests and acts of retribution followed. One such clash produced the final chapter in the long conflict between cattle and sheep ranchers, and will be described in the closing pages of this book.

* * *

Stockmen began to be firmly established in the Pacific Northwest in the 1850s, and for years open-range sheep production was the primary economic activity in many areas. When railroads were built, large numbers of farmers were attracted, many of whom raised small herds of cattle. These small-scale cattlemen quickly began complaining that "sheep threaten to eat up every spear of grass in sight." Hundreds of thousands of sheep were trailed to winter ranges in the Big Bend, Palouse, Scablands, and Yakima areas of Washington every year, and widespread resentment grew among cattle raisers about the "absolute possession" of grasslands by sheepmen.[15]

Strong tensions existed by the 1890s. In 1893 a horse rancher named Moore ran his stock through a flock, killing 200 sheep belonging to a grazier named Hewitt. Cattlemen formed an organization declaring the Channeled Scablands off-limits for sheep, although Archie and John McGregor, Phil Cox, Joseph Escallier, and other woolgrowers continued to use this area for winter grazing. A state law meant to keep sheepmen from trespassing on the unfenced land of homesteaders was misused to restrict grazing on millions of acres of unclaimed land in Washington. The Northern Pacific Railroad, which held vast tracts of land, formulated a model grazing lease program for the Columbia Plateau and brought graziers together to work out a compromise.[16]

Problems continued to surface, however, during the next few years. Cattlemen again organized and announced deadlines against sheep, while it was rumored that sheepmen would retaliate. Threatening letters were sent to farmers who sold hay to sheepmen, with matches enclosed to emphasize the prospect of arson. There were indeed a few incidents of haystack burnings, incendiary attacks on sheep camps, and damage to flocks by shooting, clubbing, dynamiting, or rimrocking. When the McGregor brothers fenced in the major watering holes on their winter pastures, open-range cattlemen cut fences and tore out gates, throwing them into the Snake River. Repairs were made and no further incidents occurred, but because they could not afford to fence in leased range in Adams County, the McGregors paid a horse raiser to take his animals off their land.[17]

Trouble in Oregon was more violent and of longer duration. By the mid-1890s there was conflict between sheep and cattle graziers in Crook, Gilliam, Grant, Lake, Morrow, Sherman, and Umatilla counties. Competition for available range was intensified by the enforcement in 1896 of a federal ban on sheep grazing in the Cascades.

Cattlemen of the Izee area, in southwestern Grant County, organized to oppose the presence of sheep in the Snow Mountain summer ranges. Boldly calling themselves the Izee Sheep Shooters, the cattlemen descended upon a few sheep camps, blindfolded and tied the herders to trees or fence posts, then proceeded to their avowed business of shooting sheep.

Cattle ranchers in the Paulina district of eastern Crook County viewed the Izee Sheep Shooters with admiration, and in July 1896 a representative of the Sheep Shooters rode over to help foster a similar organization. More than thirty cattlemen congregated beneath a pine tree on Wolf Creek, six miles from tiny Paulina. Gathering around a bonfire, the cattlemen met until midnight, grimly fashioning a document regarding the killing of sheep.

Although three men refused to associate themselves with the group, everyone else agreed to shoot herders, if necessary to kill sheep, and to bury the victim "where he falls." If an attacker were to be slain, he would be brought home for burial, "and nothing is to be said about the manner in which he met death." If any member of the association were to be brought to trial, "other members must be willing to go on the witness stand and swear to lies to obtain an acquittal." Members vowed secrecy, agreed upon deadlines, and marked the designated limits by blazing a saddle blanket notch on various pine trees (half a century later, loggers noted a number of these large blazes). During the next decade an estimated 8,000 sheep were killed in Crook County.[18]

In 1897 the Morrow County Wool Growers Association collected $1,000 from its members to hire stock detectives "to ferret out and prosecute the persons who have been shooting sheep." In 1898 the Morrow County Wool Growers offered a $500 reward "for the arrest and conviction of the person or persons who killed A. B. Thomson's sheep," as well as $100 "for the arrest and conviction of any person robbing and burning sheep camps."[19]

When a sheep camp in northeastern Oregon was attacked by night raiders armed with rifles, the owner headed for cover. "It's not worth getting killed over," he shouted to his herder. "Head for the brush." But the herder seized a rifle and opened fire, and the raiders galloped away. Although the camp had been knocked about by the horses, the herder had averted serious damage by his courageous defense.[20]

A recurring feature of Oregon's cattlemen-sheepmen conflict was the burning of hay. Of course, sheep camps and sheds also were burned, but hay was desperately needed for winter feeding, and stacks often were torched in the field. One sheepman in Wheeler County suffered heavy winter losses because the rancher who had promised to provide him hay had given in to threats from cattlemen.

In July 1903, eleven Crook County cattlemen from the Prineville area rode south on what would become one of Oregon's most destructive raids. In recent days Lake County sheepmen from the vicinity of Silver Lake had separated their wethers from their winter flocks and moved them north to Benjamin Lake, leaving a herder and camp tender in charge of 2,700 sheep. The Crook County cattlemen, armed with rifles, sixguns, and clubs, blackened their faces and rode into the camp.

The herders placed a sack over the sheepherder's head and tied him to a tree. Leaving one raider with their captive, the other riders went in search of the camp tender. The man soon was chased down in the sagebrush, and he was bound and blindfolded. Then the raiders methodically slaughtered 2,400 sheep.[21]

Sheepman Guy McKune, who headquartered at Silver Lake in northeastern Lake County, left a flock of 3,000 animals in the care of a lone herder. On the night of February 3, 1904, five riders, masked and heavily armed, moved into the camp after the sheep had been placed in a corral. While one raider guarded the herder, the other four men climbed into the corral. Using guns, clubs and knives, the raiders destroyed the flock, then warned the herder that any other sheep attempting to use the range would also be attacked.[22]

In 1904 two sheepmen named Grube and Parker placed a flock forty miles south of Silver Lake, just below the Washington-Oregon line. On Thursday, May 5, ten masked raiders struck the camp, tied up the two herders, then killed more than 2,300 sheep. About 150 miles to the southeast, a struggle had developed for use of the Blue Mountain ranges. Sheep owners from Antelope called a meeting of stockmen, especially Crook County cattle ranchers, to try to hammer out an agreement, but no division of the range could be concluded. Indeed, on June 13, just after the unsuccessful meeting, a flock was attacked fifteen miles east of Prineville, on Mill Creek. Raiders shot sixty-four sheep belonging to Allie Jones.[23]

Eight days later, on June 21, the Central Oregon Wool Growers' Association gathered in large numbers at Antelope. Rewards totaling $1,500 were offered for the arrest and conviction of any parties guilty of shooting or harming any member, or employee of a member, of the organization. A three-man committee was appointed to visit the site of any trouble and to negotiate with cattlemen.

Apparently, an anonymous group of cattle ranchers and cowboys responded by secretively banding together as the Crook County Sheepshooters Association. In January 1905, six masked riders struck a flock near the home of Fred Smith, at his ranch outside Paulina. The herder was bound and blindfolded, then the raiders began operating their rifles, methodically gunning down 500 sheep. Later in the year, as flocks were moved to summer range in the mountains, snipers fired into bands on the trail, camps were destroyed, and stampede attempts were made during the nights. Then a "report of the proceedings of the year" was sent to the Portland *Oregonian,* seemingly under the auspices of the Crook County Sheepshooters Association:

> We recently extended our jurisdiction to cover a wide territory of the desert heretofore occupied by sheepmen, and we expect to have to sacrifice a few flocks of sheep this coming winter . . . Our annual report shows that we have slaughtered between 8,000 and 10,000 head the last shooting season. We have burned the usual number of camps and corrals this season, and also sent out a number of important warnings which we think will have a satisfactory effect. We have just received a shipment of ammunition that we think will be sufficient to meet any shortage which might occur on account of increase of territory requiring general protection.[24]

But Roscoe Knox, who had migrated to Crook County in 1885 and who raised both cattle and sheep, apparently was the author of this and other "Sheepshooters" letters to arouse public opposition to sheep raiders. State officials and most of the decent citizens of Oregon took these letters seriously, fostering a widespread demand to halt the Crook County Sheepshooters Association and the general lawlessness on the range.

Although public clamor lessened the strife between sheep and cattle graziers, a final tragic incident occurred in the northeastern part of Lake County. Two stockmen moved 2,200 sheep onto range northeast of Silver Lake; in charge of the flock was Phil Barry, a recent immigrant from Ireland. Although Barry soon was approached by masked riders who advised him to drive the sheep off the range, the Irishman naively shrugged off the visit as Wild West horseplay. But two weeks later, in April 1906, the masked men came back, chousing the flock toward a cliff. Hundreds of sheep tumbled over the edge and died on the rocks below, after which the raiders opened up with rifles on the animals which had slipped away from the cliff. A total of 1,800 sheep were killed.

Outraged state officials demanded investigative action, and local officers discovered that the raiders had purchased rifle cartridges from Creed Conn's mercantile in Silver Lake. But Conn disappeared; his corpse was found several miles outside town. He had been shot to death, and it was speculated that he was murdered so that he could not reveal who had bought the cartridges. The flock owners were in San Francisco when the famous earthquake struck on April 18, and they did not learn of the raid until their return to Oregon.[25]

The range war in Oregon had persisted for more than a decade, despite growing public demands that the hostilities stop. In immediate response to the Lake County raid, the federal government announced that it would enforce grazing restrictions in national forests. Regulation of grazing in vast federal reserves had been provided by law in 1902, but had not been put into effect until continued conflict over grasslands made restrictive measures necessary to curb tensions. On November 15, 1906, a meeting was held in Canyon City, where each stock raiser with a prior history of grazing in the Blue Mountains was assigned a range allotment. Carefully designated boundaries were displayed on maps, and enforcement of specified grazing areas finally concluded the defusing of Oregon's longstanding range conflict.

* * *

Trouble between cattle and sheep graziers in Idaho began at about the same time as conflicts in Oregon and Washington. In 1892 a sheepman named Porter brought a band of sheep into the Lehmi Valley, in north central Idaho, but cattlemen promptly ran Porter and his sheep out of the valley. A few years later, two more bands were placed on range near old Fort Lehmi. Again cattlemen of the region responded decisively. One band of sheep was driven up Agency Creek and across the state line, then scattered across isolated, mountainous Montana country. When the owner of the second band announced his intention to resist, cattlemen dynamited his newly erected sheep sheds. The sheepman's resistance melted at the sight of shattered sheds, and he left the valley with his flock.[26]

In 1908, Mrs. Emma Yearian brought 1,200 lambs into the Lehmi Valley. She was threatened by cattlemen, but when she stayed they resorted to legal tactics rather than exercise violence against a woman. In 1875 cattle interests had prevailed upon the territorial legislature to pass an act which prohibited sheep grazing where cattle and horses previously had grazed. (At the turn of the century the Idaho Supreme Court had stated that without the 1875 statute, Idaho would become just a huge sheep range with no human inhabitants.) Mrs. Yearian recalled being "arrested pretty often" under both laws. "I was the most unpopular belle of the range brawl," she reminisced. But Mrs. Yearian persisted stubbornly, thereby encouraging other woolgrowers to enter the valley, and eventually she became known as the Sheep Queen of Idaho.[27]

The worst conflict in Idaho was a range war in Cassia County which climaxed in a tragic shooting and one of the most dramatic trials in western history. Cattle were first brought to southern Idaho in 1871, and ranching boomed for a decade and a half. But by the mid-1880s, Idaho cattlemen fell upon the same hard times as other open-range cattle graziers, while sheepmen enjoyed unprecedented success.

Ensuing tensions came to a head in vast Cassia County, bounded on the south by the Nevada and Utah lines and on the north by the Snake River. Railroad routes bypassed the county, which sprawled over almost 5,000 square miles but had a population that totaled merely 3,500 in the 1890s. The county's largest ranch was the Shoe Sole, owned by cattle barons John Sparks and Andrew Harrell, who held a string of spreads from the Shoe Sole to the Humboldt River in Nevada. These ranch units covered 300,000 acres and held 40,000 head of cattle, including the famous Alamo herd, perhaps the West's finest herd of Herefords.

For years Cassia County stockmen had maintained a deadline, the north-south divide separating Goose Creek on the east and Salmon Falls Creek and Deep Creek on the west. Cattlemen stayed on the eastern side, which held most of the county's population, including Albion, the county seat.

But by 1895 Cassia County sheepmen had begun to cross over the deadline and graze their flocks on the west side of the divide. Cattle ranchers had complained for years that large numbers of sheep in the eastern part of the county were being taken to Utah's Salt River Valley for winter grazing — so that they could not be taxed in Idaho. Already irritated with sheepmen over this unfair practice, cattle ranchers had no intention of permitting woollies on the west side of the deadline.

John Sparks began to hire gunmen. Billy Majors and Fred Gleason signed on as "outside men" who did not perform regular ranch work. Paid fifty dollars per month, plus bonuses for night riding, they were instructed to keep the sheep back. They were to use whatever measures they thought were best. Although admonished to shoot only to wound, they were assured that if killing proved necessary, the Sparks-Harrell corporation would provide money and staunch backing.

In July 1895 another "outside man" was added to the Sparks-Harrell payroll, a mustachioed widower in his twenties named Jackson Lee Davis. Davis was a braggart who had worked as a hardrock miner and as a cowboy, and when he once prospected in vain for a diamond field, he had become known as "Diamondfield Jack." Diamondfield Jack spoke with a stammer and claimed a romantic military past which no one believed.

Perhaps to prove that he was no blowhard, Diamondfield Jack immediately took an aggressive stance with the sheepmen of Cassia County, patrolling the deadline area on horseback and frequently engaging in abrasive encounters with herders. Announcing that he was on "fighting wages," Diamondfield Jack threatened those herders who had slipped their sheep across the deadline ("If the sheep come any farther you'll be facing the muzzle of a Winchester"), and he issued dire warnings to those who had not yet ventured over to the cattlemen's side ("I'll kill the next sheepherder who crosses that ridge"). He crowed about his prowess as an outdoorsman ("Jesus Christ himself couldn't track me"), and proclaimed that he intended to kill someone or be killed himself before the end of the summer. In one instance he threw down on a herder, and repeatedly he uttered mortal threats to herders against sheepmen who were not present.[28]

Diamondfield Jack's blatant antagonism understandably put the sheepmen on edge. Cattleman J. H. Foxley encountered several sheepmen and said hello — only to find himself looking into the muzzles of drawn sixguns. "We thought you were Diamondfield," explained sheepman E. R. Dayley as the revolvers were holstered.

Sheepman Bill Tolman, who had been the frequent subject of threats by Diamondfield Jack, determined to confront his erstwhile adversary face to face. On November 15, 1895, riding with his Winchester at the ready, Tolman found Diamondfield Jack at a Shoe Sole line shack in the Shoshone Basin. After an exchange of words, Diamondfield Jack palmed his .45 and drilled Tolman in the shoulder. Sudden pain erased Tolman's hostility, and Diamondfield Jack shouted at sheepherders on a nearby hill to come over and help. The herders had no intention of coming closer to Diamondfield Jack, so the gunman assisted his wounded victim to the sheep camp. Now proven as a shootist, Diamondfield Jack left the scene of trouble, probably to avoid legal repercussions. He rode south to Wells, Nevada, long a source of liquor and feminine companionship for Sparks-Harrell riders.

Sobered by the shooting of Tolman, sheepmen pulled their flocks back to the east side of the divide. But within a few weeks it was apparent that Diamondfield Jack no longer was patrolling the range, and sheep again began to cross the deadline, pressing almost to the Salmon Falls River near the western edge of Cassia County.

Diamondfield Jack stayed for a time at the Middlestacks, one of the Sparks-Harrell ranches on Salmon Falls Creek across the line in Nevada. He spent a lot of time engaging in target practice with Fred Gleason, plunking away until he ran out of ammunition for his Colt .45. On Saturday night, February 1, 1896, Diamondfield Jack and Gleason were prowling around the countryside several miles into Cassia County when they came across a sheep camp. Although the gunmen may not have known it, the flock was owned by Oliver Dunn, one of the sheepmen Diamondfield Jack had threatened.

Diamondfield Jack triggered a Winchester round, but herders Joseph and Loren Wilson grabbed their rifles and began shooting into the darkness. Proving to be not much of a gunman, Gleason spurred away without firing a shot. Diamondfield Jack worked his buckskin in a circle around the camp, keeping up his fire but managing only to kill a horse. Each side fired about a dozen rounds before Diamondfield Jack broke off the fight and caught up with Gleason. Apparently, Diamondfield Jack bore no grudge about Gleason's desertion under fire, because both "outside men" soon were bragging about their skirmish with sheepherders.

Diamondfield Jack and Gleason had recently headquartered at Brown Ranch, another Sparks-Harrell unit located on Salmon Falls Creek a few miles north of the Nevada-Idaho border. At daybreak on Tuesday, February 4, 1896, the two gunmen rode away from Brown Ranch, stating that they were heading south to the Middlestacks, but inquiring about a ford a couple of miles to the north. They took their midday meal at the Boar's Nest, the first Sparks-Harrell unit below the Nevada-Idaho line.

Apparently on the same date, two sheepherders, John Wilson and Daniel Cummings, were shot to death at their camp in rugged country about fifteen miles northeast of Brown Ranch. They were last seen alive by herder Davis Hunter on the morning of February 4, cooking breakfast in their wagon, with their sheepdogs tied to the wheels. Twelve days later, on February 16, another sheepherder, noticing a

DIAMONDFIELD JACK COUNTRY

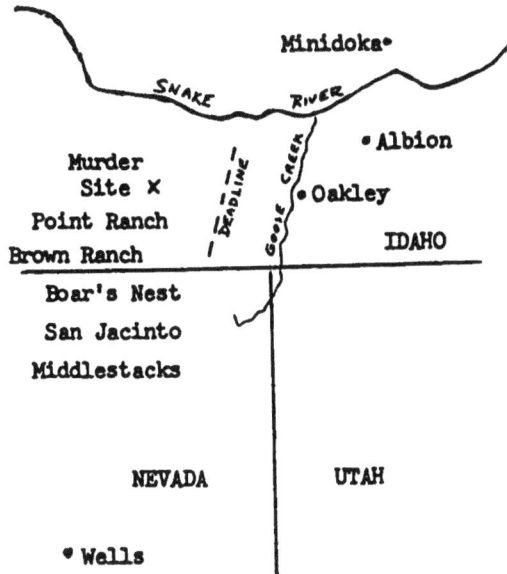

scattered flock, investigated their camp. The dogs, weak and emaciated, were still tied to the wagon wheels, and the decomposed bodies of Wilson and Cummings were inside the wagon.

While word was being relayed cross-country to authorities in Albion, sheepherders apprehensively stayed away from the shooting site, although Davis Hunter returned on February 17 to release the dogs (the starved animals were nursed back to health). Sheriff Harvey Perkins, a sheepman by profession, and Dr. R. T. Story, the county coroner, reached the camp on February 18, accompanied by a party of concerned sheepmen.

Three discharged .44 cartridge cases were found near the wagon, along with a corncob pipe and other clues. The only weapon in camp was a .45-.70 rifle which had not been fired since it had been cleaned. The sheriff was assured that the dead men were Mormons who never smoked. Each man had been shot once, but two other bullets had hit the wagon. Wilson had been shot through the chin, and his face and hands showed powder burns. Cummings, struck in the stomach, had scrawled a note before he expired: "If I die, bury me. Take care of my sisters."

Dr. Story concluded that Wilson, shot at point-blank range, had died quietly, but that Cummings might have lived as long as a day and a half. Sheepmen moved freely through the camp and handled the evidence at will. Furthermore, the sheriff was inexcusably careless with the evidence, losing the note and two of the cartridge hulls, while the corncob pipe was taken away by one of the onlookers.

Resentful sheepmen were certain that Diamondfield Jack had murdered Wilson and Cummings. On March 20, 1896, Diamondfield Jack and Gleason were charged in Albion with the double murder. The two gunmen had left the country, but rewards totaling $4,600 were posted for their arrest by the State of Idaho, Cassia County, the Idaho Wool Growers Association, the Cassia County Wool Growers, and private individuals. Most of these sources — as well as the Mormon Church in Salt Lake City, according to rumor — accumulated a large war chest to employ detectives and attorneys. William E. Borah, a thirty-year-old Boise lawyer destined to win six terms in the United States Senate as a Republican, was hired to lead the investigation and prosecution. Borah donned range clothes and rode through the country, talking to sheepmen and to Sparks-Harrell employees.

Early in 1897 it was learned that Diamondfield Jack had shot a dog and brawled with officers in Congress, Arizona, and had been sentenced to a year in Yuma Territorial Penitentiary. As a convict he spent a lot of time in solitary confinement and once managed to escape. Prison officials readily turned him over to Cassia County officers. Gleason was arrested in Montana at about the same time, and the two gunmen were incarcerated in Albion. They were scheduled to be tried in district court in Albion in April 1897. Borah was named special prosecutor to assist Cassia County's prosecuting attorney, John C. Rogers. The prosecution was further strengthened by the employment of another special prosecutor, O. W. Powers of Salt Lake City, considered by many as Utah's best criminal attorney.

Against this formidable array of legal talent the Sparks-Harrell company lived up to the promise to provide every support for their "outside men," spending a fortune estimated from $30,000 to $100,000 during the next several years. James Hawley of Boise was engaged to lead the defense. During his career Hawley, who was fifty-one in 1897, was involved in more than 300 murder cases as prosecutor or district attorney. A legendary trial lawyer, he also engaged in politics, winning a term as governor in 1910. Hawley worked on the Diamondfield Jack case with his resourceful young partner Will Puckett and with Kirtland I. Perky, a former law partner of William Jennings Bryan. Perky was practicing in Cassia County, and his knowledge of the local situation would prove invaluable.

Diamondfield Jack Davis was arraigned for the murder of John C. Wilson on Monday, April 5, 1897. The courthouse was a two-story frame building, originally constructed as a hotel. The jail in which Davis was incarcerated stood across the street to the south. The jury was selected in a day and a half and was composed entirely of men from the east side of the deadline, but Hawley was confident that any fair-minded jury would have to acquit his client. His confidence proved misplaced. The trial opened on Thursday, April 8, and lasted until the following Thursday.

It was established that on the presumed day of the killings, Davis and Gleason had left Brown Ranch a little before 8:00 in the morning and had arrived at the Boar's Nest around midday. Davis and Gleason claimed to have ridden directly from Brown Ranch to the Boar's Nest, while a surveyor established that the distance from Brown Ranch to the murder site to the Boar's Nest was fifty-three or fifty-four miles. The countryside was rocky and broken, and travel by horseback would have been further slowed by winter weather conditions. In addition, Gleason's horse was lame at the time, capable of making only three miles per hour. For Davis and Gleason to have committed the killings would have involved a seemingly impossible ride.

Wilson and Cummings had been killed with a .44-caliber gun, but Davis carried a .45 and was known to be out of ammunition. Only one of the .44-caliber cartridge cases found at the shooting site was available (Dr. Story, the coroner, testified that he thought his young daughter had been playing with the shells), and the firing pin had struck the cartridge dead-center. When a .44-caliber cartridge was test-fired in a .45 revolver, the firing pin struck off-center, indicating that Davis had not triggered the fatal bullets.

Cummings's note also seemed to be missing. Later a note was introduced as evidence, but there was doubt that it was the actual message scrawled by the dying man. Considerable doubt was raised about other factors, including the identity of Davis or Gleason by several witnesses. Hawley did not allow Diamondfield Jack to testify in his own behalf, because he was too unpredictable to risk cross-examination by skillful prosecution attorneys.

During the closing arguments, the defense pointed out that all of the evidence was circumstantial and that the burden of proof was on the prosecution. The jury retired at 7:30 on the evening of April 15, deliberated for three hours, then returned that night with a guilty verdict. When the judge asked Diamondfield Jack if he had any remarks to make before sentencing, the gunman rambled angrily for an hour about the pro-sheepman bias in the community, the lack of evidence, and assorted other injustices. At last the judge seized the opportunity to sentence Diamondfield Jack to be hanged at the Cassia County jail on June 4, 1897.

Defense attorneys promptly filed a motion for a new trial, confident that their knowledge of prosecution strategy and the completely circumstantial case against Davis would result in a reversal by a higher court. The same legal personnel tried Fred Gleason in the same April session of the district court. Gleason was a local youth who had not oppressed sheepmen as Diamondfield Jack had, and he was tried on charges of aiding and abetting the murder of Cummings. Hawley won acquittal for Gleason, while charges against him in the murder of Wilson eventually were dropped.

In subsequent maneuvers regarding Diamondfield Jack, attorneys for each side tested .44 shells in .45 revolvers, and conducted test rides over the route supposedly taken by Davis and Gleason. Hawley also produced a doctor who stated that the dogs could not have survived thirteen days without food and water, raising the possibility that the killings had occurred after February 4, when Davis's whereabouts were firmly established. But the prosecution came up with a doctor who stated that the dogs *could* have survived a thirteen-day ordeal.

The original motion for a new trial was overruled in January 1898, but Hawley filed new appeals with the Idaho Supreme Court. When the trial transcript was printed for use by the Supreme Court, the printing job was awarded to C. B. Steunenberg, a sheepman. The transcript was suspiciously edited and altered in favor of the prosecution's case. After several months of studying the transcript, the Idaho Supreme Court upheld the original verdict, and Hawley turned to the State Board of Pardons in a last-ditch effort to save Diamondfield Jack from the hangman's noose.

In the meantime, Hawley and Perky had become convinced that information was being hidden from them. The lawyers began to ride the backcountry trails of Cassia County, trying to find someone who would unlock the mystery, and Hawley wrote to John Sparks asking that the real killers be revealed. It had been determined that on February 4, 1896, the respected Sparks-Harrell superintendent, James E.

Bower, and cowboy Jeff Gray had been riding together in the vicinity of the shootings. After Hawley pressured Bower, emphasizing that an innocent man was about to hang, the veteran stockman confessed the true story of the killings.

On October 13, 1898, Bower and Gray made sworn statements relating that they had ridden into the sheep camp of Wilson and Cummings at midday on February 4, 1896. Bower climbed into the sheep wagon to talk, but when he pointed out that the flock was grazing on the wrong side of the deadline, the conversation grew heated and a scuffle broke out between Bower and Wilson. As the two men grappled, Bower pulled a revolver from his shoulder holster, but the sheepman clutched the gun. Suddenly, Gray opened fire, pumping .44 slugs at the wagon from just behind Bower. Bower claimed that he thought Wilson's chin wound was superficial and that he did not know that Cummings, who had picked up a rifle, was hit. Gray reloaded his revolver, and the two cattlemen rode away, soon parting company.

Bower realized he had lost his corncob pipe during the scuffle, but he did not learn until three days after the shooting that the sheepmen had died. Bower and Gray told several cattlemen the story, but the truth was kept secret even after Diamondfield Jack and Gleason were arrested and tried. Bower believed an innocent man could never be hanged. Finally, two and a half years after the shooting, Bower realized that an innocent man indeed was about to be executed. Bower notified Gray that he was going to confess, and Gray decided to add his own statement.

Diamondfield Jack received a reprieve, but Hawley still could not secure a pardon, and Davis was rescheduled to hang on February 1, 1899. Calmly, Diamondfield Jack watched his gallows tested in the jail yard, and he fashioned horsehair ropes and trinkets for children who had visited the jail. Hawley finally managed to secure a stay of execution from the U.S. Circuit Court of Appeals in San Francisco.

The stay arrived in Boise the day before the hanging, but the nearest telegraph line to Albion was in Minidoka, twenty-eight miles north of the execution site. There was an unreliable telephone line to Albion, but even if it worked Hawley feared that vengeful sheepmen might intercept the message. Diamondfield Jack had openly persecuted sheepmen, and it was clear that a resentful sheepmen's faction intended to see Davis dead, despite the confessions of Bower and Gray.

Hawley dispatched Will Puckett on the afternoon train to Minidoka, while arrangements were made for three horses and two riders to meet the train. Fearing that sheepmen might set an ambush, Puckett and the other two men rode separately to the south. Pushing hard through a cold winter's night, Puckett arrived before dawn on February 1, galloping past the new teachers' college on a hill north of town and seeking out the sleeping sheriff to deliver the stay of execution. The other two riders soon came in unmolested.

A couple of weeks later, Albion experienced the drama of another murder trial as Jeff Gray was brought to the little courthouse. With Hawley again leading the defense, Gray was declared not guilty, and Bower was acquitted after a short trial in the fall. Hawley had obtained statements from eleven of Gray's jurors that he had been declared innocent of murder because he had killed in self-defense. But even though it had been established legally that someone else had committed the shootings, Diamondfield Jack remained under sentence of death.

Desperate legal maneuvering continued to try to avert an obvious miscarriage of justice. Diamondfield Jack, who sometimes issued tirades to newspapers and who wrote a ninety-three-page letter to the governor, received a total of eight reprieves during his years of incarceration. But the eighth reprieve, delaying the date from July 3 to July 17, 1902, was not issued until the morning of the hanging. At 10:05 A.M. on July 3, a telegram was sent from Boise to the Cassia County sheriff. In Minidoka copies of the telegram were handed to two cowboys who had been hired by Sparks-Harrell lawyers as gallopers. Fresh relays of horses were waiting at two points, and the cowboys raced separately — still fearing ambush by sheepmen — all the way to Albion. The sheriff had scheduled the execution for late in the day, hoping that a stay would arrive, and the cowboys thundered down into town with the welcome reprieve.

Hawley went to work again. On July 16, 1901, the day before Diamondfield Jack was to be hanged, the Idaho Board of Pardons commuted his sentence — to life imprisonment. Incredibly, even though he had been acknowledged to be innocent of the killings, Diamondfield Jack was taken to the Idaho State Penitentiary outside Boise. Hawley finally persuaded "Honest John" Sparks, soon to win election as governor of Nevada, to admit to the Board of Pardons that he and Harrell had kept Bower's terrible secret to avoid the ruin of a valued employee and friend. But not until December 17, 1902 — and then only by a two-to-one vote — did the board award Diamondfield Jack a pardon. Ignoring overwhelming evidence, including two confessions, that Diamondfield Jack had spent six years behind bars for a crime he did not commit, numerous Idaho newspapers railed that freeing the hired gunman was a miscarriage of justice.

Diamondfield Jack wisely left Idaho, turning up in the boomtown of Tonopah, Nevada. Soon he struck it rich as a prospector, becoming president of the Diamondfield Triangle Gold Mining Company and founding a mining town he named Diamondfield. He consorted with the famous dancehall proprietress, Diamond Tooth Lil (who had nine husbands during her colorful life), he sued *The Saturday Evening Post* for defamation of character, and he dabbled in the Mexican Revolution along the border. Although his fortunes declined, he continued to prospect likely claims, and in 1945 Diamondfield Jack and Diamond Tooth Lil were reunited in a Las Vegas casino. He died on the second day of 1949, after being struck by a taxi in Las Vegas.

Diamondfield Jack was one of three gunmen hired by a large cattle ranching corporation to harass sheepmen, and Davis hounded herders with a vengeance. When two other employees of the corporation fought with two herders and killed them, sheepmen readily blamed Diamondfield Jack and sought his execution with vindictive persistence. Even after Diamondfield Jack was proven innocent, vengeful sheepmen still hoped to have their onetime tormentor hanged or at least imprisoned indefinitely. The malignant animosity with which each side battled the other was characteristic of the strife which erupted from time to time between cattlemen and sheepherders in scattered locations across the West.

6

War in Wyoming

We begin to fear (they the sheepmen) will ---- up the range.
— George B. McClellan, manager of
the Red Bank Cattle Company

Despite the protracted clash between cattlemen and sheep ranchers in Texas, regardless of the homicidal viciousness of Arizona's Pleasant Valley War, violence in Wyoming between cattle and sheep interests featured a greater variety of conflict than that found in any other western state or territory. Cattle were first ranged permanently on Wyoming grass in 1868, and pioneer cattlemen promptly recognized the superb grazing capabilities of the territory. Cattle ranching became the primary industry of Wyoming, which soon was dominated economically, politically, and socially by cattle barons. The Wyoming Stock Growers Association became a powerful force in territorial affairs (in 1885 the WSGA operated on a budget of $52,796, while the entire territorial budget was just over $38,000). Although North American cattle ranching originated in Texas, the cattle kingdom attained its most impressive stature in Wyoming during the 1870s and 1880s. Wyoming cattlemen and cowboys would defy the encroachments of sheep graziers with unparalleled determination and resourcefulness.

But Wyoming sheepmen proved equally determined and re-

> **THE SHEEP QUEEN OF WYOMING**
>
> Lucy Morrison brought 2,000 sheep, three daughters, and an invalid husband into Wyoming from Idaho in 1882. She had been harassed by cattlemen in Idaho Territory, but her move to Wyoming brought even more trouble.
>
> Settling near isolated South Pass, she lost all but 200 of her sheep during the first frigid winter. Tying her daughters to sagebrush so they would not wander off, she tended her little flock closely. When a mountain lion attacked her sheep, she put ground glass inside a baited lamb's carcass and killed the predator. When Indians approached her cabin, she doused the walls with pungent camphor and scattered the potential attackers by announcing that her children had smallpox. Ravaged by dysentery, she cured herself by subsisting solely on ewe's milk.
>
> Cowboys rode in to burn her wagons and scatter her expanding flock. Undaunted, she gathered her sheep on foot. After her husband died she married a sheepman named Curtis Moore, but Lucy Moore continued to develop her own property and flocks. Eventually, the "Sheep Queen of Wyoming" acquired title to 6,000 acres of land, as well as thousands of acres of leased land, and her flocks were among the largest in the state.

sourceful. Sheep were being raised in Wyoming by the late 1860s, and the Durbin brothers, who ranched four miles from Cheyenne, shipped the first sheep by rail out of the territory in 1872. Sheep ranchers conceded nothing to cattle interests and struggled resolutely for the right to use Wyoming pasturage. Battlegrounds included courtrooms as well as rangelands; Wyoming legal struggles as well as shootouts proved to be landmark episodes.

For years, however, there was little conflict between sheepmen and cattle ranchers, primarily because Wyoming's vast ranges could comfortably accommodate all of the livestock present in the territory. Federal census figures indicated that in 1870 there were only 9,501 head of cattle in Wyoming, alongside just 6,409 sheep. There was a dynamic cattle boom during the 1870s, but by 1880 Wyoming cattle still numbered merely 273,625 head, while sheep totaled 140,225. There was plenty of room in the territory for both cattle and sheep. By 1886 the number of sheep had increased to 368,997, and cattle totals likewise soared during the early 1880s.[1] But the disastrous winter of 1886–87 devastated Wyoming's cattle industry, while the despised woollies successfully withstood the bitter weather, partially because they were more carefully supervised than cattle, and because sheepmen already had begun the practice of winter feeding.

Many Wyoming cattle ranchers were forced out of business, and the Wyoming Stock Growers Association was staggered. Membership dropped from 416 in 1886 to just 68 in 1890, despite a cut in annual dues to five dollars, and many functions of the organization were taken over by the territorial government. Sheep ranchers quickly filled the void on the range, while not a few cattlemen turned to raising sheep, especially after passage of the Dingley Tariff of 1897, which had the effect of increasing the value of ewes from about a dollar and a half to four dollars per head. By 1900, more than five million head of sheep were being raised in Wyoming.[2]

But cattlemen stubbornly regrouped. The Wyoming Stock Growers Association was reorganized, and cattle numbers expanded to 670,000 by 1900. These resilient cattle ranchers were proud and courageous, and as Wyoming ranges became crowded they resisted the encroachments posed by sheepmen and "nesters." Nesters were far more numerous than sheepmen, and always obtained title to their land, often through the Homestead Act. Although 160-acre homesteads were infinitesimal in contrast to the rangelands used by sheep and cattle ranchers, these farms frequently controlled streams and were enclosed by fences. Furthermore, farmers often ran a few head of cattle, and big ranchers suspected that many of these animals were rustled from their herds.

At its zenith in the 1880s, the Wyoming Stock Growers Association employed twenty-five range detectives, and the association systematically assigned mavericks during the sanctioned roundups. But control of rustling dropped drastically after 1886, when the association's membership and activities were severely curtailed. Even if the unauthorized branding of mavericks had been widespread prior to 1886 — and there is no way of knowing — a few missing head of cattle were hardly noticed by the big operators of Wyoming's open-range heyday. After 1886, herds were dramatically reduced, and losses became obvious and resented. Nesters and small ranchers often built their little herds with long loops and hot irons, but public opinion was against the cattle barons, who found it difficult to produce sufficient evidence for court action. Cattlemen therefore began to take direct action against rustling.

In Sweetwater, Ella Watson, a buxom young woman known as "Cattle Kate," and her partner Jim Averill flouted the ire of cattlemen. Cattle Kate ran a bawdy house and apparently traded her favors for rustled beeves, while Averill condemned cattle barons in fiery letters to the editor. Cattle Kate and Averill were warned to leave the country, and Jim was accused of rustling. On July 20, 1889, Kate and Averill were taken out of her establishment and hanged from a tree.

More serious trouble arose in Johnson County, which featured a strong congregation of cattle thieves. Nate Champion, called "King of the Rustlers" by big ranchers, fought off an attack by four gunmen at a line shack on the Powder River on November 1, 1891. Frustrated cattlemen, working unofficially through the Wyoming Stock Growers Association, began to plan an invasion of Johnson County, hiring gunmen and compiling a list of seventy men targeted for assassination, including Sheriff Red Angus.

On April 5, 1892, at the conclusion of the annual spring meeting of the Wyoming Stock Growers Association in Cheyenne, a special Union Pacific train headed north. On board were nineteen cattlemen, five range detectives, twenty-one gunmen from Texas (hired for five dollars per day, plus fifty dollars for any man on the target list they killed), one Idaho gunman, and six observers. Three baggage cars carried horses, wagons, munitions, and equipment. The "Regulators" debarked at Casper and struck out on horseback for Johnson County, 100 miles away.

Led by Maj. Frank Wolcott, on April 9 the Regulators attacked the KC Ranch, recently leased by Nate Champion and Nick Ray, who were included on the assassination list. Both men were killed, although Champion put up a valiant fight. When word of the invasion reached Buffalo, the seat of Johnson County, Sheriff Angus led a posse of 200 angry citizens south to meet the Regulators head-on. Angus and his army besieged the invaders for two days, April 10 and 11, at the TA Ranch fourteen miles south of Buffalo. The U.S. Cavalry arrived from Fort McKinney, outside Buffalo, just in time to save the Regulators from being overwhelmed. The cavalrymen escorted the beleaguered Regulators to Fort D. A. Russell near Cheyenne, but the "prisoners" were given free run of town. Key witnesses disappeared, while the legal expenses and incarceration costs exhausted the Johnson County treasury. The case finally came to trial in January 1893, but charges were dismissed.[3]

An aroused populace had taken to arms against the cattlemen's invasion, and retribution looting of the cattle ranches had been so widespread in the wake of the clash that twelve troops of cavalry and a federal marshal's posse were dispersed to control the lawlessness. Cattlemen who had backed the invasion reportedly lost $100,000. There also were political repercussions against Acting Governor Amos Barber and Senators Francis E. Warren and Joseph M. Carey, Republicans who had intervened to save the Regulators. Although several of the participating cattlemen were Democrats, political power in Wyoming for a time swung from Republicans to Democrats and Populists.

Despite these problems, it was apparent by 1893 that cattlemen and gunmen who had participated in the invasion would suffer no legal punishment. It seemed clear that cattle interests still remained above the law, while sheepmen demonstrably did not enjoy such immunity. On June 7, 1893, a shootout near Sheridan resulted in the death of cattle rancher John D. Adams at the hands of sheepman William Jones. Adams had ordered Jones to keep his sheep away from the ranges near the Adams ranch. When Jones refused, Adams came after the sheepman, and an argument ensued which led to the fatal gunfight. But despite Jones's claim of self-defense, the sheepman was convicted of second-degree murder and sentenced to twenty-two years in the state penitentiary.[4] The killers of Nate Champion and Nick Ray must have smiled, and Wyoming cattlemen surely were emboldened to take action against sheepmen.

In 1893 and 1894 there were several raids on sheep camps in Converse County. Cattlemen announced deadlines, and when sheepmen violated those deadlines raiders wearing gunnysack masks struck hard. On different occasions the gunnysackers shot and clubbed sheep, burned sheep wagons, and wounded or otherwise mistreated some of the herders. No legal action resulted, although within a few years certain of the most virulent gunnysackers, swayed by economics, entered the sheep business. In 1893 cowboy Virgil Turner, who had killed a fellow ranch hand two years earlier, quarreled with a sheepherder. Armed with a rifle, the sheepherder took cover behind a rock. Turner pulled his revolver, spurred his mount, and charged the herder. The sheepherder was shot to death, and Turner was acquitted on grounds of self-defense.[5]

In March 1894 a dance at Lonetree was interrupted when a brawl broke out between a cowboy and a sheepherder. The two antagonists whaled away at each other for half an hour, until they were so battered and exhausted that they could not continue. During the fight several scuffles broke out between friends of the two men slugging it out in the main event. During the following June, a Saratoga sheepman named Jones issued a call to area sheep and cattle ranchers to meet together and determine a deadline which would be enforced by a joint committee of these rival parties. Both groups apparently ignored Jones's idea, and no action was taken.⁶

Jacob Ervay ran a ranch eighty miles west of Casper in Natrona County. On Friday afternoon, February 22, 1895, Ervay rode to a nearby sheep camp established by George E. Howard and William Kimberly, intending to ask them not to graze their flock nearer to his ranch. Almost immediately Ervay triggered a Winchester round into Kimberly; the bullet tore through the sheepman's arm and into his body. With surprising charity, Ervay dismounted and helped Kimberly to his bed in the tent. Ervay then leaped back onto his horse and pursued Howard, who emptied his gun at the rancher. Although struck in the hip, Ervay shot Howard in the arm and put a bullet through his cap.⁷

Trouble between cattlemen and sheepmen broke out in the Henry's Fork region of southwestern Wyoming in 1894. Cattlemen of the area increasingly resented the wintering of sheep in the lush area south of Henry's Fork. One cattle partisan rhapsodized that before the intrusion of sheep, "Springs were to be found bubbling from our hillsides, wild flowers bloomed in profusion, and succulent bunch grass grew in abundance." These idyllic conditions supposedly continued even after cattlemen drove herds into the valley and fenced in their ranches. But as the cowboy eulogized, "now this once beautiful country is so badly beaten down with sheep that there is scarcely enough grass to support a sage hen." Some cattlemen sold out or moved their herds out of the valley, while those who remained were "crowded to the foothills of the Uintahs." Added resentment was caused by the fact that a majority of sheepmen made their homes in Utah or elsewhere, only coming to Henry's Fork Valley for winter grazing. Furthermore, it was claimed that sheep had been ranged right up to the doorsteps of the cattlemen, and that woollies sometimes were driven into enclosures on cattle ranches.⁸

On January 15, 1894, eighteen cattlemen rode forth to force all sheep bands out of the valley. At first they encountered no resistance, but when they surveyed John Forshey's outfit, it was decided to round up reinforcements. In the meantime, Forshey rode to nearby Carter and sent a telegram to Green River, imploring the sheriff of Sweetwater County to ride over and halt the trouble.⁹

During the next couple of days more than 100 cattlemen and cowboys gathered together and drove flocks from the region, even forcing two sheepmen named Blake and Beckstead to vacate their own ranch. Any herders who seemed reluctant to move were told to get out and "d--- quick." Forshey was outraged when he received an anonymous note:

> Burnt Fork, Wyoming
> January 16, 1894
>
> Notice to John Forshey:
>
> We the people of Henry's Fork Valley from head to mouth do hereby notify you as we have all the sheep herds, to keep out of this valley, and from five to six miles to the north of Henry's Fork.
> No objection to sheep kept in your inclosure.
>
> Respectfully the People

Forshey rode through the neighborhood, but he could find no one who would admit any connection with the warning. Through a letter to the newspaper, Forshey stated his regrets over the range troubles, insisted that his sheep had not strayed onto grassland owned by other ranchers, and wryly thanked the cattlemen for permitting him to run his own stock in his own "inclosure."

After a brief investigation, the sheriff returned to Green River without taking any action. One cattleman wrote to the newspaper contending that as recently as 1889 the region north of the Union Pacific Railroad had supported 50,000 head of cattle on superb grasslands. But now, within just five years, it was claimed that half of these animals had died, and if the trend continued for five more years "one man and a blind mare with a colt following will be all that any cattleman in this part of the country will need to round up and handle his herd." This calamity could be blamed on "the little tinkling sheep bell which has sounded the death knell of the cattle industry in this vicinity."

Cattlemen issued a call for a meeting to be held at Fort Bridger on April 15 to arrange a fair division of the range between cattle and sheep ranchers. All sheepmen holding flocks on Henry's, Smith's, and Black's forks of the Green River were invited to attend. But of the fifty ranchers who met at Fort Bridger, only Thomas Taylor was a sheepman. Cattlemen condemned sheep and sheep ranching with all of the customary arguments, while Taylor courageously defended his occupation.

Then cattleman William Summers, who had been accused of leading the original eighteen-man party, introduced a resolution to create a deadline. Henry's Fork cattlemen had enlisted the support of cattle ranchers in adjoining regions: the deadline would apply to an area approximately fifty miles long and twenty-eight miles wide, encompassing 1,540 square miles and 985,000 acres — a region larger than Rhode Island and five times the size of Henry's Fork Valley. Thomas Taylor provided the lone dissenting vote to the deadline resolution.

Sheepmen countered with a meeting at the courthouse in Evanston on May 5, 1894. Thirteen sheep raisers came to the courthouse, elected John Forshey chairman, and voted to join with the Sweetwater sheepmen's organization to form the "Woolgrowers Association of Uinta and Sweetwater Counties." Five days later, a large number of sheep ranchers from Uinta and Sweetwater counties gathered at the courthouse to adopt a constitution and by-laws, and to frame a resolution for publication:

> Resolved by this association that while we do not believe in or justify the herding of sheep at or near private ranches, still we are determined to enforce our rights to free and unrestricted range upon the public domain and with that end in view this association will assist, aid and defend any member hereof in the full and complete enjoyment of his rights within the law.[10]

Newspaper criticism soon focused upon Utah flockmasters, who seasonally used Wyoming grass without generating any tax revenue for the state. In 1890 the Wyoming State Legislature had passed a quarantine law, prohibiting the entry of diseased sheep and requiring that any local sheep infested with scab be quarantined and clipped. A sheep inspector was provided for each county to enforce these provisions, but in 1894 Roney Pomeroy, inspector for Uinta County, was roundly criticized for failing to enforce the laws against "scabby Mormon sheep." The Mormon flockmasters also were regarded as scabby, and religious prejudice again took its place alongside racial overtones as a motivation of sheepmen-cattlemen conflict.[11]

Sheep graziers seem to have agreed to keep their flocks north of the cattlemen's deadline, because there was no more trouble for a time. During the middle and late 1890s, the same pattern prevailed elsewhere in Wyoming: tensions would develop between the two factions, cattlemen would insist upon a deadline, and trouble would die down when sheepmen complied. In 1897, for example, Park County cattle ranchers around Meeteetse and the upper Greybull River decided to persuade "the sheepmen to come to an agreement regarding a line on a reserved country for the cattlemen." Otto Franc and another cattleman named Pearce were delegated to approach the sheepmen. Franc and Pearce rode from ranch to ranch in a buckboard and succeeded in persuading area sheepmen to honor the cattlemen's deadline.[12]

But when sheepmen ignored deadlines, cattlemen proved increasingly inclined to resort to violence. In November 1894, cattlemen in the Big Piney region of the upper Green River Valley heard reports that sheepmen were planning to move their flocks north of the Union Pacific Railroad into the valley. During the next few months, tensions grew between sheep and cattle owners, and on April 10, 1895, a well-attended meeting was conducted at Big Piney to discuss the problem. Sheepmen and cattlemen mutually agreed to observe a deadline. At a second meeting a month later, on May 10 in Evanston, a division of the ranges in question was worked out.[13]

However, within a few weeks, in June 1895, several sheep owners combined their flocks, hired a dozen armed guards, and moved their sheep onto rangeland near Big Piney which had been designated for cattle grazing. When no resistance ensued, the sheepmen apparently let down their guard. Within a few nights raiders struck the camp, surprising the sheepherders as they slept. The herders were tied and blindfolded, then the raiders spent the balance of the night clubbing sheep. Some 2,000 sheep were destroyed, and when daylight came the sheepherders were driven back across Bridger Pass with what remained of their flocks and a warning never to return.[14]

Unchecked by the law and increasingly crowded by sheep, cattle ranchers across Wyoming turned with growing frequency to extralegal pressure against sheepmen. In May 1897 cattlemen of the Jackson Hole region established a "committee of safety" and published a notice that "no sheep would be permitted to pass through Jackson's Hole . . . under any circumstances."[15]

For more than a decade, the Big Horn Basin would be the scene of repeated conflict between sheepmen and cattlemen. In 1897 George B. McClellan, manager of the Red Bank Cattle Company, wrote to Governor W. A. Richards, a fellow cattleman: "We begin to fear (they the sheepmen) will ---- up the range." Cattlemen in the region met and drew up a deadline which angled from ranch to ranch, roughly from Kirby Creek to Ten Sleep. McClellan, Joe Emge from Ten Sleep, Dave Pickard, and a cattleman named Shaw were designated to meet the sheepmen "to divide the range in some manner agreeable to both [parties]." (When Emge switched sides a decade later, there would be tragic consequences in Ten Sleep.) Apparently no agreeable arrangement was made, because in September 1897 gunshots were fired into the tents of sheepmen who disregarded the deadline. Trouble was not confined to the Big Horn Basin; in August 1899 four horsemen killed 150 sheep belonging to Senator Francis E. Warren in the Cheyenne area.[16]

As Wyoming entered the twentieth century, sheep raising became more popular. Ranchers continued to turn from cattle to sheep, or at least ran flocks of sheep with their cattle herds. A substantial number of diehards, though, remained proud throwbacks to the days when cattle barons ruled the range and scorned sheep. In 1901, in the Henry's Fork region, a sheep outfit owned by Sam Butterfield was raided. When the raiders began to club his sheep, Butterfield tried to resist but was shot in the heel. Reportedly, Butterfield drove his sheep from the area. At about the same time, sheepman Aaron Garside drove a flock of sheep onto grasslands at Hickey Mountain near Lonetree. Garside ignored the protests of nearby cattle ranchers, but soon was killed under mysterious circumstances. No indictments were handed down, but neighborhood citizens assumed that a cattleman had assassinated Garside.[17]

In July 1902 about fifteen bands of sheep owned by men of the Rock Springs area crossed a deadline in the New Fork region of Green River Valley. Cattlemen launched a massive raid, with 150 masked riders descending upon the sheep camps. A herder was killed, 2,000 sheep were destroyed, the surviving herders were driven out of the country, and the remaining sheep were scattered, perhaps to fall prey to predators.[18]

At the same time that deadlines were being pronounced and defended, that gunnysackers were clubbing sheep and shooting herders, contests for Wyoming ranges also were being waged in courtrooms. For example, Price Martin was a cattleman who filed a homestead claim near Glendo and grazed his herd on public domain in Laramie County. He acquired no other land, by purchase or lease, and by 1890 other graziers had moved onto ranges Martin earlier had used exclusively. Martin soon learned that lands around him had been leased by J. M. Wilson, manager of the Platte Valley Sheep Company. The president of the company was DeForest Richards, the Republican governor of Wyoming. Martin complained to the State Land Commission that he had been discriminated against as a Democrat, and that he was at a distinct disadvantage because the president of the leasing company was governor. The commission denied Martin's complaint, contending

> ## THE GREATEST SHEPHERD SINCE ABRAHAM
>
> *Francis E. Warren, who became "the greatest shepherd since Abraham," was born in Massachusetts in 1844. He enlisted in the Union army at the age of eighteen, won the Congressional Medal of Honor at Port Hudson in 1863, and moved to the wild frontier village of Cheyenne in 1868. A shrewd, physically impressive man with a gifted capacity for friendship, Warren excelled at varied business ventures.*
>
> *Warren entered ranching in 1874. "Live stock raising is the safest and most remunerative industry now known to the American people," he stated enthusiastically. In 1883 he organized the Warren Live Stock Company, one of Wyoming's first corporations. By 1885 the company listed assets of $491,512, including 24,023 sheep, 1,908 cattle and 460 horses, plus 270,868 acres of land owned or controlled. In 1893 the number of sheep had increased to 93,000, and from 1901 until 1907 he served as president of the National Wool Growers Association.*
>
> *Warren's prominence as a sheepman cost him little political popularity in Wyoming, and was an indication of the increasing appeal of sheep raising. He was appointed territorial governor in February 1885, serving until the presidential administration changed in November 1886. When Wyoming became a state in 1890, he became the first elected governor, although he quickly chose to accept a seat in the United States Senate. He served thirty-seven years in the Senate, long a record tenure, and it was a fellow senator who compared him to Abraham. He died in 1929, but the Warren Live Stock Company still is a thriving operation.*

that he had had ample opportunity to have applied for a lease.[19]

The Platte Valley Sheep Company then began to fence in its lease lands, thereby enclosing several sections of public grazing lands. Martin next insisted upon his right to pass through the fences to graze his cattle on public lands and to water his stock at the Platte River. But in 1900 the Platte Valley Sheep Company obtained an injunction from the district court forbidding Martin to allow his cattle to enter or cross any portion of the leased land. Martin appealed the injunction to the Wyoming Supreme Court, contending that his cattle could derive no benefit from the public lands because they were excluded from the only available water supply.

The state supreme court modified the injunction so that Martin could graze his livestock on public lands within the enclosure, but his cattle could not drift onto leased sections. Although the leased lands had been illegally enclosed, the Wyoming Supreme Court held no jurisdiction over this aspect of the case, since the fencing had been in violation of *federal* laws. Martin therefore could utilize the lands in question, but he would have to hire cowboys to stay with his herd and see that his cattle did not drift onto leased areas.

A less intricate case was *Cosgriff vs. Miller.* In 1898 cattleman I. C. Miller leased lands near Rawlins from the Union Pacific Railroad. When sheep belonging to the Cosgriff brothers were driven onto the leased ranges, Miller obtained $6,500 trespass damages in district court. There were no fences, but the court ruled that fencing was not required to separate leased lands from adjacent public domain. Survey markings were considered sufficient, and the Cosgriff brothers had been warned to keep their sheep off of specific ranges. Cosgriff attorneys appealed the judgment to the Wyoming Supreme Court, but an 1899 decision upheld the lower court.[20]

Far more famous than *Martin vs. Platte Valley Sheep Company, Cosgriff vs. Miller,* or any other case involving litigation between cattle and sheep interests, was a homicide trial. It dealt with one of the most infamous murders in the history of western violence, involving one of the West's most notorious killers: Tom Horn.

7

Tom Horn in Wyoming

Killing is my specialty. I look at it as a business proposition, and I think I have a corner on the market.
— Tom Horn

Tom Horn was one of the most mysterious and fascinating characters of the Old West, and the notorious climax of his adventurous career resulted from the heinous murder of Willie Nickell, adolescent son of a sheepman. The brutal ambush of young Nickell crystallized a permanent change of attitude toward unbridled violence over western rangeland, as signaled by the dramatic trial and execution of Horn.

Born in 1860, Tom Horn was reared on a Missouri farm, where he became addicted to hunting, fishing, and outdoor life. Tom was a habitual truant from school, and after a whipping by his father, the rebellious fourteen-year-old ran away to the West. He worked as a railroad laborer, teamster, stagecoach driver and cowboy, but by 1876 he was employed in Arizona by the famed scout Al Sieber, and in 1885 Horn succeeded Sieber as civilian chief of scouts. Horn was an important figure in the campaign which resulted in the final capture of Geronimo — although he did not play as significant a role as he later claimed. During the next few years he served as a deputy under Arizona sheriffs Buckey O'Neill and Glen Reynolds, occasionally worked a gold claim, and avidly engaged in rodeo competitions, once winning a steer-roping contest in Phoenix. From 1890 to 1894, Horn was employed by the Pinkerton Detective Agency, headquartering in Denver, but he found the work too tame.[1]

In 1894 Tom Horn was hired by the Swan Land and Cattle Company as a "range rider," or stock detective. For the next several years he worked for big Wyoming ranches, prowling the range to eliminate rustling. During his first year as a range rider, Horn single-handedly captured and took into custody the "Langhoff outfit," six rustlers and seven stolen beeves. Horn bound his captives over to the authorities in Laramie. The rustlers were tried, but five won their freedom, and the sixth received a pardon shortly after being delivered to the penitentiary.[2]

Apparently, this failure of the legal system made a strong impression upon Horn and his employers. Horn soon acquired the reputation of killing rustlers who refused to leave the country. Through the years, Horn worked closely with John C. Coble, who ran the Iron Mountain Cattle Company in rugged country northwest of Cheyenne. Coble greatly admired the famous Indian scout, but the rancher had a certain notoriety of his own. In 1890, for example, he tangled with Kels Nickell, a nester whose stock often grazed on Coble range, and Nickell cut Coble with a pocketknife. On another occasion, in 1895, Coble went on a drunken spree in the exclusive Cheyenne Club, and he was suspended after shooting up a large painting of a Holstein bull.

William Lewis, an English immigrant who held a 160-acre homestead near the Iron Mountain ranch, bragged about stealing Iron Mountain cattle. He received a warning to pull out, then in August 1895 his corpse was found on the range, riddled with three bullets fired from a range of 300 yards. It was widely rumored that Tom Horn had killed Lewis.

Not long after the death of Lewis, Fred Powell received a similar warning to leave Wyoming. A known confederate of Lewis, Powell had a homestead about ten miles away, near Horse Creek. Defiantly, Powell invited cowboys from the nearby KYT Ranch to come to his place for a supper of their own beef. Soon a rider shot Powell to death, and those who saw the big assassin were wise enough not to identify Tom Horn.

Horn now cultivated his image as a cold-blooded killer. He was a tall, powerful man who stood over six feet and weighed more than 200 pounds. When not investigating stock thefts, he worked cattle on the ranches which employed him. He always carried a forty-foot lariat and liked to show off his roping skills. Horn usually packed a revolver along with a rifle, and he also readily demonstrated his marksmanship. A cowboy for the Swan Land and Cattle Company was sometimes asked to toss tin cans in the air for Horn, who would drill them twice with revolver bullets before the can would strike the ground.[3] Horn's two primary enjoyments were participating in rodeos and drinking in a good saloon in Cheyenne or Laramie or Denver. He drank heavily whenever in a town, and when he was drunk he talked boastfully, often about his murders and gunfights.

Much of his drunken boasting was classic frontier exaggeration. But this murderous braggadocio doubtless added to his sinister reputation. Horn roamed widely through much of Wyoming and Colorado, "working the pastures." The range was mostly fenced, but he would be out for a week or two at a time, riding through the vast "pastures" of his employers, and checking the much smaller pastures of the nesters who were likely to brand mavericks or rustle branded cattle. "Of course," testified Horn, "it is just the least bit embarrassing . . . to ride into a man's pasture and look over his pasture and have the man come along."[4] But Horn sometimes spent the night with men whose pastures he would check, although customarily he tried to stay out of sight, riding cross-country rather than on public roads.

He traveled light, carrying only a little bacon and bread, and often going without food if he could not shoot a jackrabbit. In the summers he did not even carry a slicker or coat, sleeping on the ground with only his saddle blanket to make an uncomfortable bed. But he seemed to like these duties. "I don't have any particular place to go, or any particular time. I don't work under any particular instructions at any time. I am supposed to go when I please and where I please, and how I please. The boss or foreman of the ranch, the manager of the ranch leaves that entirely to myself."[5]

Although he skulked from ranch to ranch, no one ordered him off their ranges. Horn's contemporaries understood his purpose: "He was given employment by some of the larger cattle outfits, to rid the country of rustlers and sheep men, to dispose of them in his own fashion; they called him a range rider. These large outfits by whom he was employed were very touchy and did not want it to be known who paid him or whom he was working for. Whenever rustling was evident or maverick calves were stolen and branded Tom Horn was notified so that he could go to the scene, look the situation over, and, when the guilty party or parties were identified by him, he at once disposed of them in such a way that they would never bother again."[6]

Governor William A. Richards, who owned a large number of cattle in the Big Horn country, interviewed Horn in the Wyoming Stock Growers Association office in the capitol regarding a solution to rustling problems. "Whenever anything else fails," stated Horn, "I have a system that never does." Horn went into specifics about his fee, but when he pointed out that there should be no limit regarding the number of men who might have to be gotten rid of, Governor Richards became visibly uncomfortable and indicated that the interview should end. Horn politely excused himself. "So that is Tom Horn!" exclaimed Richards to President Charles B. Penrose of the WSGA, who had arranged the meeting. "A very different man from what I expected to meet. Why, he is not bad looking, and is quite intelligent; but a cool devil, ain't he?"[7]

It is likely that Horn's chilling reputation greatly facilitated his work, persuading rustlers who received warnings to leave the country rather than risk a visit by the mysterious rider with a deadly rifle.

Horn interrupted his career as a range rider to join the army during the Spanish-American War, serving in Cuba as a chief mule packer. When he returned to Wyoming he was welcomed back by big ranchers, increasingly pressured by nesters and sheepmen. In 1900 he ventured into Brown's Park in the northwestern corner of Colorado. Still isolated even today, at the turn of the century Brown's Park was a notorious haunt of outlaws, from Butch Cassidy and the Wild Bunch to rustlers who regularly relayed stolen livestock. Horn rode into the valley, which is surrounded by vast mountains and dotted with marshy lakes. Even in outlaw country, Horn proved to be a formidable figure, later bragging that "I stopped cow stealing there in one summer."[8]

Indeed, within three months Horn assassinated two suspected rustlers in the Brown's Park area. On July 8, 1900, Matt Rash stepped outside his cabin and was staggered by three rifle bullets. A fourth round killed his sorrel mare. While Horn raced off to establish an alibi in Denver, Rash stumbled inside and collapsed on his cot. He dipped a finger in his own blood and tried to write on an envelope, but he died before he could make any legible markings. On October 3, Horn established a sniper's position 200 yards from the cabin of "Nigger Isom" Dart, a black cowboy regarded as a rustler by Horn's employers. After eating breakfast, Dart and five friends emerged from the cabin and walked toward the corral. Horn fired two rounds from his .30-.30

rifle, and Dart dropped dead with a head wound. Dart's companions fled inside, where they cowered all day before sneaking away after dark.

By 1901 John Coble and other large cattlemen were thoroughly disgusted with Kels Nickell. Nickell was born in Kentucky in 1858, but in 1863 his father was murdered by guerrilla raiders. From 1875 to 1880, Nickell served a hitch in the Fifth Cavalry, then took up a homestead on Iron Mountain. Married in Cheyenne in 1881 (he was divorced from his first wife in 1877), Nickell raised nine children on his little spread. By the 1890s he had accumulated more than 1,000 head of cattle, but naturally he was suspected of rustling some of the animals. As the range became fenced in, his still small holdings could not support such a cattle herd. Contentious by nature, in the spring of 1901 Nickell brought sheep to his range.[9]

For more than a decade John Coble, who had tried unsuccessfully to file charges against Nickell after the 1890 knifing, had looked for the opportunity to oust the disagreeable nester. Now Nickell had introduced sheep to the Iron Mountain country and was grazing his band "on the cattle range and watering them out of water holes which had always been used for cattle." Ora Haley and the Swan Land and Cattle Company joined Coble in resenting the intrusion of sheep onto range that had traditionally been used by big cattle operations. "This caused a great deal of agitation among the cattle men," observed a Swan rider, "which resulted in Tom Horn being notified of the condition."[10]

On July 16, 1900, John Coble wrote to his partner about the situation: "The Iron Mountain, Wall Rock and Plumbago pastures are filled with sheep and look wooly. Our she cattle are in Iron Mountain and they are doing fine, like in a meadow. When the sheep men attempt to drive or handle our cattle I will at once have them arrested. But they are scared to death, are hiring all the six-shooters and bad men they can find. I want Horn back here [Horn was in Brown's Park]; he will straighten them out by merely riding around."[11]

Horn heard not only from large cattlemen but from small ranchers as well, who said that it "was not right," and said so "in very strong terms."

"They say if [Nickell] started in the sheep business," pointed out Horn, "it would be different. Being in the cattle business and deliberately selling his cattle and putting sheep in for no other reasons than to spite the neighbors about it," would prove intolerable to those neighbors. The consensus of opinion among area cattle ranchers, according to Horn, was that only "the kind of man Nickell is, troublesome and quarrelsome, [a] turbulent man without character or principle," would bring sheep into a cattle haven.[12]

Adding to the tensions was the fact that Nickell had wrangled for years with another small rancher named James Miller, whose home was about three miles northeast of the Nickell homestead. Willie Nickell, one of Kels's sons, fought with Miller's sons, Gus and Victor. Even though Gus was two or three years older than Willie, young Nickell was large for his age, and he whipped Gus — much to the chagrin of James Miller. Indeed, in 1900 the senior Miller bullied thirteen-year-old Willie, beating him with a whip and threatening him with curses and a cocked sixgun. Kels Nickell had Victor and Gus arrested for fence cutting. "They go to the other neighbors with their trouble and tell what kind of ornery people they are," testified Tom Horn. "They are both the same kind of people . . . neither one has good reputations." James Miller began carrying a shotgun. When the weapon discharged accidentally in a wagon, killing one of the younger Miller boys and wounding a daughter, the embittered Miller blamed the tragedy on Kels Nickell. His reasoning was that he carried the gun only because of the feud with the Nickells. Nickell added to Miller's resentment by grazing sheep close to the Miller house. "I wonder how the son-of-a-bitch feels about it because I left them right in his door yard," Nickell told Horn. Horn said that he had heard of Miller offering a $500 reward to anyone who would kill Nickell.[13]

In mid-July Tom Horn rode out from John Coble's headquarters to spend several days inspecting the range on behalf of his employers. After a few days he stopped at the Miller ranch, partly to see Glendoline Kimmel, a schoolmarm who roomed with the Millers and who was quite taken with the famous frontiersman. On Monday, July 15, 1901, Horn slept with the Miller boys in a big tent in front of the house. On Tuesday he rode off to locate the Nickell sheep. He found them in one of Miller's pastures, then returned for another night in the tent. While at the Millers he fished a bit, yarned with the boys, visited with Glendoline, and engaged in target practice. He carried a .30-.30 Winchester but no belt gun. Horn left the Miller ranch on Wednesday morning, July 17, later testifying that he spent another couple of days checking Swan and Coble ranges before returning to the Coble ranch and on into Laramie for a spree.

On Thursday morning, July 18, thunder and rain slashed across the Iron Mountain country. Breakfast at the Nickell homestead was served before 6:00. Surveyor John Apperson and Mrs. Nickell's brother, William Mahoney, were on hand to help Kels survey fence lines a mile or so east of the house. Fred Nickell, Willie's younger brother, was assigned to drive a hay wagon to a distant barn. Willie was told to fetch a sheepherder; on Wednesday an Italian herder had stopped by looking for work, and overnight Kels had decided it was a mistake to have sent him away.

Willie was directed to ride his father's saddle horse, and because of the stormy weather he donned Kels's coat and hat. Willie, now fourteen, owned a .22 rifle, but he left on his mission unarmed. Kels led the surveyor and his brother-in-law to the east immediately after breakfast. Fred Nickell drove the hay wagon to the west, passed through a wire gate, and drove past a concealed rifleman. Fred would return home by another route.

A few minutes later, Willie rode west about a mile, then dismounted to open the wire gate on his way to Iron Mountain Station, where it was thought the sheepherder had gone. In a cluster of rocks 300 yards in front of the gate, the hidden assassin took aim. The sniper squeezed off three rounds. One bullet slammed into Willie's back and tore out his chest. The stricken youth dashed away from the gate, but another slug ripped through his body. Dying, he fell onto his face. The killer came out to check his work. He turned Willie onto his back and opened his bloody shirt to look at the wounds, then rode away.

Kels Nickell, Mahoney, and Apperson heard the three shots echo across the countryside, but they assumed someone was hunting deer. Although Willie did not return by nightfall there was no particular alarm, since he might not have been able to find the sheepherder. The next morning, Friday, young Fred Nickell drove the milk cows west to pasture. When he reached the open gate, he was horrified to find the bloated, discolored body of his older brother. Fred raced back to the house screaming out the terrible news, "Willie is murdered!"

At first it was thought that Willie's murder was a result of the family feud, and the Millers were questioned. But soon many people began to feel that Kels Nickell might have been the target — the always menacing presence of Tom Horn in the vicinity, coupled with the dislike of John Coble for Nickell and his sheep, were incriminating factors — and suspicion of Tom Horn began to grow. He was questioned, but he provided an alibi, as he usually did when under suspicion.

Kels Nickell received an anonymous note warning him to leave the country with his sheep or suffer the consequences. The bereaved father ignored the warning. But on August 4, 1901, seventeen days after the murder of Willie, Kels was fired upon by concealed riflemen. It was estimated that thirteen to seventeen bullets were triggered. Kels sprinted for his house 600 yards away, zigzagging under fire. He was hit three times, most seriously by a slug which shattered his left elbow, but he escaped with his life. After he disappeared, four riders went to find a band of 1,000 sheep owned by other men but pastured by Nickell. The raiders ran off the Italian sheepherder, then opened up on the sheep, killing about seventy-five animals. Kels Nickell was taken to Cheyenne for medical care, while his sheep ran untended for several days. Nickell accused the Millers, and James, Gus, and Victor were arrested, then released when they provided an alibi. Mrs. Nickell cowered with her children in the ranch house, afraid of the next attack that might come.[14]

The Laramie County sheriff's office engaged the services of an experienced detective, Joe LeFors. LeFors was born in Texas in 1865, moved with his family first to Oklahoma, and then, in 1875, to the Texas Panhandle. As a teenager Joe carried the mails and worked as a bullwhacker and as a cowboy. In 1885 he helped drive a herd of Texas cattle to Buffalo, Wyoming, and soon hired on with a Montana outfit. Then he was offered a job as a livestock inspector, with the assignment of locating stolen Montana stock in Wyoming. His efforts were highly effective, and he moved to Newcastle, Wyoming, in 1895. LeFors even penetrated the lawless Hole-in-the-Wall country, rounding up nearly 1,200 head of stolen livestock in 1897. After a brief stint in private business, LeFors became a deputy U.S. marshal, tracking train robbers and counterfeiters and various other lawbreakers.[15]

On August 5, 1901, LeFors arrived by train in Cheyenne to deliver a prisoner. But Laramie County Sheriff Shafer was suffering from a fatal illness, and LeFors was asked to begin an investigation of the Nickell shootings. The following morning LeFors and another officer took a train to Iron Mountain, then rode horseback seven miles to the Nickell place. LeFors found Mrs. Nickell barricaded inside the house, with three crying children clinging to her skirts. After LeFors calmed her, Mrs. Nickell showed the lawman the bloody coat worn by Willie when he was killed, and the jacket Kels was wearing two days earlier when he was wounded. "We are being shot and killed off one at a time," cried Mrs. Nickell, "and all day yesterday not an officer came."[16]

Mrs. Nickell flatly stated that the cause of the trouble was sheep. She told LeFors about the anonymous letter, and LeFors inspected the dead sheep in the pasture. Back at the office in Cheyenne, he related that Kels Nickell had the only sheep from the Iron Mountain country south to the Union Pacific Railroad, sixty-five or seventy miles. LeFors said that it was a cattleman-sheepman war for the available government range, and that any officer could determine the guilty parties by riding through the area and checking the cattle brands to "see for himself who was immediately interested."[17]

During the fall, Kels Nickell recovered from his wounds, then sold his ranch and sheep. Nickell moved his family into Cheyenne and found a job as a night watchman with the Union Pacific Railroad. On September 1, 1901, Tom Horn competed in Cheyenne's Frontier Days, winning "first honors in the riding and roping contests." Later in the month Horn helped deliver horses for rancher John Kuykendall to Denver. There Horn engaged in a saloon brawl, suffering a broken jaw which hospitalized him for three weeks.[18]

After he recovered, Tom Horn, along with almost everyone else in the Iron Mountain district, testified at the lengthy coroner's inquest. Results of the proceedings were inconclusive, but there was a growing public demand to find the killer of Willie Nickell. Pinkerton detectives were engaged, including a female agent who spent several weeks doing undercover work in the Iron Mountain area. Little concrete evidence was found, but Tom Horn was overheard talking about the Nickell killing during his drinking sprees. LeFors had a conversation with a cattle rancher who admitted he had paid Tom Horn "for the jobs committed before" (Powell and Lewis?), and "if Horn got to talking too much they would have to bump him off themselves."[19]

LeFors showed this rancher a letter he had received from the chief livestock inspector of Montana, requesting "a good man to do some secret work." Smith offered $125 per month for several months of undercover work against rustlers, but "He will have to be a man that can take care of himself in any kind of country."[20]

The letter was passed on to John Coble, who informed Horn. Apparently, the ranchers and Horn thought it would be a good idea for him to depart the vicinity. Horn wrote to LeFors stating that he had received the letter from Coble, and the offer sounded good. "I would like to take up that work and I feel sure I can give Mr. Smith satisfaction. I don't care how big or bad his men are or how many of them there are, I can handle them."[21]

LeFors continued to act as a middleman between Horn and Smith. In another letter Horn expressed his appreciation to LeFors and stated that he would be ready to depart for Montana within the next ten days. "I will get the men sure," he said confidently, "for I have never yet let a cow thief get away from me unless he just got up a[nd] jumped clean out of the country."[22] Horn obviously was eager for the challenge of a new manhunting job, and doubtless his Wyoming employers were eager for him to leave the country.

But LeFors now was ready to spring a trap. LeFors and Horn had arranged to meet in Cheyenne at the U.S. marshal's office on Sunday, January 12, 1902. LeFors contacted Charles Ohnhaus, U.S. court reporter, and Deputy Sheriff Les Snow, developing a scheme to take down Horn's remarks. Ohnhaus, of course, would record the conversation from behind an inner door, while Snow would be a concealed witness. LeFors told Laramie County Prosecuting Attorney Walter Stoll his plans. Stoll approved and suggested that Ohnhaus bring the transcript to his office as quickly as possible after the conversation with Horn.[23]

On Sunday LeFors met Horn's train. Later, Horn would refute his "confession" as partially false and partially the empty boasts of a drunk. "I know that he was not drunk," insisted LeFors in his autobiography, but the detective admitted that Horn had been drinking.[24]

When LeFors led Horn into the marshal's office, Ohnhaus and Snow already were behind the inner door. LeFors and Horn began to discuss the Montana job, and Tom soon asked, "These people are not afraid of shooting, are they?"[25]

LeFors turned the conversation to the Nickell killing. He asked a number of leading questions, and Horn later testified that he did not take such questions seriously, answering with the kind of absurd statements that he assumed LeFors wanted. LeFors did indeed receive the answers he wanted, including the famous line from Horn about the 300-yard shot that struck Willie: "It was the best shot I ever made, and the dirtiest trick I ever done." Perhaps the dirtiest trick of all, however, was done by the men who manipulated a "confession" that would not be admitted as evidence in a modern court.

A number of other incriminating statements were made by Horn, who planned to leave for Montana by rail the next day. But Ohnhaus typed the transcript Sunday night and warrants were promptly prepared. On Monday morning Sheriff Edward J. Smalley (Shafer had died) and two other officers arrested Horn in the lobby of the Inter-

Ocean Hotel. LeFors was nearby, witnessing Horn surrender with no resistance. Horn was placed in a cell in the Laramie County courthouse jail.

Despite insistent public opinion for stern action that would halt range war violence, cattle barons exerted "enormous political influence"[26] on Horn's behalf and anted up a hefty war chest for his defense. It was widely thought that many ranchers were afraid of being incriminated by Horn. But in a larger sense the big cattlemen were fighting, through the trial of Tom Horn, for the continuation of their dominance of the range, and for the continued employment of any means necessary to perpetuate their way of life.

The best available legal talent was engaged for Horn's defense. Judge J. W. Lacey would lead the defense, along with T. E. Burke, U.S. district attorney for Wyoming, and Burke's partners, Edward T. Clark, R. N. Matson, and T. Blake Kennedy. The obscure Walter Stoll, even though assisted by H. Waldo Moore and Clyde Watts, was given little chance of obtaining a conviction.

The preliminary hearing was held on January 24, 1902, before a packed courtroom. In the afternoon session Stoll stunned the defense — and the onlookers — when Joe LeFors was examined. The Horn "confession" had been kept secret, but LeFors now related the conversation in detail. This testimony, plus circumstantial evidence, determined the decision to try Tom Horn for murder in district court. Despite a lengthy plea by Lacey, Horn was ordered to be held without bail until the trial.

Stoll had performed superbly well, but the defense attorneys went to work, conferring with Horn almost every day. T. Blake Kennedy, youngest member of the defense team, spent weeks inspecting the murder site and surrounding area. Horn was visited frequently by friends, and he spent a great deal of time braiding hackamores, lariats, and other tack. These items were masterfully done, and were treasured gifts to his friends.

There were few legal maneuvers during the spring and summer of 1902, but both sides competed at length over the selection of a jury. A majority of the jury members were small ranchers who would naturally be opposed to large cattlemen, but Horn personally approved half of the men who would hear his case. When the trial finally began on Friday afternoon, October 10, an eager crowd jammed the courtroom (many spectators would not vacate the room during lunch breaks and other recesses, for fear of losing their seats). More than 100 witnesses had been assembled, and journalists added to the throng. The daily progress of the case was described on front pages across the nation.

One of the West's most famous trials would last for two weeks. The trial transcript seems to reveal that Stoll, tenacious and resourceful, outdueled his vaunted legal opponents. The defense failed to emphasize Horn's service to his country, nor did they stress the extent of cattle rustling in Wyoming, and there was an insufficient effort to refute the transcribed document of LeFors.

Stoll opened the trial on Friday afternoon with a masterful address to the jury. On Saturday photographs and measurements of the murder site were introduced, and Willie's wounds were described in graphic detail. Witnesses included Willie's parents, who offered pathetic descriptions of the discovery of their murdered son.

On Sunday the jurors were permitted to attend church services, and the trial resumed on Monday. As the trial gained momentum, business virtually came to a standstill in Cheyenne. During the early part of the week, exhaustive attempts were made to prove the caliber of the murder weapon. The Miller family appeared as witnesses, and Kels Nickell and his wife were recalled to the stand. On Tuesday the courtroom was electrified when a witness testified that on the day of the murder he had seen Horn galloping toward Laramie from Iron Mountain on a lathered, exhausted horse.

The trial on Wednesday featured two witnesses who told of an October 1901 drinking bout with Horn in Denver's Scandanavian Saloon. A drunken Horn reportedly bragged about the Nickell shot, said the killing of Willie was the dirtiest work he had ever done, stated that many Cheyenne men were involved, and asked that his drinking partners keep all of this information secret. Then Joe LeFors testified, arousing the spectators as he related details of the transcribed conversation with Horn. Deputy Sheriff Les Snow and Charles Ohnhaus added their testimony, and other witnesses swore that Horn was not drunk when he went to the marshal's office with LeFors.

The next day, Thursday, October 16, the defense provided several witnesses who testified that Horn had been drinking heavily and was "loaded" prior to meeting with LeFors. Various other witnesses appeared on Thursday and Friday. Then silence fell over the courtroom as Tom Horn took the stand in his own behalf. Judge Lacey questioned Horn at length about his occupation and his activities during the period of the murder. Horn testified that he was hospitalized in Denver when he supposedly was in the Scandanavian Saloon bragging about committing the murder.

Horn was to be cross-examined by Walter Stoll on Saturday morning, and people began trooping to the courthouse in the dawn chill to make sure of having a seat. They were rewarded with a relentless grilling of Horn by Stoll. At one point Stoll pressed Horn regarding a question the defendant earlier had answered vaguely. Stoll asked Horn if he could not "speak more clearly" as to his whereabouts. "I certainly can," replied the beleaguered Horn, "because I have had several things to refresh my memory. The simple fact of your questioning me so closely . . . has certainly had a tendency to refresh my mind on the subject."[27]

But when Stoll quizzed Horn about what he was wearing when he returned to Laramie shortly after the murder, Tom dryly commented, "I change clothes sometimes anyhow." The courtroom broke into laughter. Horn brought even more laughter from the spectators with his next remark.[28]

Stoll continued to bear down, repeatedly asking Horn if he was sober enough to remember this or that conversation. "I knew perfectly well what I was saying," replied Horn. The defendant insisted that he had "a distinct recollection" of a certain point, and he stated emphatically, "I remember everything that occurred to me in my life." Regarding "the young gentleman, Charlie Ohnhaus, who took down the conversation in short hand," Horn was surprisingly charitable: "I have every reason to believe that he took it down as accurately as he could, and he didn't make any mistake that I know of, and I certainly don't think that he made an intentional mistake."[29] Stoll, by extracting a repeated insistence from the defendant that he always was in control of his faculties, may have caused jurors to feel that even if Horn had been drunk while talking to LeFors, the transcribed statements were not empty boasts.

Horn also admitted making a number of statements, some peppered with profanity ("I am given in a natural way to profanity"), but he insisted that he was just swapping "stories."

Over and over Stoll asked Horn if he had made this or that statement under the influence of alcohol. To one such question Horn replied affirmatively, adding, "I would have said anything else that pleased him." To a similar question he admitted, "I had been drinking considerably, of course, but as far as that influencing anything I had to say, I knew perfectly well what I was saying." Horn had told LeFors that his horse was far away at the time of the murder, and Stoll asked if that conversation had occurred as stated: "It did and the horse was a long ways off at that time," Horn said pointedly, "and I was with the horse also."[30]

Although Horn continued to insist that he had never killed anyone, Stoll hammered at him throughout Saturday. Sunday brought a day of recess, and on Monday Joe LeFors and Les Snow were recalled to the stand, followed by a series of miscellaneous witnesses. Judge Richard H. Scott delivered instructions to the jury on Tuesday morning, then Walter Stoll spent the balance of the day reviewing the evidence and delivering his summation. On Wednesday, T. E. Burke spoke at length for the defense, followed by Lacey. Lacey concluded his impassioned plea on Thursday, then Stoll began his closing argument to the jury. Stoll dramatically concluded his presentation on Friday morning, and the fatigued jury filed out at 11:30.

The crowd dispersed, betting enthusiastically about the verdict. Joe LeFors "fully believed that the jury would find a verdict of not guilty," and Horn's friends planned a party to celebrate his expected acquittal. But at 4:20 in the afternoon a voice called down from the jury room that a verdict had been decided upon, and spectators scurried back to the courtroom. Horn was pronounced guilty and was sentenced to hang on January 9, 1903.[31]

Attorneys for the defense soon filed a motion for a new trial, citing twenty-three reasons for their motion. The prosecution blocked the motion for a new trial, but the defense filed a petition of error and won a stay of execution. Ensuing legal maneuvers would cause a stay for at least six months, until the state supreme court could offer a ruling. Many citizens, already appalled at the enormous cost of the long trial, predicted that another trial would bankrupt the county. Although Horn was dismayed at the prospect of several more months in confinement, the defense was optimistic, and in many quarters it was cynically assumed that the cattle barons would ultimately prevail over the law again. But Stoll resoundingly won reelection in November 1902, an indication of the public's opposition to Horn and his high-powered lawyers.

Rumors of escape plots began to circulate, causing Sheriff Smalley to take precautions. Extra arms were placed in the sheriff's office, anyone entering the cell block was carefully inspected, steel gratings were placed over the windows to the sheriff's office, and a heavy steel door was installed at the corridor entrance to the jail area. In January 1903 an elaborate plan to liberate Horn with a dynamite explosion was exposed by Hubert Herr, a cowboy from Coble's Iron Mountain ranch who had been jailed as an inside man to facilitate the scheme. Herr fled west on a train, fearing for his life. He told a newspaper reporter — in exchange for travel funds — that he had "overheard a conversation between Horn and another man, in which the deal was arranged for the murder of Kels P. Nickell." Horn's lawyers must have cringed at the revelation of a plan which could only swing public opinion further against Horn.[32]

Legal activities continued through the spring and summer of 1903. Desperate for freedom, Horn was relieved of a concealed length of pipe in July. Then Horn and fellow inmate Jim McCloud, who was under indictment for bushwhacking a sheepherder, overpowered a guard on Sunday morning, August 9. The two escapees made their way outside, where McCloud galloped off on the only horse in the jail corral. He was caught and subdued after a brief chase.

Horn, fleeing on foot, was charged by a citizen named O. A. Aldrich. Aldrich fired several pistol shots, one of which grazed Horn in the head. Horn was unfamiliar with the revolver he had seized and could not release the safety, and Aldrich wrestled him to the ground. A swarm of officers beat Horn into submission and dragged him back to jail. Mobs threatened to lynch Horn, further evidence of the turn of public opinion. (However, when Kels Nickell tried to harangue a mob, he was silenced by Sheriff Smalley, who threatened to put him into the cell with Tom Horn.) For his efforts O. A. Aldrich was granted permanent license to run his concession, a merry-go-round, free of charge in Cheyenne.

Horn's escape attempt damaged his chances for another stay of execution. On October 1, 1903, the Wyoming Supreme Court affirmed the verdict of the trial court in an opinion that required two hours to read. Horn would be executed on November 20 — the day preceding his forty-third birthday — on a complex gallows designed in 1892. As Horn's lawyers mounted a last-ditch legal effort, rumors again abounded that cattle barons would sponsor an escape attempt. Butch Cassidy and the Wild Bunch were mentioned as leaders of the jailbreak. A machine gun from Fort D.A. Russell was set up at the jail, with a sergeant to operate it, and a large arc light was strategically placed to discourage a night attack.

Every possible legal device was attempted by the defense lawyers, but to no avail. Horn wrote numerous letters and finished an autobiography which would be published posthumously by John Coble. The book closed with 1894, "since which time everybody else has been more familiar with my life and business than I have been myself."[33]

No rescue attempt was made, and on the day of the execution Horn faced his fate stoically and with admirable courage. John Coble broke down as he said farewell, but other cattlemen, holed up at the Cheyenne Club, were rumored to be apprehensive to the last that Horn might talk. But Horn denied to the end that he had killed Willie Nickell, and he disdained to divulge any information about his employers.

By dawn a crowd began gathering which soon numbered in the hundreds, while two troops of the Wyoming National Guard were deployed to maintain order. A plank fence had been erected to shield the gallows area from public view, and only a small number of law officers, journalists, and friends of Horn were permitted to view the execution. Horn ate a hearty breakfast, smoked a final cigar, and met his end impressively. That night cattlemen in the Cheyenne Club celebrated with relief that Horn was dead and that no further revelations would be forthcoming about their involvement.

Many students of the murder trial remain unconvinced that Horn killed Willie Nickell. "I don't think there's anyway Horn did it," said Will Henry, the noted western author who wrote *I, Tom Horn,* and who carefully studied the trial transcript. "Not only does the evidence not support it — it wasn't the kind of thing he would do. Horn could've recognized this *boy* wasn't his big ol' dad, and he would never have shot a kid."[34]

After reading the trial transcript and considering other aspects of the case, one is tempted to conclude that a member of the Miller family murdered Willie Nickell. On the day of his execution Horn wrote John Coble that when he spent the two nights at Miller's ranch, James Miller and another cattle rancher, Bill McDonald, told him they intended "to kill off the Nickell outfit and wanted me to go in on it." Two other ranchers would pay Horn, but Tom declined. The next day Horn was asked again, and when he once more turned down the offer, McDonald said, "Well, we have made up our minds to wipe out the whole Nickell outfit." When Horn heard of Willie Nickell's murder, "I felt I was well out of the mix up." Several weeks later, he again saw McDonald and Miller, "and they were blowing to me about running and shooting the sheep of Nickell." Horn went on to refute the "supposed confession" on several points of testimony: "Ohnhaus, La Fors and Snow . . . all swore lies to fit the case." He closed his final letter with a ringing statement: "This is the truth, as I am going to die in ten minutes."[35]

Whether or not Horn was guilty of the murder of Willie Nickell, there was general certainty that he had killed four other men as a hired killer, along with rumors — which he had done nothing to discourage — that he had slain many others in the course of his work. There was a sense that Horn was a throwback to a more primitive and lawless era, and that Wyoming was well rid of the noted assassin.

A decade earlier, the cattlemen's faction had suffered no significant legal discouragement from a large-scale effort to invade Johnson County with hired gunmen. But by the beginning of the twentieth century a civilizing transformation had been wrought in Wyoming, as profoundly evidenced by the conviction and execution of Tom Horn. Wyoming cattle barons had committed hundreds of thousands of dollars to Horn's defense, they had exerted immense political pressure to secure his release — and he had been hanged. Such efforts several years earlier surely would have resulted in the exoneration of a hired gun of the big ranchers. In 1902 and 1903 the message had been forcefully delivered that lawlessness on the open range must come to an end. But would even this deadly message be strong enough to overcome the profound hatred of Wyoming cattlemen for sheep?

8

More Wyoming Hostilities

Graze them anywhere you d--- please.
— William Maxwell, sheep rancher

Despite the firm set of public opinion early in the twentieth century against warfare on Wyoming rangelands, many cattle ranchers and cowboys retained their traditional hatred of sheep and sheepmen. Although large cattle ranchers reluctantly submitted to the requirements of the law in their disputes with sheepmen and nesters — indeed, cattle barons increasingly turned to sheep as a profitable source of ranch income in the twentieth century — violence continued to be directed against sheepherders and their flocks. Across Wyoming, sheep camps were still raided, sheep were destroyed and herders were shot — not by the hired gunmen and crews of cattle barons, but by cowboys and small ranchers who were too proud and stubborn to tolerate the presence of the hated woollies.

A. A. Spaugh was typical of the old-time cowboy-cattleman who turned to sheep raising rather than continue to fight the trend of economics and public opinion. As a young cowboy, Spaugh helped trail a herd of Texas longhorns to Wyoming in 1874. He caught on as manager of Wyoming's Converse Cattle Company, and in time went into business for himself. He bought the 77 and Horseshoe ranches, along with other spreads. But by the turn of the century his ranges were being crowded by sheepmen. Rather than resort to violence, which by then was being regarded with disfavor by the public, in 1902 Spaugh bought out the sheepmen who had surrounded him. Spaugh, a cowboy and cattleman for three decades, became a sheep rancher.[1] In 1904 the historic Swan Land and Cattle Company, one of the large outfits which had employed Tom Horn, switched to sheep.

Many cowboys and ranchers across Wyoming, however, refused to adapt to changing times. William MacLeod Raine published an article, "The War for the Range," in *Frank Leslie's Popular Monthly*, in which he related that a Sheridan sheepman recently had suffered losses when dynamite was thrown into his flock while the animals were feeding. Raine also pointed out that sheep ranchers around Laramie and Cheyenne "have been annoyed greatly by sudden attacks from cowboys," who would drive bands into nearby hills to be destroyed by coyotes and mountain lions.[2]

In 1902 in the Wood River country southwest of Meeteetse, two wether bands were rimrocked by marauders. Two days later, John Sayles trailed a yearling band into the area. Confronted by thirteen masked riders, Sayles boldly stated his intentions to graze the sheep during the summer on public lands, and his show of firmness worked. But even though Sayles was left alone, other sheepmen in the vicinity continued to bear the brunt of violence. Harry Webb, Ezra Nostrum, and Herb Brink, a cowboy with a vicious hatred of sheep, shoved a herder's wagon off a knoll and saw it go "tail over double-trees into a coulee." Sheepman Jim Duncan and a herder named Richmond were sleeping in a sheep wagon when their camp was raided by cowboys. The raiders killed thirty or forty sheep, then warned Duncan to move back across the Crow Creek deadline "or else."[3]

Worse violence occurred when William Minick moved his sheep into a large basin between Black Mountain and No Water Creek during the winter of 1902–03. Minick planned to winter his flock in the basin, an area that had always been cattle country, and deep animosity was aroused among cowboys and ranchers. In the spring of 1903 Minick's brother Ben, about twenty years old, was tending the camp, now located between Thermopolis and Meeteetse. Ben was aided by a one-armed herder. Emil Thoren, a sheepman from Copper Mountain, purchased some bucks from Minick and stayed overnight in the camp. But Thoren was aware of the hard feelings in the neighborhood, and early in the morning he departed with relief.

Soon after Thoren left with his bucks, a rider with a bandana over his face knocked on the door of Minick's sheep wagon. Ben opened the door. He thought nothing of the bandana because the weather was cold, and he invited the rider to come inside.

Instead the masked rider shot Minick in the back. Then the assassin, apparently realizing that his victim was not William Minick, apologized for the shooting, claimed it was an accident, and helped the one-armed herder place Minick on the bed. The masked rider climbed back into the saddle and was joined by two accomplices. The three raiders then attacked the sheep, shooting or clubbing 200 animals to death.

Down the trail Thoren had met a friend, and soon the two men heard shooting from the direction of the sheep camp. Cautiously, they approached the camp, sighting dead sheep everywhere. At the wagon they found the one-armed herder standing at the door and Minick lying on the bed.

A doctor was summoned, but Minick's spinal cord had been cut and he died that night. Charley Berger, range foreman for the Bragg cattle outfit on No Water Creek, was with Minick when he died. Berger took Ben Minick's corpse to the hamlet of No Wood, where a casket was built and the corpse stored in Bragg's warehouse until claimed by the family.

Henry Jensen and another man were employed by William Minick to skin the dead sheep. While they were at work, they were surrounded by a group of armed riders. But Jensen explained that they were simply doing what they had been hired for, and the riders left them alone. Shell casings found at the camp site were from cartridges purchased at a store in Shoshoni, south of Thermopolis. In July 1903 three men were arrested by Sheriff Jack Fenton and jailed at Thermopolis, where the National Guard had to be called in because of the threat of lynching. Despite public anger over the murder, however, no convictions resulted.[4]

One of the prisoners was "Driftwood Jim" McCloud, an outlaw who was friendly with cattlemen in the No Water district. McCloud was hustled out of Thermopolis to answer charges for robbing a post office, and he was thrown into the cell with Tom Horn in Cheyenne, where the district court would convene. McCloud and Horn soon began planning a break. For several days McCloud feigned a stomach illness, requiring water to take his regular dose of medicine. On Sunday, August 9, 1903, Richard Proctor brought a glass of water to

McCloud. As Proctor unlocked the steel door with one hand, holding the water in his other hand, McCloud and Horn slammed into the door, knocking Proctor backward. Proctor staggered McCloud with a punch but was overpowered by the two criminals.

McCloud tied Proctor's hands with a length of cord from a window blind. Horn and McCloud then seized the keys and pushed Proctor ahead of them to the sheriff's office, where McCloud found a loaded Winchester. But Proctor grabbed the rifle and the three men again went down in a desperate wrestling match. McCloud twisted the rifle out of the officer's grasp, but Proctor lunged for a pistol. As Horn piled on top of Proctor, McCloud dashed through the door. Proctor finally surrendered the Belgian-made revolver to Horn but snapped the safety on, and when Horn tried to escape he could not fire the unfamiliar weapon.

As McCloud bolted outside he pointed the Winchester at Deputy Les Snow, but the astonished lawman darted from view, then began firing his revolver and shouting an alarm. McCloud found a horse in the courthouse barn, but as he tried to mount in an alley, Sheriff Ed Smalley ran up and opened fire. McCloud used the horse as a shield, led the animal down the alley, then mounted up and rode into Eddy Street.

McCloud immediately encountered Patrick Hennessey, a mail clerk who had snatched up a double-barreled shotgun when he heard the alarm. "Tom Horn has escaped!" shouted McCloud to Hennessey. "Have you seen him?"

"No," said Hennessey, lowering his shotgun. "Which way did Horn go?"

McCloud whipped his horse with the reins and galloped away from the confused Hennessey. But armed men were in hot pursuit, and McCloud galloped into an alley between Twentieth and Twenty-first streets. With aroused citizens at the other end of the alley, McCloud leaped off his horse and hid in a barn. There two men cornered him, and McCloud surrendered and was hauled back to jail, where Horn had already been taken. Driftwood Jim was sentenced to a long prison term at Leavenworth. After serving several years he was released, turned up for a time in Basin, then disappeared.[5]

At about the same time that Ben Minick was murdered in Hot Springs County, similar action was contemplated against Mormon sheepmen a couple of hundred miles to the south. In southern Wyoming, feelings remained high against "poaching sheepmen" who drove their flocks into the state for seasonal pasturage. On Friday morning, March 20, 1903, sixty-one cowboys and cattle ranchers rode against four Mormon outfits which were using winter pasturage in the Sweetwater country. The riders intended to drive the sheepmen back into Utah "or to destroy their outfits."[6]

But the big posse was caught in a raging blizzard. For three days there were savage winds, frigid temperatures, and blinding snowfalls. Most of the riders were caught in the storm and forced to endure a miserable night, and virtually everyone repeatedly became lost while groping their way back to their homes. It was determined that five men did not make it back, but not until March 23, when the storm finally subsided, could search parties be sent out. The countryside was scoured, but after three days the searchers lost hope of finding their comrades alive. Apparently, the Utah sheepmen weathered the storm with little difficulty.

During that same troubled month, cattlemen rode successfully, if illegally, against a sheepman in the eastern part of Wyoming. Forty miles north of Lusk a sheep camp was struck by seven masked men. The herder was tightly bound and his wagon burned, then the raiders destroyed his horses and 500 sheep.[7]

The isolated atrocities against sheepmen continued in 1904. Lincoln A. Morrison, a prominent sheep rancher, was assassinated on Kirby Creek, below the village of Kirby. In the spring of 1904 a large number of sheep passed through the rocky, timbered country along the Wyoming-Colorado border below Laramie, "killing the grass untimely." Angry cattlemen in the region "demanded that no sheep be permitted to graze on the range." Unknown persons trailed 500 sheep owned by Fred Henderson of Casper into the mountains and held them until they were hungry enough to eat poisoned feed. Although it took two or three days to administer the poison, the entire flock was destroyed.[8]

"Graze them anywhere you d--- please," was the directive of William Maxwell, a sheep rancher at Tie Siding. He was not at all intimidated by cowmen, and supposedly he instructed his herders to take their flocks to any range in the district. According to one area cattleman, Maxwell arrogantly added that "if the ---- -- ------- kicked he would graze them in their door yards."[9]

For years Maxwell had owned about 1,000 acres of rangeland south of Tie Siding. (In 1887 a rancher lost 2,600 sheep when a fire of apparently accidental origins consumed an entire flock penned in a plank corral four miles west of Tie Siding, but there were persistent rumors that cattlemen had intentionally incinerated the animals.)[10] Maxwell fenced in his deeded property and several thousand acres more, applied to the State of Wyoming for a lease to the land he did not own, and began charging rent for pasturage rights. Maxwell ran a few hundred head of cattle on the land he did not own, but in 1903 he sold his herd and brought in at least 8,000 sheep and several herders. Dr. Henry L. Stevens, a prominent Laramie physician, was part owner of the flock, and many cattlemen of the Tie Siding area felt that he was sole owner and that Maxwell was merely his manager. The cattlemen grumbled that "Maxwell's interest if he has any is either in wind or on paper."[11]

Dr. Stevens was quoted as saying that when he became interested in sheep he "was told that Mr. Maxwell had land enough to graze them on."[12] But beginning in September 1903, nearly twenty area cattlemen reported finding Stevens-Maxwell sheep — or sheep *sign* — on their land, and they began to watch their pastures carefully for fear that the sheep would trespass. Maxwell shrugged off complaints from the neighbors, and Dr. Stevens was assured that his sheep were being grazed either on government range or Maxwell's property. But the cattlemen detested the presence of sheep and repeatedly insisted that the woollies were encroaching on their range. Occasionally, cattle ranchers riding near a flock threatened the herders that if the sheep trespassed on their land "they would kill them off." William Keyes, Westley Johnson, and other ranchers had fields of rye trampled by trespassing flocks, and in April, Maxwell's foreman received a warning to take the sheep out of the county.[13]

Maxwell and Stevens had leased range from a Mrs. Weaver seven miles below Tie Siding, and a large number of sheep were moved to the land. On Monday, April 25, dogs at the Weaver ranch were poisoned and the sheep outfit's horses were driven away. That night at about 11:00, sixteen masked riders surrounded a sheep wagon on the Weaver place. Asleep inside the wagon was a Mexican herder who was in charge of a band of wethers. Jostled awake, the herder was pulled from the wagon. His bedding was tossed out behind him, then the wagon was filled with firewood and set ablaze.

Hauling the terrified herder with them, the masked riders proceeded to another camp half a mile away. The foreman and a herder were asleep in the wagon, while a night herder tended 3,000 ewes. The night herder heard the riders approaching and ran to the wagon to waken the others. When the sixteen riders came into sight under a bright moon, the three sheepmen broke for the nearby brush. But the masked men fired shots over their heads and shouted at them to throw up their hands. The sheepmen stopped and raised their hands. They were tied up, then shoved to a fence and bound to the posts. The Mexican herder taken at the first camp was left untied because he seemed too frightened to offer resistance. When the foreman asked their purpose, the masked men announced that they intended to kill as many of the sheep as possible — and the herders, too, if they made any trouble or attempted to escape.

The raiders then threw firewood into the second wagon and burned it. While one masked man guarded the herders with a Winchester, the other fifteen produced clubs and walked toward the flock. Hitting the sheep on their heads or breaking their backs, the raiders felled more than 200 animals. Finally, they mounted their horses and rode away into the night.

The Mexican herder quickly untied the other three, and the foreman, Cyrus Engbrson, hiked seven miles to Tie Siding, where he caught a train to Laramie. He found Dr. Stevens, told him the story, and estimated that 300 sheep had been destroyed. Engbrson also told Dr. Stevens that he had recognized several of the raiders as neighboring cattlemen: William Keyes, when his mask had been blown up by the wind; his son, Harry Keyes, by his reddish hair; and Frank Carroll and Westley Johnson, by their general appearance.

Dr. Stevens took Engbrson to the sheriff's office, and soon a party was on a train to Tie Siding. Sheriff Alfred Cook and Deputy Sheriff McKay visited the sheep camp, along with County Attorney Thomas H. Gibson and County Surveyor Edward A. Buck. Unaccountably, many of the injured sheep had not yet been put out of their misery. Gibson reported that the sight "was most sickening." Some 225 dead sheep were counted, and a pick handle that had been used as a bludgeon was discovered. Buck found indications where the sheep had grazed outside of their boundaries, "but to no great extent."[14]

Stevens and Maxwell announced their determination not to be driven away and to "fight as long as there is any thing to fight about."[15] Warrants were sworn out for the suspects, and provisions and camp equipment were sent to the Weaver place. Sheriff Cook and his deputy arrested William and Harry Keyes at their ranch and Frank Carroll at Tie Siding, then brought them to Laramie on the train.

For years these incidents had been front-page news across the country, but national wire services often fed their readers exaggerated accounts of western violence. In the case of the Tie Siding raid, national readers were informed that fifteen sheepherders (there were four, of course) were captured and tied up "all night," while 3,000 sheep were killed (225 were destroyed). Tensions in the aftermath of the raid were described with greater accuracy: "Further trouble is expected, as the sheepmen say they will refuse to be run out. All parties are armed, and a clash may occur at any moment."[16]

A preliminary hearing was set for May 9, and Westley Johnson soon was charged. The men posted $500 bail apiece, and both sides secured former judges as legal counsel. The trial opened on Tuesday, May 31, 1904, and continued through the following Saturday. The wives of the three older defendants, and the mother of Harry Keyes, swore that the men had been at their homes on the night of the raid. There were no non-family members who could substantiate the alibis, and a neighbor of Johnson's testified that he had seen him out that evening. The jury retired at 4:15 Saturday afternoon, then returned to the courtroom at 9:30 that evening to deliver a not-guilty verdict. The defendants were enthusiastically congratulated by a crowd of friends and neighbors.[17]

Occasional depredations continued in the Big Horn Basin. The home ranch of sheepman Jess D. Lynn was located at the mouth of Shell Creek, a few miles north of the town of Basin. Most of the cattlemen in the Shell Creek area gathered together to strike a band of 3,000 sheep pastured on Trapper Creek, several miles east of Lynn's headquarters. Lynn's two herders wisely offered no resistance, but at gunpoint they were forced to wade into the icy stream while the entire flock was rimrocked into Trapper Creek. The identity of the raiders was common knowledge, but law officers made only a perfunctory inquiry into the incident, and there were no arrests.[18]

The lack of legal pressure strengthened the resolve of Shell Creek cattlemen, as Louis A. Gantz would discover. Gantz and his brother were sheep ranchers who headquartered near Casper. In the summer of 1905, Gantz leisurely trailed a large band northwest, generating complaints that the pace was so slow that the sheep were destroying all range in their path. When Gantz camped on Shell Creek, area cattlemen again decided to launch an attack. On the night of August 24, ten masked men struck furiously. The raiders shot, clubbed, and dynamited 4,000 sheep, then killed a team of horses. Next Gantz's sheep dogs were tied to the wagons, and three wagons were burned, roasting the dogs. All camp provisions and equipment were destroyed, along with a large supply of grain.

The stunned Gantz telephoned Thomas Long, manager of the Garland Mercantile, in which the sheepman owned an interest. The Garland *Guard* vehemently decried the "UNKNOWN DEVILS" who had committed the vicious assault, and the *Guard* accurately headlined: "LAW ABIDING BE DAMNED!" Again no legal action resulted, and Gantz died within a few weeks of the devastating raid.[19]

Later in the year, a more direct murder was committed. Joseph Earl Cleveland was a herder for Senator Francis Warren's livestock company. On October 6, 1905, Cleveland's body was found beside a spring about 100 yards from his sheep camp. He had been shot in the back, the bullet entering behind his left hip and emerging above his heart. Curiously, there were no holes in his clothing, nor did his garments show bloodstains. For some inexplicable reason, the killer had stripped Cleveland, then put fresh clothes on the corpse.[20]

Ora Haley, a cattle baron who had staunchly resisted the encroachments of sheepmen — and who had heavily stocked all range near his famous Two Bar Ranch with cattle to keep sheep off — at last acknowledged the pressures of economics and invested in sheep. He ran large flocks in Utah as a silent partner with a man named Saunders. But in 1905 a gang of cowboys rimrocked the Haley-Saunders sheep, effecting heavy losses. Haley received the news at his splendid home in Laramie. Called away from the dinner table, he talked with Saunders by long-distance telephone, then returned to the table, picked up his napkin, and resumed eating. When the family learned the nature of the call, they asked Haley if he was not disturbed by the losses. "I never look at my losses," shrugged Haley, "or let them bother me. I always look ahead."[21]

* * *

Under the pressure of sporadic raids and deadlines, sheep ranchers tried to band together, in the same way that cattlemen had organized in the 1870s against rustling. Of course, the Wyoming Stock Growers Association also had wielded great political influence. Sheepmen recognized the need for lobbying power in Cheyenne and Washington, D.C., and already had formed county associations (Crook, Fremont, and Laramie were the only Wyoming counties without a sheepman's association), but they were unable to form a state association. As raids against sheep camps continued, however, sheepmen finally responded to the obvious necessity of cooperative action.

The Wyoming Wool Growers Association was formed in Cheyenne during four days in April 1905. There were forty charter members; Dr. J. M. Wilson was elected president, and the board of trustees included one representative from each of Wyoming's thirteen counties. The association held its second meeting in Casper just eight months later, and the number of members in attendance ballooned to 271. By January 1909 membership had doubled, to 541, and a year later reached 646, the all-time peak. The association could report that Wyoming led all states in wool production by 1908, and during the period 1908 to 1910, sheep husbandry was the state's leading industry.[22]

In December 1906 fifteen cattlemen who ranched on Owl Creek, northwest of Thermopolis, signed a formal deadline against sheep. Woollies were to stay south of Owl Creek, and the deadline involved approximately 250 square miles of range.[23] With a growing sense of power, sheepmen ignored the deadline. With a growing sense of disgust, cattlemen rode to the attack. Early in March 1907, a flock belonging to a sheepman named Wisner was struck. Raiders burned the camp and killed 400 head of sheep. A week later, twelve masked riders attacked a big camp near Owl Creek. The herders were driven away and 4,000 sheep belonging to Hugh Dickey were destroyed.[24]

The Wyoming Wool Growers Association, at their annual meeting in April, responded forcefully to the recent raids. The association offered a $1,000 reward for the conviction of any sheep camp raider, then began raising a fund of $50,000 to lobby against "Pinchot's forest reserve policy and President Roosevelt's land leasing policy" — and, most importantly, to use against sheep camp raiders.[25]

The united stand of the sheepmen, who now were entering their most prosperous period in Wyoming, caused a temporary cessation of hostilities. But many diehard cattlemen refused to be intimidated, as they would prove in 1908. Sheepman J. W. Blake of Lander, undeterred by a 1906 raid on one of his camps which had resulted in the destruction of 300 sheep, had placed a drop band on leased land inside the Shoshone Indian Reservation. The pasturage certainly was regarded as safe from raiders. Robert Meigh was in charge of the band, and he was aided by two herders.

Early in April, Meigh and his herders bedded down outside, while a drunken visitor was sleeping off his liquor in one of the wagons. It began to rain, but a worse disturbance came at midnight, when a group of mounted raiders fired a volley of shots into the air. Startled from an uneasy slumber, the three sheepmen were told to pull on their boots and move to the sheep wagons. One herder found his boots frozen, and as he hopped and cursed he caused some of the raiders' mounts to shy. Warning shots quietened the unruly herder.

The raiders tried to burn the wagons, despite the slumbering presence of the drunk, but it was too wet to start a fire. Instead wheel spokes on one were chopped with an ax, and the wagons were turned over. As dawn began to break, Meigh and his men were chased out of camp with gunfire. Then the raiders opened up on the sheep.

Meigh and the herders returned to camp when the raiders left. Incredibly, the drunk still slept in an overturned wagon. The raiders had killed or wounded 350 sheep; grieving ewes stood over their dead offspring, while orphaned lambs were bleating helplessly beside their dead mothers. After a hasty breakfast, Meigh and his men righted one of the wagons and fashioned makeshift spokes for the damaged wheels. Carcasses were loaded into the wagon to keep the flock together, then the outfit retreated to town. In Lander it was learned that J. W. Blake had just died. Now in charge, Meigh issued revolvers to his men before taking the flock back to pasture.[26]

In Crook County in 1908, the cattleman-sheepherder conflict took a fraternal turn. Fraternal orders were popular at the turn of the century. Following the trend, several cattlemen met at a lonely country school house on the night of July 20 to organize a secret society. Most fraternal orders of the day were founded for purposes of philanthropy and fellowship, but the Crook County cattlemen swore a death oath to drive the Gutherie and Rodney King sheep companies out of the district. It was solemnly agreed "that any party thereto who betrayed the others should be executed for his disloyalty."[27]

The first move against the sheep companies occurred on Monday, August 31. The cattlemen split into two groups and raided two widely separate ranches on the same night. The greatest damage was done at the Berry ranch on Kara Creek, where Fritz Reison and his son Edouard were sleeping in a sheep wagon. Five riders opened fire on the wagon, riddling the vehicle and grazing Edouard. Fritz and Edouard bailed out of the wagon but were roughly manhandled and tied up by the raiders. The raiders set fire to the wagon and ranch buildings, then rode away into the night. Fritz Reison quickly managed to work his way free. He untied his son, and the two men attacked the flames. The sheep wagon already was ablaze, but the Reisons saved the house and outbuildings.[28]

A month later, October 1, 1908, a sheep wagon was burned near

Mule Creek by a solitary raider. At the end of the month, on October 29, seven raiders struck the Matt Shoe ranch on Deer Creek, burning 100 tons of hay. On November 7 another double raid was executed: twenty tons of hay were burned on a spread operated by a Mrs. Hulett on Kara Creek, while several miles of fence were cut in the same vicinity. The next night raiders again struck the Berry ranch, this time burning to the ground the buildings that had been previously damaged.

Each of these raids had been directed against property owned by either the Gutherie or Rodney King sheep companies, and these concerns, staunchly backed by the Wyoming Wool Growers Association, decided to put range detectives into the field. Joe LeFors was the most notable detective who was employed, and the raiders ceased their activities. But LeFors quietly amassed evidence, and on December 23 Orin Squires and George Martin were confronted with the case against them. Before the day ended, Squires and Martin confessed, implicating several members of their "association": Samuel, Andrew, and Isaiah McKean, Stanley Baugh, Jefferson Mulholland, Dan Mosberger, and Henry Zimmerschied. Martin was placed behind bars in Sundance, the county seat, while Squires was sent to jail in Basin, the seat of Big Horn County, in order to segregate these two key witnesses. On December 24 the seven individuals they had named were served with warrants, but these men immediately posted bail. Martin refused bail, fearing that his confederates would kill him, and for a time no one knew the whereabouts of Squires, who also feared retaliation.

The case filed on December 31 charged the defendants with burning two dwellings, a barn, and 2,000 feet of lumber, and with the attempted murder of Edouard Reison. The whereabouts of Squires finally was leaked. He was assured that the original death pact of the raiders would not be enforced against him. Squires accepted bail, then promptly disappeared. Soon Martin was bailed out, and he, too, vanished. The prosecution found itself in an embarrassing position: although the confessions of Squires and Martin were on file, the men who had confessed were gone.

The case came up in Sundance's ornate Victorian courthouse on May 8, 1909. Motions were filed for a month and subpoenas were issued every few days, but before the case came to trial the dispute was settled out of court. On June 8 it was announced that the nine cattlemen had consented to pay property damages and court costs. Approximately $5,000 was paid for property destroyed or damaged during the raids, and court costs were enormous: prosecution fees included special attorneys, detectives, witness expenses, and jury costs. Payments totaled more than $25,000, and the defendants also "agreed to never again molest sheep or sheep outfits on the disputed range."[29]

The sheepmen and their association had put forth an all-out effort within the law, and they had scored an impressive victory. But before the case was resolved, another Wyoming sheep camp had been struck, resulting in one of the most vicious tragedies of the entire cattlemen-sheepmen conflict.

9

Turning Point at Ten Sleep

Who in hell are you? Get them hands up!
— Herb Brink, raider

The little community of Ten Sleep is located just east of the Nowood River, "ten sleeps" from Fort Laramie, according to the Indians. Ten Sleep grew up in vast Big Horn County; today the entity is divided into three counties (Ten Sleep now is in Washakie County), but originally Big Horn County was 110 miles wide and 150 miles long. The Nowood River Valley angles basically north to south, with most of the ranching in the eastern part of the valley. There is very little water west of the river, and most of the tributaries run into the Nowood from the east. As a result, the area between Ten Sleep and Worland, thirty-five miles to the west, is a barren waste accurately known as the Badlands. Although moisture, primarily from snow accumulation and spring rains, nourishes a light spread of grass in the Badlands, area cattlemen were quick to point out that these meager grasslands had been cropped to the ground by sheep.

Indeed, there were hard feelings throughout the Big Horn Basin between cattle and sheep interests. In the spring of 1903 sheepherder Ben Minick had been shot to death, and the following year Lincoln A. Morrison, a prominent sheepman, was assassinated in the southern

TEN SLEEP, WYOMING, APRIL 2, 1909

THE VICTIMS

Joe Emge: Cattleman-turned-sheep rancher. Rumored to have raided sheep camps himself. Abrasive personality and generally disliked.

Joseph Allemand: Longtime sheep rancher popular even with cattlemen.

Joe Lazier: Youthful French sheepherder.

Pete Cafferal: Middle-aged French sheepherder who served as camp tender on ill-fated drive, and who slugged it out with two cowboys in a saloon brawl before drive began.

Bounce Helmer: Adolescent son of cattle rancher. His divorced mother had remarried another cattleman, but Bounce had signed on for his first sheep drive.

THE RAIDERS

Herb Brink: Itinerant cowboy who loudly proclaimed his hatred of sheep.

Albert E. Keyes: The raiders met at his ranch.

Charles Farris: Neighbor of Keyes who would crumple under legal pressure.

Ed Eaton: He should have been more careful with his mask.

George Saban: Owner of the Bay State Ranch.

Tommy Dixon: His alibi made no sense.

Milton Alexander: Finished off the wounded Allemand with a shovel.

---

part of the county. During the next few years, especially in the Nowood section, sheep camps were burned and sheep were dynamited, rimrocked, and clubbed to death. Ax handles or rolling pins were used and discarded on the spot, but cattlemen would shrug and offer the opinion that neighborhood women had killed the sheep.[1]

Joe Emge was a bachelor cattleman who ran a spread on Spring Creek several miles southeast of Ten Sleep. Emge was noted for his gold teeth and his hatred of sheep. He erected a wire fence which ran ten miles north to south and which blocked sheepherders (or cattlemen disliked by the belligerent Emge) from grazing in the Big Horn Mountains to the east. Emge and his employees filed claims on the land covered by the controversial fence, but court action disallowed these claims and mandated removal of the fence. Then the cattlemen resorted to an arbitrary deadline, precisely designated by a long plowed furrow, which denied use of fragile Badlands grazing to sheep. Joe

THE TEN SLEEP DISTRICT, 1909

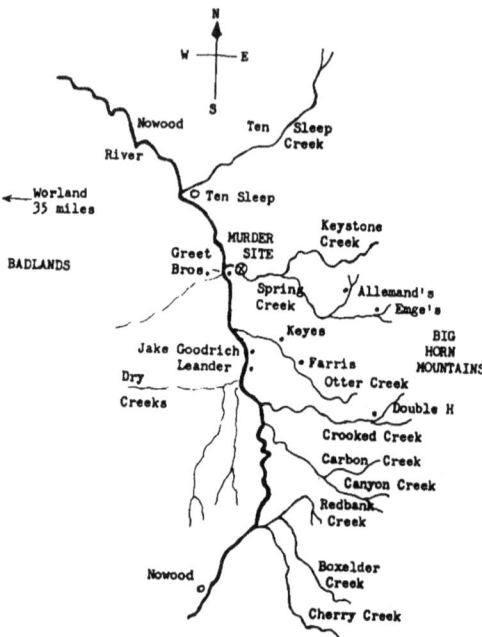

Emge helped to plow the furrow, and it was rumored that he participated in at least one or two of the sheep raids.[2]

But Emge, of all people, finally became converted by the economics of the sheep industry. He dissolved his partnership with a cattleman named Mann, sold his herd, and entered into a sheep operation with a neighboring rancher, Joe Allemand. Although Allemand, a Frenchman, had run sheep in the area for several years, he was an amiable man, well-liked even by the cattlemen. Many locals believed that Joe Emge once had been involved in a raid against Allemand's flock. But after Emge made up his mind he became an instant convert, driving his first sheep across the Badlands with a heavily armed crew. Area cattlemen, of course, regarded Emge as a turncoat: some of his friends tried to talk him out of switching to sheep, while others issued threats. The abrasive Emge had clashed in the past with several fellow cattle ranchers, and he took a perverse pleasure in irritating these men. When his sister reacted tearfully to warnings against him, Emge informed her, "There are some fellows I want to get even with."[3]

Late in March, Emge and Allemand journeyed to Worland to pick up 2,500 head of sheep that had wintered in the area. Allemand left behind his wife, an eight-year-old son, and a newborn infant, but he expected to be back around the first of April. From a camp near Worland, Emge and Allemand assembled an outfit for a trail drive through the Badlands: by ignoring the deadline and traveling across thirty miles of "cattle country," Emge and Allemand would cut their drive almost in half. They gathered two sheep wagons, one for each band, as well as a supply wagon, a buckboard, saddle horses, and sheep dogs. In addition to Emge and Allemand, there were two Frenchmen, young herder Jules "Joe" Lazier and middle-aged Pierre "Pete" Cafferal, an old hand who would act as camp tender during the drive. Neither men spoke English well (Lazier had been in the United States less than a year), nor did they know many people in the Ten Sleep district. Rounding out the crew was Bounce Helmer, an adolescent participating in his first sheep drive. His father, known to everyone as "Double H," was a prominent cattle rancher, and Bounce's divorced mother had married cattleman Jake Goodrich. Bounce had worked roundups before and knew every cattleman in the neighborhood. But now he lived with his mother at the Goodrich place alongside the Nowood River south of Ten Sleep, and he signed on with Emge and Allemand, whose spreads lay just a few miles to the northeast.[4]

The proposed Emge-Allemand sheep drive aroused ominous threats from the cattlemen. Pete Cafferal, during a visit to Charlie Worland's saloon, was jumped by two cowboys. Cafferal had been to Worland before, and he had been insulted by cowboys before, but the insults had been good-natured and cowboys sometimes had bought him a drink. This time, however, Cafferal did not know the cowboys who provoked him while he was drinking. Cafferal slugged one of the cowboys, knocking him off his feet. The cowboy's nose caught the end of a foot scraper as he went down, and blood spurted brightly. The other cowboy seized a whiskey bottle from the bar, but the bartender clutched him for a moment, then pressed his bar rag over the bleeding nose and sent the cowboys toward the doctor's office. The barkeep took money from Cafferal to pay the doctor, then told Pete to get out. Cafferal obeyed but continued to worry about the incident.[5]

Emge shrugged off the saloon brawl and the threats, but he made certain that the expedition was well-armed: he carried two rifles and an automatic pistol, and Allemand also had a rifle. On Monday, March 28, the party set out from Worland, heading east — directly across the forbidden Badlands.

Emge, on a saddle horse, kept a lookout and directed the flock.

LAST CAMP, APRIL 2, 1909

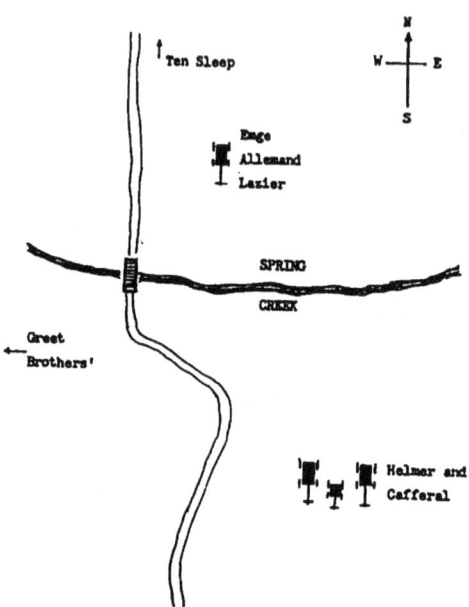

Allemand drove one of the sheep wagons, while Lazier kept the lead band together. The other band trailed a short distance behind: young Helmer drove the supply wagon, and Allemand was in the other sheep wagon, with the buckboard hitched behind. Emge maintained a constant vigil, refusing to bed down the last night in Worland and the four nights the outfit made camp in the Badlands.[6]

The drive was unhurried; the sheep were allowed to graze leisurely at midday, and they were not pushed hard as they crossed the Badlands. But on March 31 or April 1, Allemand found a telephone and called his wife, apparently telling her that he would be at home by April 2. (A telephone line had been strung across the area; anyone who wanted to be connected would purchase a telephone set and hook onto the line. Therefore, the entire system was a party line, and it was always thought that an eavesdropper had listened in and become convinced that Allemand would be safe at home on the night of April 2.)[7]

But it was not until Friday, April 2, that the outfit hit the Nowood River and turned south on the public road. As the drive passed by Ten Sleep, Bounce Helmer slipped into town to buy a .22 rifle at the Walt Fiscus store, where he also picked up a bundle of clean clothes left for him by his mother. The outfit moved on to its final camp at the mouth of Spring Creek. Allemand parked his wagon on a little knoll just north of the creek. The other vehicles were grouped 1,300 feet to the south. A quarter of a mile to the west, just across the Ten Sleep road, was the log cabin owned by Fred and Frank Greet, who were cattlemen and friends of Emge. Indeed, Emge arranged for his party's horses to be pastured that night at the Greet ranch. Visiting overnight at the ranch were John Meredith from Ten Sleep and Porter Lamb from Worland.

Fred Greet walked over to eat supper with Allemand, Emge, and Lazier at the north wagon, expressing his worries about a raid. But Emge and Allemand were just a few miles from home, and felt safe now that they had passed the cattlemen's deadline. Emge walked over to the Greet brothers' ranch house to make a phone call, perhaps to his sister. "I've not slept for five nights," he was overheard to say, "I can sleep tonight; I'm almost home. I'll never go through this again."[8]

Emge, Allemand, and Lazier crawled into the wagon on the north to sleep. Cafferal and Bounce Helmer had made their supper at the south camp. Cafferal bedded down inside his wagon, while Bounce rolled into his blankets beneath a little tent nearby. It was a chilly night with the usual breeze, but every man slept soundly now that they were in safe territory. No one heard seven riders advance cautiously from the east at 10:00.

On Thursday, George Saban and Milt Alexander had ridden to the ranch of Albert Keyes on Otter Creek. These men had joined the angry talk of cattlemen who had fumed about the sheep drive across the Badlands. Several diehards had determined to raid the sheep camp, and word was spread to meet at Keyes's ranch. George Sutherland, a veteran of the Johnson County War of 1892, intended to go, but company arrived at his ranch and he stayed home. Herbert Brink, rumored to have raided sheep camps in Colorado, had been the most outspoken against Emge and Allemand, even though he was just a drifting cowboy who had ridden the grub line all winter and who owned no property or cattle. On Friday, Brink arrived at the Keyes ranch, along with Charles Farris, Ed Eaton, and Tommy Dixon. Everyone had gathered by 7:00 in the evening, and although each man was armed, Keyes and Farris understood that there was to be no killing. The sheepmen were to be held under guard while the wagons were destroyed and the sheep driven over a gully.[9]

The seven raiders rode out after 7:00 on that Friday night. A quarter of a mile from the camp they dismounted and tied their horses to tall sagebrush. They walked together under a bright moon about 200 yards, then split up. Saban and Dixon moved toward the wagons on the south, and the other five crept toward the lone wagon where Emge, Allemand, and Lazier slept. The raiders donned masks they had fashioned from gunnysacks.[10]

Bounce Helmer had been roused when his dog, Smoke, began to bark, probably after smelling the approaching riders. Bounce quietened his dog, then went back to sleep. A sudden outbreak of gunfire jolted him awake. He leaped out of his blankets and, barefoot and clad only in his underwear, he shouted a warning to Cafferal and broke into a run. But two armed men wearing masks blocked his way. Bounce was ordered to halt, then he was told to climb into the sheep wagon and light a lantern, which would illuminate anyone inside. As Bounce did what he was told, he heard the men discussing him, acknowledging that they knew him.[11]

Bounce crawled into the wagon and lit a lantern. He came out, followed by Cafferal. They were made to raise their hands and turn their backs to the north wagon, while shooting continued from that direction. Finally, they were allowed to dress. Cafferal was escorted by a gunman into the sheep wagon, and when he came out he was again lined up beside Bounce. Then Bounce and Cafferal were walked to the road, where they turned north and were taken across the bridge. About fifty yards from the knoll where the second sheep wagon was parked, Bounce and Cafferal were forced to lie face down on the ground. When they lay prone they were frisked for weapons, then Bounce was asked where the coal oil was located.[12]

Two of the raiders later claimed that Joe Emge came to the door of his sheep wagon and fired a rifle. The hard-bitten Herb Brink loudly ordered the men inside the wagon to light a lantern. He threatened to open fire if a light did not show by the time he counted to three. Then he quickly counted to three and cut loose with an automatic rifle. Another rifle also opened up, and bullets could be heard ricocheting off the go-to-hell stove.[13]

Emge and Lazier were fatally wounded by the fusillade and died inside the wagon. Allemand, struck in the arm, staggered out of the wagon. "Who in hell are you?" asked Brink derisively. "Get them hands up! This is a hell of a time of night for a man to come out with your hands up!"[14]

Brink then cold-bloodedly shot Allemand, who fell to the ground moaning in agony. Milt Alexander finished off Allemand with a blow to his throat from the cutting edge of a shovel. Raiders gathered around Allemand, surprised that the Frenchman was present. The raiders quarreled among themselves; there was a suggestion that Bounce and Cafferal be killed, but this idea was shouted down. Bounce and Cafferal finally were told to get up and head down the road to the south without looking up.[15]

By this time the raiders had piled sagebrush beneath the vehicles, splashed coal oil on the wagons, and set them ablaze — including the north wagon with the bodies of Emge and Lazier inside. South of the ravine the buckboard was pushed into the flames of the burning wagon. As Bounce and Cafferal passed the blazing vehicles south of the ravine, young Helmer sneaked a look to his left. One raider, who stood between Bounce and the burning wagons, was throwing a harness and a saddle into the fire. Illuminated by the blaze and a bright moon, the raider stooped over — and a breeze momentarily fluttered the mask away from his face. Bounce instantly recognized cattleman Ed Eaton, under whom he had worked on a roundup. Smoke, Bounce's dog, headed toward his master, but one of the raiders raised his rifle. Four sheep dogs already had been shot, and Bounce desperately shouted: "Goddam you. Don't you shoot my dog." The man with the rifle asked Bounce if it was his dog, and when the answer was affirmative the masked man lowered his gun. Then Bounce and Cafferal were turned off the road and told to leave and keep their mouths shut.[16]

Across the road to the west, the Greet brothers, Porter Lamb, and John Meredith stood outside the log cabin. When the shooting started, the four men had dressed and armed themselves, then went outside, staying in the shadows of the ranch house. A warning shot was fired over their heads and they made no move to intervene, but watched for two hours as gunfire erupted and flames blazed high.[17]

Cafferal, Bounce, and Smoke struck out cross-country, hiking through the sagebrush prairie toward Jake Goodrich's spread, several miles away. They arrived at Bounce's home between 1:00 and 2:00 A.M. Bounce and Cafferal blurted out their nightmarish story, but overnight visitors were present, and Bounce said nothing about recognizing Ed Eaton. Although Jake Goodrich had installed a telephone, it proved impossible to call authorities because the line to Ten Sleep had been cut.[18]

But word had reached Ten Sleep by Saturday morning, and even though the main phone line to Basin also had been cut, it soon was repaired. Sheriff Felix Alston was called in Basin at 10:00. Alston then telephoned Deputy Sheriff Al Morton, who lived near Ten Sleep, directing him to keep onlookers from obliterating tracks and disturbing other evidence. Alston and County Attorney Percy Metz, Deputy Sheriff Ed Cusack, and Coroner Dr. C. Dana Carter then climbed into a buckboard and headed for the murder site. They made the sixty-mile journey by the end of the day, and at dusk Alston and the other officials inspected the burned-out sheep camps.[19]

Sheep were scattered all over the area, grazing aimlessly. Two dozen sheep lay dead on the bed grounds, and several animals were dying from shots in the belly or leg. Four sheep dogs also lay dead. At the south camp, smoke still circled upward from the blackened remains of the two big wagons, while one wheel and part of an axle were all that stood of the buckboard. At the north camp Joe Allemand lay on his back, staring vacantly at the sky. Curled on his chest lay a fuzzy puppy whose mother had been killed Friday night, and another puppy was snuggled beside him. Two severely burned bodies were in the charred remains of the sheep wagon, along with the go-to-hell stove, tipped on its side. The trunks of both corpses were burned crisp, little was left of the arms and legs, and the faces were unrecognizable. One skull had split open and the baked brains were visible; a gold tooth was nearby. Three rifles were found, the stocks burned off.[20]

Porter Lamb, John Meredith, and the Greet brothers told the sheriff what they had seen, and Fred Greet insisted that the bodies had to be Joe Emge and the French youth, Lazier. It was speculated that the corpses of Bounce Helmer and the other Frenchman might be lying in some ravine. As darkness gathered the bodies were moved across the road to the Greet cabin. Sheriff Alston announced over the county telephone line that the corpses would be on public view the next day: he hoped to achieve a positive identification, and perhaps to detect some sort of lead among the crowd.[21]

Although six inches of snow fell Saturday night, early Sunday morning Sheriff Alston carefully examined the murder site. There was a bloody shovel near the spot where Allemand died, and Alston found another gold tooth. He collected a great many shell casings of common calibers, as well as a number of .35-caliber cartridge hulls. Boot prints at the .35-caliber shooting site showed a pair with one worn-off heel and one that had been half-shod; Alston traced the size and shape of these prints on a piece of paper. Other tracks indicated to Alston that there had been as many as eight raiders. He found where the horses had been left, and he saw that the raiders had ridden off to the west, toward the Badlands, but these tracks could not be followed far because of the snowfall.

As expected, a large crowd gathered throughout the day to view the bodies and to walk around the burned-out camps. Among the early arrivals were Bounce Helmer and Pete Cafferal, who were intensively questioned by the sheriff. Although Sheriff Alston insisted that Helmer must have recognized some of the raiders, Bounce stated that they all wore gunnysack masks — he never mentioned Ed Eaton. Alston circulated among different groups around the Greet cabin and corrals, but everyone was tight-lipped. The sheriff also had no luck in spotting a .35-caliber rifle nor a pair of badly worn boots. Deputy Morton organized a coroner's jury, which ruled that the deceased "came to their death unlawfully, by shooting."[22]

Jacques Allemand, brother of the murdered sheepman, arrived from his home in Buffalo. After the bodies were released by the coroner, coffins were secured and the deceased were taken to the Allemand ranch. Another French herder was employed, and the sheep were rounded up and pastured. On Tuesday, April 6, a large crowd assembled at 2:00 P.M. on the Allemand ranch to attend funeral services for the three murder victims. Allemand was a Mason, and the Masonic graveside ritual was performed. The three men were buried side by side, with simple wooden crosses marking the graves beside Spring Creek. That night, after the crowd had left, a lone rider appeared within view of the Allemand house. Watched by the widow and others who were staying overnight, the rider maintained a long vigil from a hill southeast of the house, but Mrs. Allemand refused to be frightened into leaving.[23]

★ ★ ★

There was a groundswell of outraged reaction to the "ATROCIOUS AND COWARDLY CRIME," and there was talk of organizing vigilantes to track down the killers. The Big Horn County Wool Growers' Association immediately offered a reward of $1,000, and the Wyoming Wool Growers Association added another $1,000. The National Wool Growers Association soon offered an additional $2,000, the Big Horn county commissioners offered $500, and Jacques Allemand, bitterly vowing that he would "never rest until the guilty men have been brought to account," pledged another $1,000 — bringing the reward total to $5,500.[24]

Sheriff Alston and Deputy Cusack spent days separately riding from ranch to ranch, questioning everyone for possible clues, including information that might have been overheard on the party line. Alston instructed his deputy to talk to the ranch wives about the need to avoid further violence, but the women remained as tight-lipped as the men. Porter Lamb, however, told Alston that when he rode toward the Greet ranch from the south on the Friday afternoon of the raid, he had encountered Herb Brink and Tommy Dixon on Otter Creek. A week into his investigation, Alston was told by cattleman Ed Brandt that he had unexpectedly seen Milt Alexander only a mile or so from the Greet ranch on the previous Friday.[25]

When Alston stopped at the ranch of Albert Keyes, he found the young rancher to be peaked and "bilious." Telephone gossip already had revealed Charles Farris also to be ailing. At every ranch where he stopped, Alston unobtrusively looked for badly worn boots, and he said he was trying to buy a .35-caliber carbine. At the Keyes spread he was told that Farney Cole, who rode for Keyes, had such a gun. When Cole came in from the range he reported that his carbine had disappeared the day after April Fool's Day. On that day Herb Brink, Tommy Dixon, Milt Alexander, George Saban, and Ed Eaton had turned up at the ranch, while Cole had spent the night at the hamlet of Hyattville. Cole expressed his intention to question Brink and the others about the disappearance of his rifle.[26]

The next day Alston rode twenty miles to Hyattville. Cole's alibi checked out, and the sheriff could find no trace of the missing carbine. Suspicious of Herb Brink, a vociferous opponent of sheepmen, Alston next rode to Billy Goodrich's ranch, where Brink was staying. There he met a six-foot-six cowboy named Bill Garrison — who owned a .35-caliber carbine and whose boot heels were badly run over. But when the sheriff checked Garrison's tracks against the paper tracings he had made at the murder site, the towering cowboy's boots proved too large. Alston asked Garrison if he would sell his carbine, but Garrison replied that his father had the gun at his home in Manderson. The sheriff rode to Manderson, asked to see the gun, and discovered that the firing pin was broken and rusted over. The senior Garrison told Alston that the firing pin had snapped off three years earlier. Although Alston's efforts seemed fruitless, he had collected a certain amount of evidence and suspicions, and soon he received notable reinforcement — the Wyoming Stock Growers Association engaged Deputy U.S. Marshal Joe LeFors to help with the investigation.[27]

Soon after the murders, newspapers had predicted "arrests which will startle the state because of the prominence of the persons involved." Alston must have realized that he was getting close when he found an anonymous note in his pocket warning him to stop searching for the Ten Sleep murderers. Other sheepmen reportedly received warnings that they should leave the country "or meet the fate of Allemand, Emge, and Lazier."[28]

But Alston, his deputies, and LeFors continued their questioning and the search for the .35-caliber rifle. Bounce Helmer, questioned frequently, soon revealed that he had seen the face of Ed Eaton. On Monday, April 12, Alston sent two deputies to arrest Eaton, a former bartender who had left saloons to work as a cowboy. The officers found Eaton and four other drovers at Lake Creek with a bull herd. Eaton offered no resistance to arrest, and the deputies took him to the rickety county jail in Basin. Word spread that wealthy cattlemen had paid retainers to all lawyers in the general vicinity, so that special legal help would be unavailable to the prosecution. Joe LeFors slipped into Billy Goodrich's bunkhouse and found the runover boots and Farney Cole's rifle wrapped in Herb Brink's bedroll, and soon Brink joined Eaton in jail.[29]

Attorneys were readily available for Eaton and Brink. Young Percy Metz enlisted his father, William S. Metz, a former judge, and the county attorney was further reinforced by E. E. Enterline of Sheridan and William L. Simpson of Cody, attorneys provided by sheep raisers' associations. Percy Metz empaneled a grand jury, which first met on Thursday afternoon, April 29. Basin teemed with spectators; sheepmen and their families camped in one area, cattlemen camped in another area, and everyone jammed into the ramshackle courthouse.[30]

Saturday was spent in a gruelling examination of Bill Garrison, who apparently had been told about the raid by at least one participant. The big cowboy was grilled throughout the day, questioned again after supper, then told to be ready to answer more questions when called. Garrison was visibly uncomfortable on the witness stand. Filled with the westerner's typical loyalty to his friends, he was tormented by the prospect of revealing the terrible information he had been told. Outside at last, he met Billy Goodrich, paid off a debt of $6.50, then asked Goodrich for the loan of his gun. Goodrich replied that the gun was at Joe Henry's home in Basin. On Sunday, Garrison encountered Henry, who told the cowboy he needed rest and invited him to go to bed at his home. Garrison complied, but while he was at Henry's he found Goodrich's automatic.

That evening Garrison was seen in downtown Basin. On Monday morning he turned up at the Voss ranch near Manderson. He restlessly stayed by the haystacks for a long period, finally coming to the house at 1:00 to ask for dinner. After eating he requested a pencil and paper, which he took with him to the haystacks. The ranch owner last noticed him at 4:00. Three hours later, his body was found near the haystacks. Goodrich's automatic was in his left hand; two rounds had been fired. Garrison had shot himself in the left side, but when the wound did not prove fatal he fired a second bullet into his left temple. Two penciled notes were found on the body.[31]

When word reached Basin, it was thought that the notes would reveal the identity of the Ten Sleep raiders. Concerned cattlemen saddled up and galloped toward the Voss ranch. But Coroner Carter borrowed an automobile and beat the horsemen to the ranch by rocketing along at speeds of up to twenty miles an hour. The first note read: "When found, notify John C. Garrison, Thermopolis, Wyo." The second note was no more dramatic, directing the First National Bank of Buffalo to turn over all his credits to his brother, John C. Garrison.[32]

Garrison's body was brought to Basin that night, and the next day a coroner's jury was formed: County Commissioner Ira Waters, who had loaned his car to Coroner Carter; Billy Goodrich, whose gun had been used by Garrison; and Joe Henry. The death was ruled a suicide, and the funeral was held at the Methodist Church of Basin on Thursday. Burial followed in the local cemetery. The grand jury recessed for the funeral, but these men had been busy.[33]

Most of the grand jury members were veterans of the range, and they could not get around the claim of Tommy Dixon that on the day of the raid he had been helping Herb Brink hunt strays. The alibi of Dixon and Brink made no sense: why would Dixon, who worked for another ranch, ride with Brink? It became clear that seven men for unexplained reasons had been in the vicinity of Spring Creek on the date of the raid. A short time after the funeral of Bill Garrison, the grand jury issued indictments for three counts of murder for Brink and Eaton, who were already in jail, and for Albert Keyes, Charles Farris, Tommy Dixon, George Saban, and Milt Alexander. The latter five men, like almost everyone else in the district, were in town, perhaps so that suspicion would not be aroused by their absence. During the evening of Thursday, May 6, these men were located and arrested by Sheriff Alston, Deputy Cusack, and several special deputies. Sheriff Alston ordered a four-man guard at the jail around the clock.[34]

Keyes and Farris spilled out full confessions, maintaining that they had participated in the raid only because of assurances that no one would be killed. On Sunday Keyes and Farris were moved from the county jail to the city jail. Two lawyers employed by cattle interests tried to see them, but Keyes and Farris refused to meet with the attorneys. Instead, on Monday they petitioned District Judge C. H. Parmalee to be transferred out of Basin. In the afternoon they were whisked out of town by Joe LeFors, and the party turned up in Sheridan at 2:00 in the morning. The prisoners were not handcuffed but immediately placed in the county jail. At about this time, Bounce Helmer disappeared. It later developed that Sheriff Alston had sent his key witnesses — Helmer, Pierre Cafferal, and Billy Goodrich — to the state of Washington for safekeeping. Judge Parmalee refused to release the prisoners on bond.[35]

It was rumored that cattlemen raised a war chest of $200,000, and ranch owners in the Big Horn Basin contributed $100 to $500 apiece. A platoon of noted lawyers was engaged to represent the defense in court. (Not to be outdone, sheepmen later claimed that their legal forces had been guaranteed financial support up to $250,000.) Large crowds, including armed cowboys, continued to throng Basin, and early in June eight members of the Wyoming National Guard arrived from Cody. Commanded by a Lieutenant Williams, the detachment pitched camp in the public square near the jail. The guardsmen set up two Sibley tents and a cook tent, and engaged an old-timer known as Dad Payne as camp cook. As in the Tom Horn incarceration of 1903, there were rumors of an attack on the jail to free the defendants. But the guardsmen had been sent primarily to alleviate the cost of guards to Big Horn County, and the men stayed for months.[36]

When Judge Parmalee called the district court to order on the third Monday in October, Basin again became crowded with curious citizens. Every spare room in the town of 1,200 was jammed. A large cattlemen's encampment was established on the west side of the river, complete with tents and chuck wagons.

George Saban was the first defendant to face the court. His lawyers, discovering that the list of jurors had not been properly prepared, filed a plea of abatement against the indictments that had been filed against all seven defendants. Several days later, Judge Parmalee ruled that the indictments be quashed, but Percy Metz filed for new indictments — three for murder and one for arson against each defendant. A new list of 2,600 jurors was scrupulously compiled, and nine farmers, a sheepman, an undertaker, and a barber were quickly empaneled as a new jury. Proceedings were moved to the local opera house to better accommodate the crowds, and additional guardsmen arrived as a precaution.[37]

Charles Farris took the witness stand, told the story of the raid, stated that he understood there would be nothing worse than rimrocking sheep — then declared flatly that Brink had shot Allemand when the victim had his hands up. Albert Keyes provided further details, emphasizing that he had fired no shots and had not even been told of the deaths until the day after the raid. Further damaging testimony came during the afternoon of November 8, when Billy Goodrich took the stand. Like Bounce Helmer and Pete Cafferal, Goodrich and his wife had been sent out of the area, visiting Washington and Montana before being escorted back to Basin to testify. Goodrich said that on the Sunday after the raid, when several men were riding back from the scene of the murders, Brink suddenly had blurted out: "Alston was wrong when he said there were eight men in the party: there were only seven." Brink then went on to describe various aspects of the crime, and Goodrich, astounded, said, "You must have been there."[38]

"I was," said Brink. Trusting in the discretion of fellow cattlemen, Brink went on to describe the killings in detail, according to Goodrich, and he named four other participants. Other witnesses testified to having seen Brink riding up to the Keyes ranch on the day of the raid. Similar testimony was delivered from a number of witnesses about other defendants, naming the time of day that these men had been seen prior to the raid. Witnesses also recalled conversations in which Brink had threatened the sheep drive. Deputy Sheriff William Gibson identified a rifle he had found wrapped in a gunnysack in a chicken coop at Billy Keyes's ranch, and it already had been determined that this weapon was used by George Saban during the raid. Cole said that he had been directed to go to Hyattville, and that en route he passed the sheep drive and spoke briefly with Joe Emge. Mrs. Allemand told of receiving several phone calls from her husband during the drive, but the widow was questioned only briefly.[39]

The defense, attempting to refute the testimony of Billy Goodrich, presented witnesses who rated his veracity from "kind of bad" to "flat bad." Otherwise the array of defense lawyers had little to offer, and, to the surprise of onlookers, lamely closed their case on Tuesday,

November 9, at noon. Final arguments were presented in the afternoon, and the judge issued instructions to the jury.[40]

At 6:00 P.M. the jury was escorted to a little log cabin. Special Deputy H. L. Mead had been placed in charge of the jury, and he watched over the cabin. Groups of citizens walked up and down Park Avenue, stopping to watch the shadows of jury members silhouetted against the green shades that covered the windows. Men could be seen pacing up and down and gesturing at each other, and the muffled sound of voices could be heard outside. From time to time Mead would say, "I guess you have seen enough," and pedestrian traffic would continue to move.[41]

The jury worked through the quiet, starry night. At 8:00 on Thursday morning, jury foreman W. H. Packard called Mead to announce that the jury was ready to come in. Judge Parmalee entered a packed courtroom at 9:45, and there was no need to gavel the crowd quiet. "Deathlike silence prevailed," reported a journalist. Parmalee asked if the gentlemen of the jury had agreed on a verdict. "We have," said Packard.

"What is your verdict?" asked Parmalee.

"Guilty of murder in the first degree, as charged."[42]

Herb Brink did not show a flicker of emotion, and he was taken immediately to his cell at the county jail. Deputies and guardsmen were put on alert, in case an escape plan might be put into effect by cattlemen. Defense attorneys were expected to appeal the verdict, and county officials promptly selected a jury to try the next defendant, Thomas Dixon. But the trial of Brink had seemed decisive. "The conviction of Brink marks the end of the assassination and warfare on the open range," triumphantly proclaimed Judge W. S. Metz, senior counsel for the prosecution. "It is the first conviction ever obtained in the state for murder growing out of raids and clashes between cattlemen and sheepmen. It is significant of the beginning of a new era.... The 'gunman' has had his day in Wyoming."[43]

Defense attorneys apparently felt a grudging measure of agreement, meeting on Sunday with the prosecuting attorneys and Judge Parmalee. It was suggested that Brink, convicted of first-degree murder in the death of Allemand, would be allowed a new trial, whereupon he would plead guilty to second-degree murder and be sentenced to life imprisonment. Saban and Alexander would plead guilty to second-degree murder and be sentenced to twenty years each. Eaton and

Dixon would plead guilty to manslaughter and be sentenced to three years each at hard labor.[44]

At first the prosecution objected to anything but the death sentence for Brink, as well as to the light sentences for Eaton and Dixon. Brink valiantly offered to let his execution be carried out if it would save the other four. But they refused, and Saban declared that Brink's life must be spared or they "would all hang to the same tree." State Senator George B. McClellan, Milo Burke, and other wealthy, influential cattlemen urged the prisoners to accept the concessions that were finally offered by the State. The defendants concurred, and Judge Parmalee approved the results of the conference.[45]

Early the next morning, Brink summoned Judge Parmalee to his cell and claimed that Charles Farris had fired the shot which killed Allemand. An hour later, Brink was arraigned for sentencing and Judge Parmalee asked if he had anything to say. "I did not kill Allemand," he said. "I would not shoot a man with his hands in the air." Brink then accused Farris in court, after which Parmalee pronounced the death sentence on Brink, setting the date of execution for January 14, 1910. Of course, Brink's death sentence soon would be changed. Judge Parmalee then proceeded to hear the guilty pleas of the other four defendants, and he announced the previously agreed sentences.[46]

The five defendants met with Judge Parmalee on Sunday, November 14. They told Parmalee details of the fight, and Brink and Alexander insisted that Farris had shot Allemand. The prisoners also claimed that they were forced to shoot, because the sheepmen violated the deadline and tried to defend themselves. On the same day that this story became public, November 16, an editorial hooted that the claim of self-defense was "ludicrous" and "grotesque."[47]

On Monday, November 15, Percy Metz filed a motion dismissing criminal charges against Charles Farris and Albert Keyes. That same day, Farris and Keyes turned up at the Basin depot to be given safe conduct out of the state. Billy Goodrich, who had related Brink's confession of guilt, also was present with his wife and child, as were Farris's wife and child. Farris and Keyes were given bills of sale by the county for their holdings in the Ten Sleep area (Goodrich's sawmill on his ranch had been burned to the ground on Wednesday night, November 3). Farris, Keyes, and Goodrich were treated like lepers in the depot. When they walked into the waiting room everyone either rose and left, or pointedly looked out the windows. When they strolled up and down the platform, they did not receive a word of greeting. When they spoke to acquaintances, they were coldly ignored. Farris and Keyes were held in contempt: "guilty but by the law made guiltless because they betrayed the guilt of others; first outragers, then protectors, of society, and, finally, ostracized by society." They all left on the train for Billings, Montana, but left no word of their final destination. Keyes disappeared, Farris later became a preacher and died in Manhattan, Kansas, and Goodrich and his family eventually returned to the Big Horn Basin.[48]

On a rainy Saturday, November 20, a number of people went to the county jail to offer farewells to Brink, Saban, Eaton, Dixon, and Alexander. One friend brought a "huge" basket of fruit. A large crowd gathered at the depot when the heavily guarded prisoners were taken to the special car attached to a train that would take them to prison in Rawlins. Sheriff Alston, accompanied by deputies Cusack, Frank James, and James Johnston, as well as jailer Walter Smith, boarded the special car with the five raiders and two other prisoners. As the group walked down the platform, hands shot out of the crowd for final handshakes. Three ranking members of the Wyoming National Guard, along with the detail which had been stationed at the jail for six months, also boarded the special train. The distance from Basin to Rawlins was about 250 miles, but the train had to meander through Montana, South Dakota, Nebraska, then back into Wyoming (a direct line was built a few years later). On Tuesday, November 23, the party dined in Cheyenne, expecting to arrive at last in Rawlins at about 3:00 in the morning.[49]

Sheriff Alston refused to accept the rewards due him, altruistically stating that he was paid a salary to perform his duty. About a year later, Alston returned to Rawlins as warden of the penitentiary, and he appointed George Mead to the guard force. George Saban was made a trusty and drove a wagon on errands around Rawlins. Sent with a road gang to Cody, he continued to drive his wagon at will, and complaints were made that he was seeing his wife. He was transferred to Worland, then learned that he soon would be returned to Rawlins. Saban received permission to go to Basin on business, presumably relating to his livestock. In Basin he visited old friends, secured money for an escape, then hired a hack driver to take him to Laurel, Montana. Saban then permanently disappeared; rumor suggested that he had gone to Mexico or Cuba or South America.[50]

Milt Alexander served eight years of his term before being released. He returned to Ten Sleep and later died there. Tommy Dixon was released after three years; he was rumored either to have died insane in Montana, or to have been killed in an Oklahoma oilfield accident. Soon after his release, Ed Eaton went to Meeteetse, Wyoming, where he was bitten by a tick and died of Rocky Mountain Spotted Fever. Herb Brink was paroled in 1914. He moved in with his half sister, who was the mother of his two children, and who soon would give birth to another. Balking at family life, he broke parole and headed for Canada, where he was captured by the Royal Canadian Mounted Police and was returned to the penitentiary in Rawlins. Released as an old man, he spent the rest of his life as a ward of the State of Wyoming.[51]

A fur trapper named John Callahan became a constant source of aid and comfort to Mrs. Allemand, and the couple married in December 1909. Pierre Cafferal returned to France after the trial, but reportedly was thrown in jail. Apparently, he had been instrumental in bringing the Lazier boy to the United States, and Lazier's parents prosecuted him (the French government also obtained a large damage payment from the United States government for Lazier's death). Bounce Helmer remained in the Ten Sleep country as a bachelor sheepherder; he died in 1956.[52]

Editorial praise of the successful legal action against the Spring Creek raiders was strong and widespread. Immediately after the guilty verdict against Brink, the Cheyenne *Daily Leader* reprinted an editorial from the *Rocky Mountain News* of Denver, adding that "the existence in Wyoming of the spirit of justice and a determination to stop lawlessness has been almost as well advertised as have evil occurrences in the state heretofore." An editorial in the *Daily Leader* prophesied "that never again will the rivalry for the use of the open Wyoming range result in organized and armed attack on one faction by another."[53]

Indeed, the Ten Sleep murders and subsequent, unprecedented convictions proved to be a dramatic turning point in the range wars between cattlemen and sheepmen. It was undeniably clear that public opinion, reflecting changing economic realities, no longer would permit cattlemen to run roughshod over sheepherders without suffering severe consequences. But cattle ranchers typically were men with great pride and perverse stubbornness, who did not quit in the face of adversity — and the raids had not ended.

10

Final Troubles

Several times in the history of this country {northeastern Colorado} there has been trouble caused by the introduction of sheep, and it is not the sentiment of this association only, but of the entire country at large, to keep them out.
— Williams River Cattle and Horse Growers' Association

The Ten Sleep tragedy often is mentioned as the final important incident in the conflict between western cattle and sheep interests. But trouble persisted sporadically in Wyoming and New Mexico, and as late as 1920 shootings erupted in Colorado and Arizona, where the intrusion of sheep from Utah was a continual cause of tensions. During the second decade of the twentieth century, there were at least a dozen attacks by raiders against flocks or sheepherders, four herders were shot to death, and more than four thousand sheep were killed. But cattlemen increasingly turned to lawyers or legislators to resolve their problems, and by the 1920s not even diehard cattle ranchers resorted to violence to solve difficulties with sheepmen.

In Wyoming, despite the outcome of the Ten Sleep trial, raiders struck a flock in Sublette County in February 1912, killing sixty sheep and burning wagons owned by Albert Johnson and Charles Wilson. The Wyoming Stock Growers Association promptly offered a reward of

$2,500. Three men were arrested, but were proclaimed not guilty on May 31, 1912.¹

In New Mexico a cowboy still might resort to gunplay at the intrusion of sheepmen. On Sunday, February 6, 1916, ranchers George Haydon and Robert M. Reynolds were putting up the framework for a goat herder's shack a mile south of Pyramid Peak near Lordsburg. About 2:30 in the afternoon, Eugene "Curley" Rolland rode over from a nearby cow camp and announced that the shack was going up on property he claimed through squatter's rights. Haydon and Reynolds vehemently protested such an archaic concept, and the three men exchanged "hot words." Finally, Haydon turned on his heel to walk away. Rolland pulled his revolver and tried to fire, but the gun failed to discharge. Haydon wheeled around just as Rolland jerked the trigger again. This time the hammer fell on a live round. The slug tore into Haydon's left arm above the elbow, shattering both bones and bringing all parties to their senses.²

Ranchers in northwestern Colorado had occasional difficulties between 1910 and 1920. By 1910 several years had passed since the last trouble between sheep and cattle graziers, and George Woolley confidently brought two bands to his ranch southeast of Craig. Although area cattlemen were aggravated over the presence of sheep, Woolley experienced no repercussions. He earned a tidy profit and made plans to bring in more sheep the next year, but cattlemen held meetings in April and June of 1911 to debate the threat to their range.

In December 1911 a band of 110 rams, ewes, and lambs was wintering on Woolley's place in the care of sixteen-year-old Louis Eberle. It was widely known in the district that Woolley was in Denver, intending to purchase 3,000 sheep to winter at his ranch and to range in the forest reserves during the spring. Cattlemen had no intention of allowing such an invasion of woollies.

On the moonlit night of December 4, five raiders cut through a wire fence to enter Woolley's ranch from the public road. The telephone line was cut, but with Eberle sound asleep and Woolley's family in Craig, there was no one to sound an alarm. The raiders worked efficiently, clubbing and knifing almost all of the sheep; a ewe with a three-day-old lamb was found and killed in the barn. When Eberle came out of the house at dawn, he found 90 of the 110 sheep dead, and almost all of the others were dying of wounds.³

From 1912 to 1922, L. H. "Doc" Chivington was employed by cattlemen in northwestern Colorado to ride the state line. His assign-

Final Troubles 151

ment was to see that Wyoming sheepmen did not try to sneak flocks onto Colorado ranges between Vermilion Creek and the Little Snake River. Although Chivington had little to do besides ride his patrol line, on July 4, 1917, several hard-drinking cowboys decided to celebrate the nation's birthday by raiding a nearby sheep camp in Gunnison National Forest. They saddled up and rode toward the mountains, but forest supervisor William E. Kreutzer was warned by telephone. Kreutzer and a forest ranger climbed into an automobile and drove to intercept them. In an ugly mood, the cowboys threatened to kill Kreutzer and his ranger. But Kreutzer courageously talked the riders into following him back to town. A year later, however, raiders from the area struck a sheep camp on Oh-Be-Joyful-Creek. Nearly 2,000 sheep belonging to John Campbell were driven over a cliff. Campbell's herder was bound and thrown into a gulch, and later he refused to testify against the raiders.[4]

Utah sheepmen had begun to place their flocks across the Colorado line by 1920. Nine years earlier, area cattlemen had drawn up a lengthy resolution protesting the introduction of sheep and expressing the sentiment "of the entire country at large, to keep them out." The intervening years had not weakened the resolve of the cattlemen. On Tuesday night, April 5, 1920, seven masked and heavily armed riders struck a sheep camp on the homestead of Winfield D. Keeley in northwestern Rio Blanco County. The 350 sheep belonged to Snellen Johnson of Vernal, Utah, who had employed two herders, twenty-two-year-old William Mann and eighteen-year-old Dean Leonard. The raiders dragged Mann and Leonard out of their sheep wagon, intending to lynch them, but neither of the herders were foreigners and both young men pleaded for their lives. Bound and gagged, they were guarded by one raider, while the others clubbed every one of Johnson's sheep to death. One of the masked men growled to the herders that they intended to give Keeley "the same dose" they had given the sheep.[5]

A few days later, Johnson and Keeley trailed the seven horsemen through the mud, finding discarded clubs along the way. Tracks led to the Box Elder Ranch belonging to Frank and Thomas Berry, but Johnson called a halt half a mile from the ranch. When warrants were sworn, however, county officers refused to serve them, and Frank Berry was reported to have said, "We are going to get blood next time." Johnson contacted Colorado's governor and attorney general, and was instructed to proceed through Frank Delaney, district attorney for Colorado's Ninth Judicial District. But Delaney was noticeably reluctant to take action against cattlemen. Frank Berry later reported that "Frank Delaney said we could kill all the damned sheepherders and Mormons we pleased, and sheep." But homesteaders, fed up with intimidation from cattlemen, pledged their support to Johnson, and the sheepman took his case to investigators of the U.S. Land Office. Finally, in December 1920, six "prominent" cattlemen, including the Berrys, were indicted by the federal grand jury, with a promise from the government attorney to "prosecute to the limit."[6]

While Johnson was trying to secure legal action, blood was shed on a raid in Moffatt County. John Darnell had established a squatter's spread in 1916 in Rough Gulch, just four miles east of the Utah boundary. A married man with a child, Darnell built a cabin and two water reservoirs. Known as a good pistol shot with either hand, Darnell did not hesitate to run a flock of 1,800 sheep on "his" land.

At 3:00 A.M. on July 20, 1920, eleven cattlemen rode up to Darnell's place. Darnell had bedded down in a sheep wagon while his father-in-law, James E. Price, slept in the cabin. Awakened by the barking of his dogs, Darnell grabbed a gun and fired two warning shots. Then he lit a lantern, carelessly revealing his silhouette against the canvas. The raiders opened fire, riddling Darnell. Unaware that anyone was in the cabin, the raiders turned to the flock, fatally shooting and clubbing 686 sheep.

Price slipped from the cabin to the wagon, found his son-in-law still alive, and headed to the nearby K Ranch to seek help. The nearest doctor was in Jensen, Utah, but before the physician could be brought in, Darnell breathed his last. A newspaper in Craig speculated that the identity of the killers "will probably always remain a mystery, as have such cases in the past."[7]

During the troubled spring and summer of 1920, Colorado's final significant conflict developed between cattlemen and sheepmen. The United States Forest Service allotted summer grazing permits to Utah sheepmen in ranges of the White River National Forest, about 100 miles from the Utah border in northwestern Colorado. Cattlemen in the region had previously resisted similar allotments to Wyoming sheep graziers in the Routt National Forest, but at least flocks from Wyoming entered the Routt Forest directly, without passing across rangelands where cattle traditionally had grazed.

The most practical procedure for Utah sheepmen with summer allotments in the White River National Forest, however, was to drive their flocks east in the spring, after their ewes had lambed. The cross-country drive would bring thousands of head of sheep through more than 100 miles of cattle country. Much of the region had long been used by cattlemen for winter grazing, but the passage of sheep would crop off much of the forage needed by cattlemen. In fact, as early as 1900, Colorado cattlemen had patrolled the Utah line for fifty miles to keep sheep out of the state. Utah sheepmen responded by stampeding cattle and poisoning water holes. Cowboys from the Prairie Cattle Company destroyed 4,000 sheep, although the company later reimbursed the owner, Jesus Ma Perea, for his losses.[8]

Cattlemen insisted that Utah sheep be moved to the White River National Forest by rail. But sheepmen would have to drive their flocks to Price or some other Utah shipping point, then proceed on the Denver and Rio Grande all the way to Denver. In Denver the sheep would be transferred to a line heading west for a trip of 150 miles to tiny Yampa, then unloaded for a drive of ten or twelve miles to the forest reserves. Sheepmen, of course, protested such a roundabout and expensive journey, and claimed that by using public roads and existing driveways they could reach their allotments with little damage to cattle ranges.

The first sheepmen to attempt such a drive in 1920 were two Utah ranchers named Coltharp and Brimhall. They assembled two bands each in the Moffatt County hamlet of Sunbeam, about sixty miles northwest of the White River National Forest. Recognizing the hostility of cattlemen in northwestern Colorado, Coltharp and Brimhall asked Governor Oliver Shoup to send the Colorado National Guard for protection.

Governor Shoup instead directed Pat Hamrock, head of the state police, to safeguard the sheepmen, and a carload of officers and two motorcycle policemen were sent to Sunbeam. Although cattlemen held a protest meeting in Craig, forty miles east of Sunbeam, the sheep drive commenced with a police escort. But Ferry Carpenter, attorney for the Hayden Stockgrowers' Association, suggested an ingenious legal stopgap under a Colorado law which allocated responsibility for opening and abandoning county roads to the county commissioners.

The route of the sheepmen would take them from Moffatt County south into Rio Blanco County. Shortly after entering Rio Blanco County, the county road passed through the ranch of cattleman Jap Wyman. Rio Blanco county officials strongly favored cattle interests, and each of the three commissioners were cattlemen. Jap Wyman readily agreed to Carpenter's plan, stating that he wanted the county road through his property to be closed. Carpenter placed a telephone call to Meeker, seat of Rio Blanco County, requesting that the commissioners meet in emergency session to act on a petition by Wyman and his neighbors to abandon the road.

About fifty cowboys and cattlemen drove out to Wyman's ranch, hauling a roll of hogwire. Carpenter stayed on Wyman's phone to the Rio Blanco courthouse, while two of the commissioners were located. When the sheep approached Wyman's ranch, the state policemen spotted the congregation of cattlemen and realized that a confrontation was likely. The police car pushed through the first band of sheep and headed toward the house just as Carpenter received the news he wanted. He announced that the commissioners had voted to abandon the road, and immediately cattlemen surged across the road, unrolling the hogwire among the leading sheep and throwing a flimsy fence across the road. Carpenter informed the captain that the road had been abandoned and that the owner of the property strongly objected to the presence of sheep on his ranch.

The police captain ordered Coltharp and Brimhall to turn the sheep around, and the sheepmen complied. As the flocks backtracked, cattlemen along the way attacked any sheep that strayed from the road onto their property. About 150 sheep were killed, while one rancher broke a bone in his foot when he kicked a woolly that had ventured onto his land. Coltharp and Brimhall drove their flocks to Craig, then shipped them by rail back to Utah, suffering large financial losses.

Utah sheepmen lost little time in attempting to have a stock driveway designated across public domain to the White River National Forest. Cattlemen registered protests, and the issue came to rest with the Bureau of Public Lands within the Department of the Interior. The key official in this situation was William Spry, commissioner of the General Land Office within the Department of the Interior. Spry was a former governor of Utah who could be expected to favor Utah sheepmen, and soon he established a stock driveway 108 miles long and six to thirty-six miles wide from the Utah-Colorado border to the White River National Forest.

Although the protests of Colorado cattle ranchers brought few results in Washington, Ferry Carpenter petitioned Colorado's congressmen to oppose the driveway. The congressional delegations of Colorado and Utah engaged in political and parliamentary maneuvering for more than a year. During that time, hard feelings continued on the northwestern ranges of Colorado. In January 1921 cattlemen forced a sheepherder to hold his band of 1,600 ewes on the same bedground at Lily Park for nearly a month; cowboys then threw out poisoned corn to the half-starved sheep, killing 300 head. Finally, on April 11, 1922, Colorado Senators Lawrence C. Phipps and Samuel D. Nicholson accompanied a delegation from their state into a conference with Commissioner Spry and Secretary of the Interior Albert B. Fall. Ferry Carpenter and two other determined citizens presented the argument that Colorado cattle ranchers now had no objection to grazing privileges for Colorado sheepmen, but regarded it as "most unfair" for Utah sheep graziers to range their flocks more than 100 miles into Colorado while traveling to and from the White River forest reserves. The Coloradoans presented their case so persuasively that the permit for the controversial stock driveway was immediately revoked. Colorado's last conflict between sheep and cattle graziers was won — through decidedly peaceful means — by cattlemen.[9]

* * *

In Arizona, even though a quarter of a century had passed since the bloody Pleasant Valley War, tensions had not disappeared between cattle and sheep interests. When sheepman R. W. Brookins decided to drive his flock from Geronimo on the Gila River nine miles east to winter range at Hooker Mesa, he felt sufficiently intimidated to enlist the aid of lawmen. Early in December 1912 he moved his flock across the river under the watchful eyes of several deputy sheriffs.[10]

A consistent problem involved Utah sheepmen, who seasonally drove their flocks into northern Arizona. By 1915 Arizona cattlemen had determined to keep Utah woollies out by seizing control of public watering places. Legal action resulted, and at the trial in Prescott, the cattlemen from Arizona especially resented the testimony of J. W. Imlay. Imlay was manager of the Walnut Development Company of Hurricane, in the southwest corner of Utah. Although unsuccessful at the trial, the cattlemen bided their time. Then in the spring of 1917, when Imlay sent a flock into Arizona, 700 of his sheep were poisoned to death.[11]

At the annual meeting of the Arizona Cattle Growers' Association in February 1918, ranchers supported the efforts of the U.S. Forest Service, endorsed the leasing of "enormous areas" of state lands as a means of transition from open-range operation to fenced grazing, and requested the appointment of a federal grazing commissioner. Among other items of business was "the granting of additional driveways and grazing ground to the sheepmen." After due deliberation, the cattlemen resolved "that no more sheep trails be permitted in the state."[12]

The following April two prominent sheepmen, J. D. Newman of Flagstaff and Frank Hoctor of Springerville, quarreled over matters pertaining to their respective flocks. Long accustomed to standing up for their range rights, in January 1919 Newman and Hoctor encountered each other in the desert west of Phoenix. Again an argument broke out, and apparently Hoctor, who was in his thirties, took a shot at the older man (Newman was fifty-four). Newman unlimbered a revolver and shot Hoctor twice, then placed the wounded man in his car and headed for help. Hoctor died, however, and Newman drove into Glendale and surrendered to the police.[13]

A few weeks later, on March 5, 1919, another fatal fray between two herders erupted at a sheep camp twenty-five miles west of Wickenburg. At 10:00 A.M. a sheepherder entered the camp of Alberto Hernandez, and the two men began arguing over trespassing. The intruding herder went for his revolver, but Hernandez had his Winchester ready and felled his antagonist with a fatal round.[14]

Such unfraternal friction between sheepmen was less common than range troubles between rival cattle ranchers and, of course, was far less common than conflict between sheepmen and cattlemen. Many twentieth-century Arizona cattlemen remained opposed to the presence of woollies on the range. In the spring of 1919, for example, cattle ranchers around Oracle were angered when a Mrs. Yale leased her ranch to sheepman Herbert Boyer. Area ranchers had hoped to make use of the Yale property, which would have connected several cattle ranches with unsurveyed state lands and which would have given them access to these lands without a lease. Furthermore, the Yale ranch boasted a pump which provided a sorely needed water supply. Boyer's lease put sheep on the Yale ranch, cutting off cattlemen from the water pump, but late in April the pump was mysteriously blown up — no doubt by "displeased" cattlemen.[15]

A few months later, a cowboy found a different but effective means to harass a Basque sheepherder named Gabriel Baltaesleque. While riding deep in the Cococino National Forest, the cowboy found an antelope hide in a sheep camp abandoned by Baltaesleque (antelopes were off-limits as game). The conscientious cowboy (it is questionable whether he would have been concerned about illegal hunting of an animal by another cowboy) summoned a forest ranger, and the two men discovered the antelope's head, one foot, and a piece of meat. They presented the evidence to a deputy sheriff, who confronted Baltaesleque. The sheepherder pled guilty before a Flagstaff justice of the peace and was assessed a six-month suspended jail sentence and a $1,000 fine "as a perpetual reminder that antelope are rare and expensive meat, that the State of Arizona and Uncle Sam intends to save what few are left, and that even the migratory sheepherder can not live on such a delicacy as antelope meat with immunity."[16]

Early the next year a forest ranger killed sheepman Charles Quayle in Cococino County, forty miles southwest of Winslow. Ranger Fred W. Croxton and Quayle clashed at Quayle's ranch on Tuesday afternoon, January 6, 1920. Croxton shot the sheepman to death, then called the sheriff's office in Flagstaff with news of the killing.[17]

Later in the year Arizona cattlemen resorted to the courts in an effort to keep sheep off the range. Testing the statute that sheep had to move more than three miles per day over range where cattle traditionally had grazed, cattleman Logan Morris swore out a complaint against two sheepherders, Joe M. and B. Romero. The Romeros were herding a flock that belonged to the Piper Sheep Company. The flock was being grazed in the mountains above Cave Creek, in a region traditionally used by cattlemen, and the Arizona Cattle Growers' Association was the force behind the legal action. The Arizona Wool Growers' Association joined the battle, providing funds for the defense and lining up at least fifteen prominent sheepmen to offer testimony. The Romeros were arrested in March and brought to trial in April on a charge of "sheep trespassing." After hearing testimony from well-known sheepmen and cattlemen, the judge ruled that the Romeros were not guilty because sheep actually had been grazed in the area since 1897 without prior complaint from the cattleman.[18]

Although newspapers optimistically declared that the decision "will tend to settle a long dispute between the cattlemen and the sheep men of the state," Arizona cattle ranchers soon squared off once more against sheepmen. In June 1920 cattlemen in northwestern Arizona insisted that the state law taxing transient flocks of sheep be enforced against Utah stockmen. Vindictive Utah sheepmen from Kane County began to throw the carcasses of dead animals into Kanab Creek, which flows from Utah into Arizona and which was an important water supply for area ranchers. Arizona cattlemen from Fredonia complained about the polluted creek, and the state attorney general placed the matter before the Utah legal department. Utah Attorney General Dan

B. Shields placed the complaint with the county attorney and county commissioners of Kane County, and announced that any stockman who befouled the waters of Kanab Creek would be prosecuted.[19]

Within two months the familiar conflict again led to shooting. Two Mexican herders, employed by a sheepman named Bob Dagmans, brought a flock onto range seven miles north of Williams, near the homestead of William A. Johnson. At the end of July, Johnson ordered the sheepherders to leave, then unsuccessfully tried to have the Mexicans arrested for trespassing. At dawn on Friday, August 13, 1920, Johnson and fellow cattle rancher George Robinson approached the sheep camp with rifles at the ready. The herders warily opened fire but were gunned down by Johnson and Robinson. The ranchers rode into Williams and informed Constable George MacDougall that "there had been a shooting scrape which had better be looked into." Johnson and Robinson turned over their rifles, then accompanied officers to the shooting site. One herder still in his teens was found dead in the camp, and the other had crawled a quarter of a mile into brush, where he died soon after discovery by the posse.[20]

Cattle and sheep ranchers met together in Flagstaff in July 1920 to try to smooth out their difficulties. A bill was fashioned establishing trails for sheep moving from summer to winter ranges. The proposal also required flocks being driven to lambing grounds or from summer to winter ranges to travel at least three miles a day. Early in 1921 there was another joint meeting in Phoenix, where lawyers representing both sides carefully examined the bill and declared it to be satisfactory. But when the bill reached the Arizona legislature in February, cattlemen claimed that the wording had been altered; theoretically, sheepmen could maintain a small ranch in northern Arizona and another little spread in southern Arizona and keep their sheep moving slowly between the two ranches across cattle ranges throughout the year.[21]

The bill passed the legislature, but several sheepmen were promptly indicted for violating the three-mile law, and the first case was avidly attended by numerous sheep and cattle ranchers. In the face of a lengthy drought, however, sheepmen and cattlemen realized that they were plagued by mutual problems, and again resorted to a joint meeting to "bring to the [ranching] industry some means of solution of the serious problems with which it is now confronted." The Arizona Wool Growers' Association and the Arizona Cattle Growers' Association convened in Phoenix on July 7, 8, and 9 in "the most significant gathering of stockmen ever gotten together in the state." M. E.

Crabb, president of the Arizona Cattle Growers' Association, "announced to the cattlemen the imperative necessity of united action" in seeking relief measures in financing, reducing operation costs, and other measures.[22]

At last, Arizona cattlemen came to control their deep enmity toward sheep, as evidenced by their reaction to a situation which arose a few months after the Phoenix meeting. Utah sheepmen continued to bring their flocks south for four months of winter grazing in the Arizona Strip, the area north and west of the Colorado River. Angry cattlemen in this district did not resort to violence. Instead, Professor E. B. Stanley, livestock specialist at the University of Arizona, was brought in from Tucson to inspect the range. Stanley reported that there were 365,000 sheep in the Arizona Strip. Cattlemen were resentful that no state tax was collected on the Utah sheep. "That the range was overstocked when I was there was obvious," said Stanley, going on to relate that the cattlemen intended to seek legislative action to halt the great influx of Utah sheep.[23] A few years earlier, however, Arizona cattle ranchers would have relied upon violence rather than legislation.

* * *

By the 1920s, although resentment still existed among sheepmen and cattlemen, western ranchers finally stopped engaging in combat to settle questions of range rights. But by this time western movies were being cranked out by the hundreds, and prolific writers were producing even greater numbers of western novels. Thus the range war that had raged for half a century across the West was perpetuated for another generation on the silver screen and upon the printed page, and these fictional depictions of the cattleman-sheepherder clash accurately reflected elements of the conflict that had existed in the real West.

The noted western author Henry W. Allen (who also wrote under the names Will Henry and Clay Fisher) spent several years as a young man working in the West, including a stint in Wyoming as a sheepherder. "I didn't last long," he reminisced in a letter to the author. "Too dark at night and too empty by daylight." Although he produced an award-winning short story, "Isley's Stranger," about the conflict, he never wrote a sheepman novel: "The only reason I would ever do one would be to prove I could write anything."[24]

His sentiments apparently reflect those of most western writers, who penned far more cowboy tales than sheepman sagas. However, one of Zane Grey's finest novels was based on Arizona's Pleasant Valley War. Captivated by conflicting accounts of the Graham-Tewksbury feud, Grey spent two months in the Tonto Basin in the fall of 1918.

He returned in 1919 and 1920, and he found descendants of the feudists to be decidedly tight-lipped. "I never learned the truth of the causes of the Pleasant Valley War," he admitted,[25] but in 1921 he published a romanticized version of the range war, *To the Last Man*. Although the names of the feuding families were changed, *To the Last Man* proved to be one of Grey's most memorable works. In the opening chapter Grey narrates that "this band of sheep had left a broad bare swath, weedless, grassless, flowerless, in their wake. Where sheep grazed they destroyed."[26] A silent version of *To the Last Man* was filmed in 1923 starring Richard Dix, and a sound version came out in 1933 starring Randolph Scott and introducing to the screen four-year-old Shirley Temple. Dane Coolidge also wrote a novel about the Pleasant Valley War entitled *The Man Killers*.

Early in his career as a western novelist, Louis L'Amour wrote *The Burning Hills*, featuring a fiery Mexican girl who runs an isolated sheep ranch. She finds a wounded cowboy and falls in love with him while nursing him back to health, but the presence of sheep proves insignificant to the story line. L'Amour envisioned John Wayne as the cowboy; however, when *The Burning Hills* reached the screen in 1956, the producer, attempting unsuccessfully to reach the teen-aged market, co-starred young Tab Hunter and sixteen-year-old Natalie Wood.[27]

Indeed, John Wayne, star of more than two hundred films, never played in a cattleman vs. sheepherder western (*The Shepherd of the Hills*, released in 1941, starred Wayne as an Ozark mountaineer, not a westerner). But the opening scene of *Big Jake*, a 1971 western set in 1909, establishes the character of Wayne by having Big Jake intervene in the lynching of a "sheep farmer." A group of cattlemen prepares to hang the Scottish sheepman, but Big Jake rides up and buys the sheep for merely $400. Big Jake announces that the Scotsman and his Mexican herder go with the flock, and he menacingly intimidates the cattlemen into leaving. Even though Big Jake is the founder of a vast cattle ranch, he has proven himself to be the champion of the underdog — even if the underdog is a sheepman.

Another, even briefer establishing scene was included in the 1962 epic *How the West Was Won*. With a view of a flock of sheep, an off-screen narrator states: "A man's life was less valuable than grass." Suddenly, the sheepherder is shot in the back. In *Wild Rovers* (1971), cowboys William Holden and Ryan O'Neal whip three sheepherders in a saloon brawl. In *The Appaloosa*, a 1966 western starring Marlon Brando, the villain is cattle rancher John Saxon, whose *vaqueros* practice marksmanship by periodically sniping at sheep.

The King of the Cowboys, Roy Rogers, broke up the threat of a range war between cattlemen and a pretty sheep rancher in *Texas Legionnaires*. This 1943 movie, set in the 1940s, depicts cattlemen still hating "sheepers." A fine scene shows the villains stampeding a large flock toward a cliff, but Roy and Trigger foil the rimrocking attempt by turning the sheep. In *Roll on Texas Moon*, a 1946 film, Roy smooths out the problems between sheep rancher Dale Evans and cattleman Gabby Hayes. Gabby, of course, detests sheep, but a running gag has the cantankerous Gabby followed — then *adopted* — by Dale's pet lamb. Gene Autry tackled the classic conflict in *Springtime in the Rockies* (1937). Gene, as a ranch foreman, must defuse the resentment of neighboring cattlemen when his absentee owner, a student of animal husbandry, returns to the ranch with a flock of sheep.

During the era of western series on television, there were occasional episodes dealing with sheepherders. An episode of *Rawhide*, for example, finds the cattle drive impeded by a flock of sheep herded by Tod Stone (played by Richard Basehart). Stone wears a wool vest, hates cattle, and stampedes the herd. But when Stone is injured by Rowdy Yates (Clint Eastwood) in a fight, trail boss Gil Favor orders Rowdy to tend Stone and the flock. Yates and Stone eventually become friends, and Rowdy even has to fight cowboys who cannot tolerate his sheep smell. When Stone joins his band with the enormous flocks of his grandfather and cousins, Rowdy is amazed: "Nightmare," he mutters. "All the sheep in the world." But Rowdy comes to the same conclusion as pragmatic cattlemen of the real West: "You know, Stone, sheep ain't so bad, once you get to know 'em."

The long-running series *Bonanza* twice dealt with sheepherders. In "The Mountain Girl," Warren Oates plays a simple but steady sheepherder, complete with the requisite wool vest. A far more intriguing episode features Everett Sloane as an aggressive, murderous flockmaster. The customary roles are reversed, because cattle baron Ben Cartwright (Lorne Green) is the epitome of kindness and fair play. However, the villainous flockmaster, who has been driven off "his" range (public grassland) by cattlemen and homesteaders, crosses Cartwright's vast Ponderosa Ranch on the way to California with his sheep. Sloane, playing his character with evil gusto, kidnaps Adam Cartwright (Pernell Roberts), offers to trade the life of Ben's oldest son for 50,000 acres of land, but finally is killed by the virtuous cattleman.

The western movie which most fully deals with the cattleman vs. sheepherder conflict is *Montana* (oddly enough, there were few problems between sheep and cattle ranchers in Montana). The 1950 film starred Errol Flynn as an Australian flockmaster (Flynn was a native of Australia) named Morgan Lane. Lane wears a wool vest, his foreman is a Scotsman, and his herders are Mexican. He falls in love with a cattle baroness (played by Alexis Smith), but a sign proclaims: "WARNING — SHEEPHERDERS PASSING THIS POINT WILL BE SHOT ON SIGHT." The cattlemen argue that sheep chew up the grass by the roots, and because of their stench cattle refuse to graze after them. When a sheepherder is murdered, the sheriff shrugs: "Wal, I don't like shootin'. But maybe it'll learn 'em this is cattle country." But a banker is converted by Flynn — "We'd have two crops, wool and mutton, and the price for both is up" — and Flynn eventually marries Smith. As in the real West, the inarguable economics of sheep ranching ultimately prevail.

Ramrod, an excellent Joel McCrea western released in 1947, tensely relates a vicious range war triggered by the introduction of sheep into cattle country. "You know how sheep ruin a country for cattle," states McCrea. In 1980 Steve McQueen starred in *Tom Horn.* Although there was no focus on sheep, the film graphically portrayed the murder of Willie Nickell, the famous trial, and Horn's execution.

Another interesting movie treatment is seen in *Heaven With a Gun,* a 1968 production starring Glenn Ford as a gunfighting preacher who rides into the midst of a brutal range war. A Mexican sheepherder is ambushed, his flock is run off, a barn full of sheep is set ablaze, cowboys use a flock of sheep for target practice, and an Indian sheepherder is hanged. But the sheepmen, led by Abraham and Scotty Andrews, are well-armed and aggressive. Cowboys shear the head of Scotty Andrews, but he later stabs a villain in the throat with shears. Although cattlemen refuse to attend church with "sheepers," Ford preaches that sheep and cattle complement each other on the range. He demonstrates that they will water together, and at film's end there is a combined cattle and sheep drive to a lake.

Glenn Ford also starred in *The Sheepman,* a 1958 release that is one of the funniest westerns ever lensed. (Author Will Henry explained why he wanted to see the film: "Anybody that can get a laugh out of a sheep deserves my patronage."[28]) Ford comes to Powder Valley and deliberately antagonizes everybody in town: he hornswoggles a saddle merchant and a horse trader, then picks a fight with the town bully. After licking the bully, Ford announces that he is bringing in his stock to graze on public lands, and he would like to take care of any objections beforehand. Cowgirl Shirley MacLaine asks what kind of stock. "I was afraid you'd ask that," replies Ford. "Sheep."

Final Troubles 163

"Mister, this is cattle country," he is told. But Ford and his Mexican herder bring in the flock anyway. Ford admits that he won the flock in a poker game, but he has found an advantage to woollies: "I got tired of kickin' dumb cows around — sheep are easier to kick." And he is undismayed when the town marshal (played by Slim Pickens) refuses legal protection: "The day you elected to go to sheepherdin' is the day you gave up your rights as a U.S. citizen." Ford is able to overcome the inevitable opposition, wins MacLaine, then announces that he will sell his sheep and buy a herd of cattle!

* * *

Few western movies have been filmed in recent years, and paperback westerns have suffered a severe decline in popularity. The public appetite for fictional western entertainment is slight, and perhaps there is little new for screenwriters and novelists to say about a range conflict that ended early in the century.

But the clash between cattlemen and sheepherders produced violence across the West from the 1870s until 1921. From Pleasant Valley to Ten Sleep to the Idaho courthouse where Diamondfield Jack Davis was tried, from Iron Mountain to Tie Siding to the Holbrook dwelling where Commodore Perry Owens shot four adversaries, it is still possible to visit some of the most historic sites of this long conflict. At ranches and small western towns, an inquirer can visit with men and women whose fathers or uncles or old friends participated in the hostilities, and who still remember strong feelings against bleating woollies or overbearing cattle barons.

During five decades of irregular but vicious warfare, scores of raids were launched by cattlemen, at least twenty-eight sheepmen and sixteen cowboys were killed, and more than 53,000 sheep were shot, clubbed, knifed, poisoned, dynamited, and rimrocked. The venomous struggle between cattlemen and sheepmen was one of the major conflicts of the West. The ghosts of the Grahams and Tewksburys, of Tom Horn and more than forty unknown sheepherders and cowboys, are just as tangible in the vastness of the West as those of George Armstrong Custer and Crazy Horse and Wild Bill Hickok. The fifty-year war between cattlemen and sheepmen, waged in a magnificent arena of mountains and plains, is a classic story of murderous aggression and retribution that forms one of the great dramas of western history.

Endnotes

CHAPTER 1:   CATTLEMEN, SHEEPMEN, AND THE OPEN RANGE

1. J. Evetts Haley, *Charles Goodnight*, 466.
2. Adams, *Western Words*, 276.
3. *Ibid.*, 275.
4. *Ibid.*, 10, 275–276.
5. Literature on the western cattle industry and on cowboys is enormous. Edward Everett Dale's *The Range Cattle Industry* offers an enlightening starting point. Lewis Atherton's *The Cattle Kings* is superb, and so is *The Cowboys* of the *Time-Life* series. Charles Wayland Towne and Edward Norris Wentworth provided an interesting volume in *Cattle & Men* (Towne and Wentworth previously produced the classic *Shepherd's Empire,* while Wentworth wrote *America's Sheep Trails*). Excellent studies and fascinating contemporary accounts abound about this colorful, engrossing frontier industry.
6. In 1885 the governor of Wyoming wrote to the secretary of the interior that a man could get started in the sheep business for an investment of $5.127.14, realize a profit of $1,129.11 after one year, enjoy a second-year profit of $2,201.50, and proportionate profits thereafter. See George W. Rollins, "The Struggle of the Cattleman, Sheepman and Settler for Control of Lands in Wyoming, 1867–1910" (diss.), 242–243.
7. Bryant B. Brooks, *Memoirs of Bryant B. Brooks,* 197.
8. *Ibid.,* 196.
9. Literature on the western sheep industry and on sheepherders is scanty by comparison with that on cattle ranching and cowboys. Towne and Wentworth, *Shepherd's Empire*, and Wentworth, *America's Sheep Trails*, are standard volumes. Paul H. Carlson, *Texas Woollybacks*, offers a penetrating study of sheep in one frontier state. Virginia Paul, *This was Sheep Ranching*, has compiled an excellent pictorial history. Other books on the subject include Mary Austin, *The Flock;* Hughie Call, *Golden Fleece;* Archer B. Gilfillan, *Sheep, Life on the South Dakota Range;* George Wilkins Kendall, *Letters from a Texas Sheep Ranch, 1860–1867;* Winifred Kupper, *The Golden Hoof;* V. W. Lehmann, *Forgotten Legions, Sheep in the Rio Grande Plain of Texas;* Alexander Campbell McGregor, *Counting Sheep, From Open Range to Agribusiness on the Columbia Plateau.*
10. Barnes and Raines, *Cattle,* 306.
11. Rollins, "The Struggle of the Cattleman, Sheepman and Settler for Control of Lands in Wyoming, 1867–1910," 207–213.
12. William MacLeod Raine and Will C. Barnes, *Cattle,* 305.
13. Rollins, "The Struggle of the Cattleman, Sheepman and Settler . . . ," 213–216.

14. Harold K. Steen, *The U.S. Forest Service*, 104–105.
15. *Ibid.*, 164–165.
16. *Ibid.*, 66, 164–165.
17. Michael Frome, *The Forest Service*, 14.

CHAPTER 2: TROUBLE IN TEXAS

1. Paul H. Carlson, *Texas Woollybacks*, 169–178.
2. J. Evetts Haley, *Charles Goodnight*, 278–279.
3. *Ibid.*, 280. During the next few years, other New Mexican sheepherders apparently were coerced to abandon Panhandle grazing lands, understandably causing "hard feelings." See Williams, *Texas' Last Frontier*, 245.
4. Pauline D. Robertson and R. L. Robertson, *Panhandle Pilgrimage*, 128–142.
5. Dulcie Sullivan, *LS Brand*, 23–38.
6. *Ibid.*, 38–41.
7. E. L. Yeats and Hooper Shelton, *History of Nolan County*, 49; R. D. Holt, "Sheep Raising in Texas in 1881–1882," *West Texas Sheep and Goat Raiser*, 19.
8. San Saba *News*, quoted in Austin *Democratic Statesman* (February 6, 1880); Jay Monaghan (ed.), *The Book of the American West*, 290.
9. Holt, "Sheep Raising in Texas in 1881–1882," 40.
10. R. D. Holt, "Woes of the Texas Pioneer Sheepman," *Southwestern Sheep and Goat Raiser*, 63.
11. R. D. Holt (ed.), *Schleicher County*, 14–15; H. P. N. Gammel (comp.), *Laws of Texas*, 9: 111–112, 195–196, 348–350, 1363–1365.
12. Holt, "Woes of the Texas Pioneer Sheepman," 60.
13. *Ibid.*, 40, 60.
14. *Ibid.*, 73; Monaghan (ed.), *The Book of the American West*, 290.
15. Holt, "Woes of the Texas Pioneer Sheepman," 62; T. R. Havens, "Sheepmen-Cattlemen Antagonism on the Texas Frontier," *West Texas Historical Association Year Book* (1942), 19.
16. R. D. Holt, "The Introduction of Barbed Wire Into Texas," *West Texas Historical Association Year Book* (June 1930), 65, 76, 77.
17. Holt, "Woes of the Texas Pioneer Sheepman," 62; also see Wayne Gard, "The Fence-Cutters," *Southwestern Historical Quarterly* (July 1947), and Holt, "The Introduction of Barbed Wire Into Texas," 65–79.
18. Holt, "Woes of the Texas Pioneer Sheepman," 62; and Beatrice Grady Gay, *Into the Setting Sun: A History of Coleman County*, 58–60.
19. Gard, "The Fence-Cutters," 11; Gammel (comp.), *Laws of Texas*, 9: 566–567, 569.
20. Holt, "Woes of the Texas Pioneer Sheepman," 62, 63, 74.
21. Winifred Kupper, "Folk Characters of the Sheep Industry," *In the Shadow of History*, 95.
22. Carlson, *Texas Woollybacks*, 181.
23. The following incident was related to the author in an interview with Mark and Buddy Feild at the Feild ranch in Burnet County (February 10, 1978, and on other occasions).
24. Glenn Shirley, *Shotgun for Hire*, 56.
25. Carlson, *Texas Woollybacks*, 185–186.

Notes

26. Holt, "Woes of the Texas Pioneer Sheepman," 72.
27. Clayton W. Williams, *Texas' Last Frontier*, 338–339.
28. Holt, "Woes of the Texas Pioneer Sheepman," 72.
29. *Ibid.*
30. *Ibid.*
31. *Ibid.*, 63, 72.
32. *Ibid.*, 74.
33. Harrell, "Arthur G. Anderson, Pioneer Sheep Breeder of Texas," *Southwestern Sheep and Goat Raiser* 13; Barry Scobee, "Highland Country Once Strictly Cattle, Now Vastly Changed," *Sheep and Goat Raisers' Magazine*, 11.

CHAPTER 3: COLORADO CONFLICTS

1. Las Animas *Leader*, quoted in Virginia Paul, *This was Sheep Ranching*, 47–48.
2. *Ibid.*, 48.
3. Jay Monaghan (ed.), *The Book of the American West*, 290.
4. Charles W. Towne and Edward N. Wentworth, *Shepherd's Empire*, 194–195.
5. Denver *Republican* (January 2, 1897).
6. Edward N. Wentworth, *America's Sheep Trails*, 532; Monaghan (ed.), *The Book of the American West*, 290.
7. John Rolfe Burroughs, *Where the Old West Stayed Young*, 67–68; George W. Rollins, "The Struggle of the Cattleman, Sheepman and Settler for Control of Lands in Wyoming, 1867–1910" (diss.), 279–280.
8. Cheyenne *Daily Leader* (May 23, 1895).
9. *Ibid.*, (June 8, 1895).
10. Burroughs, *Where the Old West Stayed Young*, 140.
11. Craig *Courier* (September 14, 1895).
12. *Ibid.*, (March 7, 1896).
13. Burroughs, *Where the Old West Stayed Young*, 141; and Craig *Courier* (May 30, 1896).
14. Burroughs, *Where the Old West Stayed Young*, 136.
15. *Ibid.*, 136–137; and William MacLeod Raine, "The War for the Range," *Frank Leslie's Popular Monthly*, 436.
16. Paul, *This was Sheep Ranching*, 38.
17. Burroughs, *Where the Old West Stayed Young*, 142–143.
18. *Ibid.*, 143–144.
19. Wentworth, *America's Sheep Trails*, 536.
20. Cheyenne *Daily Leader* (May 22, 1909).

CHAPTER 4: ARIZONA'S PLEASANT VALLEY WAR

1. Bert Haskett, "History of the Sheep Industry in Arizona," *Arizona Historical Review*, 3–50; and George H. Tinker, *A Land of Sunshine, Flagstaff and Its Surroundings*. The Daggs brothers drove 4,500 sheep across the Mohave Desert into Arizona in 1875, locating where Flagstaff would be built. By the mid-1880s they were shipping an annual wool clip in excess of a quarter of a million pounds, and they ranged sheep across much of northern Arizona into New Mexico and Colorado.
2. Frank C. Lockwood, *Pioneer Days in Arizona*, 257; Stanford incident recounted in John Henry Cady, *Arizona's Yesterday*, 99–101.

3. William MacLeod Raine, "The War for the Range," *Frank Leslie's Popular Monthly*, 435–436.

4. R. D. Holt, "Woes of the Texas Pioneer Sheepman," *Southwestern Sheep and Goat Raiser*, 74; and Edward N. Wentworth, *America's Sheep Trails*, 525.

5. Will C. Barnes, *Apaches and Longhorns*, 128.

6. Ibid., 129.

7. Ibid., 128–129.

8. Ibid., 128.

9. The most complete account of the Pleasant Valley War is Earle R. Forrest, *Arizona's Dark and Bloody Ground*. Will C. Barnes was a cattle rancher headquartering in Holbrook during the range war; he knew most of the principals and was an eyewitness to the incredible battle when Sheriff Commodore Perry Owens shot four men. See Barnes's "The Pleasant Valley War of 1887," *Arizona Historical Review* (October 1931 and January 1932), and his descriptions of events in *Apaches and Longhorns*. Another contemporary observer was Joe T. McKinney, who wrote his "Reminiscences" in the *Arizona Historical Review* (April, July, October, 1932). I have two accounts by Col. James H. McClintock, who knew many of the principals: "Pleasant Valley War," a seven-page typescript of an article printed in *Arizona Cattleman* (March 11, 1918); and "The Bloody Pleasant Valley War," a similar version included in McClintock's *Arizona*, 2: 484–487. O. D. Flake, writing from memory, produced a lengthy and informative reminiscence in the *Arizona Republican* (April 10, 1940). Clara T. Woody and Milton W. Schwartz fashioned an excellent account of the "War in Pleasant Valley" in their book *Globe, Arizona*. A long manuscript by Drusilla Hazelton on "The Tonto Basin's Early Settlers" is indispensable to studying the Pleasant Valley War. Also see Joseph Fish's manuscript "Autobiography of Joseph Fish, 1840–1926, Revised and Enlarged by Himself From His Journal." Contemporary newspaper accounts found on microfilm in the Arizona State Archives include the *Arizona Gazette* (August and September, 1887, and August 1892) and the Tombstone *Epitaph* (August, September, and October 1887). I based my account of the Pleasant Valley War on these sources and other sources as cited.

10. Earle Forrest discovered that William and George Graham were charged with larceny, but he speculated that "George" Graham was actually Tom. See Forrest, *Arizona's Dark and Bloody Ground*, 42–44.

11. Dane Coolidge visited Pleasant Valley in 1916. Although the people "were still carrying guns and walking softly," he heard a first-person account from Jim Gilliland. See Coolidge's chapter on the Pleasant Valley War in *Arizona Cowboys*, 141–152.

12. Various accounts label the herder a Navajo or a Mexican, but Clara T. Woody, in *Globe, Arizona* (246, fn.), relates that the man was a Basque and brother-in-law of Apache County Deputy Sheriff Jim Houck. Tom Graham claimed that he more than once fired a rifle bullet into the sheepherder's frying pan or coffee pot as a warning. McClintock, "Pleasant Valley War," typescript, 3.

13. Cocōcino *Sun* (September 10, 1887). Eva Blevins, wife of John, stated that Andy "took the name of 'Cooper' when an outlaw in Texas" and kept it in Arizona. Robert Allison, "The Blevins Family," typescript, 1.

14. Barnes, *Apaches and Longhorns*, 144–146. Also see Philip J. Rasch, "Two Diamonds Bid: Two Diamonds Down," *Quarterly for the National Association for Outlaw and Lawman History*, 8–9.

15. Earle Forrest stated that Cooper had sworn to kill or drive out of the valley all of

the sheep and sheepmen in Pleasant Valley. See Forrest, *Arizona's Dark and Bloody Ground*, 54.

16. Several years later Blevins's rifle and a human skull were found on Cherry Creek, but there was no positive identification, nor could the cause of death be determined. See Barnes, "The Pleasant Valley War of 1887," 33–34; Flake, "Cattle Theft Called Start of State Feuds," *Arizona Republican* (April 10, 1940).

17. Barnes, "The Pleasant Valley War of 1887," 24–25.

18. Joseph Fish, well-acquainted with Paine, was happy to see him dead. "He was a wicked and desperate man," wrote Fish in his journal, "and we felt a relief when we heard of his death. . . . Some of my neighbors had intended to kill him the first chance and I had made a trip to Holbrook . . . to get a gun for that purpose. . . ." Fish, "Autobiography," 249.

19. Barnes, "The Pleasant Valley War of 1887," 36–38.

20. *Cococino Sun* (September 17, 1887).

21. Earle Forrest related this "well-authenticated version" in *Arizona's Dark and Bloody Ground*, 77–78.

22. William MacLeod Raine interviewed Jim Houck, who stated that he carried a warrant for John Graham. Setting an ambush for John, Houck stepped out from behind a tree as a rider came by on the trail to the Graham ranch. But the rider turned out to be Bill Graham, who pulled his gun. "Everybody was carrying a gun them days," commented Houck. Houck fired three or four rounds because "he was shooting at me as fast as he could pull the trigger." Raine, "The War for the Range," *Frank Leslie's Popular Monthly* (September 1903), 440.

23. *Cococino Sun* (September 10, 1887).

24. *Arizona Silver Belt* (October 1, 1887); Barnes, "The Pleasant Valley War of 1887," 30–31; *Cococino Sun* (September 10, 1887).

25. Barnes, *Apaches and Longhorns*, 147.

26. Flake, "Cattle Theft Called Start of State Feuds," *Arizona Republican* (April 10, 1940).

27. Barnes, *Apaches and Longhorns*, 146–147.

28. *Ibid.*, 147–148.

29. *Ibid.*, 151.

30. Explained in jury verdict as quoted by Forrest, *Arizona's Dark and Bloody Ground*, 125–128.

31. *Saint Johns Herald* (September 9, 1887); *Cococino Sun* (September 10, 1887).

32. Barnes, *Apaches and Longhorns*, 151.

33. Will C. Barnes stated that the Tewksburys sprang an ambush (see "The Pleasant Valley War of 1887," 28–29, 38–39), but Earle Forrest thought that the Graham riders attacked the Tewksburys in camp and were repulsed (*Arizona's Dark and Bloody Ground*, 139–143).

34. *Prescott Journal Miner* (September 8 and 9, 1887).

35. *Arizona Silver Belt* (October 1, 1887); Flake, "Cattle Thefts," *Arizona Republican* (April 10, 1940).

36. *Arizona Silver Belt* (October 1, 1887).

37. Barnes, "The Pleasant Valley War of 1887," 39.

38. Forrest, *Arizona's Dark and Bloody Ground*, 203, 209.

39. *Ibid.*, 215; Phoenix *Gazette* (August 3, 1974). Joe McKinney related an incident in Holbrook when Scott "backed down" Houck, who "forever afterward had an awful

grudge against Jimmy Scott." McKinney flatly declared: "Jim Houck was the cause of his demise." See McKinney, "Reminiscences," *AHR,* 203.

40. McClintock, "Pleasant Valley War," typescript, 5.
41. Forrest, *Arizona's Dark and Bloody Ground,* 251–252.
42. Barnes, "The Pleasant Valley War of 1887," 25.
43. Forrest, *Arizona's Dark and Bloody Ground,* 271–282.
44. Fish, "Autobiography," 249.
45. Tombstone *Daily Prospector* (January 14, 18, 19, 22, and 29, 1889).
46. *Ibid.*
47. *Ibid.* (January 14 and 15, 1889).
48. *Ibid.* (January 29, 1889).
49. Sources for the Berry-Rafael murders were Drusilla Hazelton's manuscript, on file at the Arizona Heritage Center in Tucson, and Charles McAdams, "Sheep Camp Murders," *Frontier Times* (June–July 1970): 6–9, 54–56.
50. Sheriff Carl Hayden to Governor Kibbey (January 22, 1908). Arizona Ranger correspondence, Arizona State Archives, Phoenix.
51. Coolidge, *Arizona Cowboys.* Fully half of Coolidge's book relates aspects of the conflict between sheepmen and cattlemen in Arizona. Specific quotes used in this paragraph are on pages 54, 58, and 74.
52. Coolidge, *Arizona Cowboys,* 54 and 68.
53. *Arizona Republican* (February 14, 1909).
54. P. P. Daggs to Mrs. George F. Kitt (May 29, 1926), quoted in Forrest, *Arizona's Dark and Bloody Ground,* 348.

CHAPTER 5: MISCELLANEOUS HOSTILITIES ACROSS THE WEST

1. Alver War Carlson, "Sheep Industry," *New Mexico Historical Review,* 37–40.
2. James F. Hinkle, "A New Mexico Cowboy on the Pecos," *Frontier Times,* 355.
3. *Ibid.,* 354–355.
4. Howard R. Lamar, "Edmund G. Ross as Governor of New Mexico Territory: A Reappraisal," *New Mexico Historical Review,* 198–201.
5. Governor Ross to E. Carlisle (February 9, 1886), cited in Lamar, "Edmund G. Ross," 200.
6. Jay Monaghan (ed.), *The Book of the American West,* 290; and Lamar, "Edmund G. Ross," 200–201.
7. Michael P. Malone and Richard P. Roeder, *Montana,* 110–119.
8. Mark H. Brown and W. R. Felton, *Before Barbed Wire,* 91.
9. Broadside cited in Lee M. Ford, "Bob Ford, Sun River Cowman," *Montana,* 43.
10. Brown and Felton, *Before Barbed Wire,* 92.
11. Lewis Atherton, *The Cattle Kings,* 89–90, 106, 218, 268.
12. The raid on Selway's flock is thoroughly examined by Lyman Brewster, "December 1900: The Quiet Slaughter," *Montana,* 82–85. The author was the son of George W. Brewster.
13. Brown and Felton, *Before Barbed Wire,* 93.
14. David J. Wasden, *From Beaver to Oil,* 142.
15. Alexander McGregor, *Counting Sheep,* 65.
16. *Ibid.,* 65–66.
17. *Ibid.,* 66, 81.

18. Phil Brogan, *East of the Cascades*, 115–116.
19. McGregor, *Counting Sheep*, 81.
20. Virginia Paul, *This was Sheep Ranching*, 48.
21. Brogan, *East of the Cascades*, 119–120.
22. *Ibid.*, 117–118; William MacLeod Raine and Will C. Barnes, *Cattle*, 260–261.
23. Raine and Barnes, *Cattle*, 259.
24. Cited in Brogan, *East of the Cascades*, 119–120. For other communications from "Sheep Shooters Headquarters," see Raine and Barnes, *Cattle*, 259–260, and Thomas Vaughan (ed.), *High & Mighty*, 32–33.
25. Brogan, *East of the Cascades*, 120–121.
26. Rafe Gibbs, *Beckoning the Bold*, 167.
27. *Ibid.*, 167–168.
28. The story of Diamondfield Jack, the murders of the two sheepherders and the subsequent trial, along with assorted background events, has been expertly researched and described by David H. Grover in *Diamondfield Jack, A Study in Frontier Justice*. The comments of J. Selby Ratt, whose father testified as a character witness on behalf of Diamondfield Jack's partner, are of interest; see John Myers Myers, *The Westerners*, 25–26.

CHAPTER 6:   WAR IN WYOMING

1. George W. Rollins, "The Struggle of the Cattleman, Sheepman and Settler for Control of Lands in Wyoming, 1867–1910" (diss.), 122–124. I found this dissertation to be extremely thorough and enlightening, not only about the conflict between cattlemen and sheepmen, but also about the background of ranching in Wyoming. T. A. Larson, in *A History of Wyoming*, also provided useful information and statistics about these subjects.
2. These statistics — and many others — may be found in the Rollins dissertation, 85–86, 139, 242.
3. The most comprehensive study of the Johnson County War was accomplished by Helena Huntington Smith, *The War on the Powder River*. Also see A. S. Mercer, *The Banditti of the Plains*. Mercer, the editor and publisher of a stock journal, despised the high-handed methods of the cattle ranchers in importing hired gunmen. When his book was published in 1894, several ranchers filed a libel suit and all copies were impounded. A number of copies were smuggled out of custody, however, and distributed from Denver. For years, members of the Wyoming Stock Growers Association and their descendants and friends destroyed any copies they could find. In 1954 the University of Oklahoma Press reprinted the book.
4. Rollins, "The Struggle of the Cattleman, Sheepman and Settler . . .," 275–276.
5. Walter, "Economic History and Settlement of Converse County, Wyoming," *Annals of Wyoming*, 295–296; Bryant B. Brooks, *Memoirs of Bryant B. Brooks*, 160.
6. Evanston *News-Register* (March 14 and June 24, 1894).
7. Edward N. Wentworth, *America's Sheep Trails*, 538.
8. Evanston *News-Register* (January 27, 1894).
9. George W. Rollins wrote authoritatively about the Henry's Fork range war in his dissertation, 255–268. Rollins was a native of the area and had access to contemporary newspaper files as well as to excellent interview sources.
10. Evanston *News-Register* (May 19, 1894).
11. Rollins, "The Struggle of the Cattleman, Sheepman and Settler . . .," 269–272.

12. David J. Wasden, *From Beaver To Oil*, 140.
13. Cheyenne *Daily Leader* (April 21 and May 14, 1895).
14. Wentworth, *America's Sheep Trails*, 539.
15. Larson, *History of Wyoming*, 132.
16. George B. McClellan to Governor W. A. Richards (October 14, 1897); and Larson, *History of Wyoming*, 132-133.
17. George W. Rollins interviewed David Hicks about the raid on Sam Butterfield's camp. Rollins was told by William Bluemel that Garside was killed about 1902, while James E. Eyre said that the killing was in 1906. No official documentation has been found. See the Rollins dissertation, 273-274.
18. Larson, *History of Wyoming*, 132.
19. George W. Rollins analyzed this case in his dissertation, 287-290.
20. Rollins also described *Cosgriff vs. Miller* in his dissertation, 290-291.

CHAPTER 7:   TOM HORN IN WYOMING

1. Lauren Paine, in *Tom Horn, Man of the West*, provides good background information on the enigmatic frontiersman. Dean Krakel, *The Saga of Tom Horn*, is a detailed chronicle of Horn's last years in Wyoming, but Horn's testimony from his trial is presented verbatim, and considerable insight about his background may be gleaned from his comments. Interesting accounts of Horn were presented by contemporary western writers William MacLeod Raine (who covered Horn's trial), in *Famous Sheriffs and Western Outlaws*, 80-91, and Dane Coolidge, *Fighting Men of the West*, 87-110. Eugene Cunningham provided a worthwhile chapter on Horn in his classic *Triggernometry*, and Dan Thrapp effectively covered Horn's Indian-fighting days in his superb biography, *Al Sieber*. Excellent biographical files on Horn are maintained at the Wyoming State Historical Society in Cheyenne, the Arizona State Archives in Phoenix, and the Arizona Historical Society in Tucson. In addition, Dean Krakel delivered an illuminating address about Horn in Cheyenne at the 1984 Rendezvous of the National Association for Outlaw and Lawman History, and he wrote "Was Tom Horn Two Men?" in *True West* (January-February, 1970), 12-17, 52-56.
2. Horn referred to his experience with the "Langhoff outfit" three times during his trial testimony, which is on 595-701 of the transcript of *The State of Wyoming vs. Tom Horn*, on file at the Wyoming State Historical Association in Cheyenne. Dean Krakel reproduced Horn's testimony in *The Saga of Tom Horn*, 103-118, 135-197. I have read the trial transcript in Cheyenne, taken notes from it, and photocopied portions of it. But because *The Saga of Tom Horn*, although out of print, is more readily available than the trial transcript, I have noted specific trial quotations from Krakel's book.
3. Henry Melton, "Recollections of Tom Horn," typescript, 3.
4. *Wyoming vs. Horn*, cited in Krakel, *The Saga of Tom Horn*, 109.
5. *Ibid.*, 110. Horn's complaint about his duties as a Pinkerton agent reveals why he liked his stock detective activities. "My work for [Pinkerton] was not the kind that exactly suited my disposition; too tame for me. There were a good many instructions and a good deal of talk given the operative regarding the things to do and the things that had been done." Tom Horn, *Life of Tom Horn*, 222.
6. Melton, "Recollections of Tom Horn," typescript, 2.
7. Krakel, "Was Tom Horn Two Men?" *True West*, 15-16.
8. Horn to Joe LeFors (January 1, 1902), cited in Joe LeFors, *Wyoming Peace Officer*, 190-191.

Notes

9. Dennis Trimble Nickell, "Who Were Tom Horn's Victims?" *Yesterday in Wyoming*, 23-38.
10. Melton, "Recollections of Tom Horn," typescript, 4.
11. Letter quoted in LeFors, *Wyoming Peace Officer*, 136.
12. J. C. Best, "More on Tom Horn," *Real West Yearbook*, 40.
13. *Wyoming vs. Tom Horn*, 291; and Tom Horn file at Wyoming State Historical Society, Cheyenne.
14. LeFors, *Wyoming Peace Officer*, 132-134.
15. LeFors wrote his autobiography, *Wyoming Peace Officer*, while Mabel Brown added considerable information in an article in the *Quarterly of the National Association for Outlaw and Lawman History* (Winter 1983-1984), 6-9.
16. LeFors, *Wyoming Peace Officer*, 132-133.
17. *Ibid.*, 133-134.
18. Laramie *Daily Boomerang* (September 1, 1901).
19. LeFors, *Wyoming Peace Officer*, 136.
20. W. D. Smith to Joe LeFors (December 28, 1901), cited in LeFors, 190.
21. Tom Horn to Joe LeFors (January 1, 1902), cited in LeFors, 190-191. Horn stated that he could guarantee Smith "the recommendation of every cow man in the State of Wyoming in this line of work." Horn asked LeFors to assure Smith "that I can handle his work and do it with less expense in the shape of lawyer and witness fees than any man in the business." Horn closed with a final suggestive remark: "Joe you yourself know what my reputation is although we have never been out together."
22. Tom Horn to Joe LeFors (January 7, 1902), cited in LeFors, 191-192.
23. LeFors, *Wyoming Peace Officer*, 138-139.
24. *Ibid.*, 141.
25. The transcript of the Horn-LeFors conversation may be found in LeFors, 140-145.
26. LeFors, *Wyoming Peace Officer*, 146.
27. Horn's testimony cited in Krakel, *The Saga of Tom Horn*, 162.
28. *Ibid.*, 169.
29. *Ibid.*, 173, 175, 179, 184, 196, 197.
30. *Ibid.*, 174-175, 178-179, 184.
31. Cheyenne *Daily Leader* (October 25, 1902); and LeFors, *Wyoming Peace Officer*, 145.
32. Tucson *Daily Citizen* (November 1, 1902, and January 24 and 26, 1903).
33. Horn, *Life of Tom Horn*, 225.
34. Will Henry, telephone conversation with the author (October 26, 1984).
35. Tom Horn to John C. Coble (November 20, 1903), cited in Horn, *Life of Tom Horn*, 240-241. In another letter to Coble on October 3, 1903 (cited in *Life of Tom Horn*, 234-235), Horn wrote of other ranchers who had made specific offers "to do something to the sheep."

CHAPTER 8:   MORE WYOMING HOSTILITIES

1. Maurice Frink, *Cow Country Cavalcade*, 122.
2. William MacLeod Raine, "The War for the Range," *Frank Leslie's Popular Monthly* (September 1903), 436.
3. Dorothy Milek, *Hot Springs: A Wyoming County History*, 63.
4. *Ibid.*, 62-63; and David J. Wasden, *From Beaver to Oil*, 141.

174   CATTLEMEN vs. SHEEPHERDERS

   5. Dean Krakel, *The Saga of Tom Horn*, 213–217; Milek, *Hot Springs*, 74.
   6. Tucson *Daily Citizen* (March 25, 1903).
   7. T. A. Larson, *A History of Wyoming*, 133.
   8. Frink, *Cow Country Cavalcade*, 119–120; Tucson *Daily Citizen* (May 6, 1904); Edward N. Wentworth, *America's Sheep Trails*, 539.
   9. Laramie *Daily Boomerang* (May 15, 1904).
   10. *Ibid.* (January 6, 1887).
   11. *Ibid.* (May 15, 1904).
   12. *Ibid.*
   13. *Ibid.* (April 27, 1904).
   14. *Ibid.* (April 29, 1904).
   15. *Ibid.* (April 28, 1904).
   16. Tucson *Daily Citizen* (May 6, 1904).
   17. Laramie *Daily Boomerang* (June 4, 1904).
   18. Wasden, *From Beaver to Oil*, 141.
   19. *Ibid.*, 141–142.
   20. Tucson *Daily Citizen* (October 7, 1905).
   21. John Rolfe Burroughs, *Where the Old West Stayed Young*, 75–76.
   22. Larson, *History of Wyoming*, 370–371.
   23. Milek, *Hot Springs*, 63.
   24. Tucson *Daily Citizen* (March 9, 1907).
   25. Larson, *History of Wyoming*, 371.
   26. Charles W. Towne and Edward N. Wentworth, *Shepherd's Empire*, 191–192.
   27. Cheyenne *Daily Leader* (June 9, 1909).
   28. This incident and subsequent events may be studied in case nos. 261–273, Criminal Docket #1, District Court Office, Crook County Courthouse, Sundance, Wyoming. Also see Cheyenne *Daily Leader* (May 26 and June 9, 1909), and Tucson *Citizen* (May 25, 1909).
   29. Cheyenne *Daily Leader* (June 9, 1909). A Guthrie foreman, Charles A. Blake, was reimbursed for a trunkful of clothes destroyed by fire. Blake recalled that during the August 31 raids "a bullet creased one fellow's Adam's apple and another grazed the right corner of my mouth and slanted across my chin." John Myers Myers, *The Westerners*, 37–39.

CHAPTER 9:   TURNING POINT AT TEN SLEEP

   1. Marvin B. Rhodes, "The Rest That Came, A History of the Ten Sleep Raid." Typescript available in the Miscellaneous Files on Ten Sleep Raids, Wyoming State Archives, Cheyenne, 10–11.
   2. *Ibid.*, 11; Jack Gage, *Tensleep and No Rest*, 7.
   3. Rhodes, "The Rest That Came," 11; and Cheyenne *Daily Leader* (November 16, 1909).
   4. A rich source of information about the Ten Sleep raid is Jack Gage, *Tensleep and No Rest*. Gage, who served as governor of Wyoming from 1961 to 1963, interviewed Bounce Helmer, Percy Metz, and other principals. Governor Gage manufactured a great deal of dialogue, presumably to make his story more readable, and the book must be evaluated with care; however, many anecdotes and nuggets of information have been uncovered by Gage which are not available anywhere else. Another useful source which featured

Notes

first-person interviews and excellent photographs, but which also must be considered with care, is Charles Kurt, "Massacre at Big Horn Basin," *Official Detective Stories* (December 1941), 26-29, 46-47.

5. Gage, *Tensleep and No Rest,* 98-99.
6. Rhodes, "The Rest That Came," 11.
7. Gage, *Tensleep and No Rest,* 154. Mrs. Allemand stated that she last saw her husband alive on March 25, but "heard from him over the telephone several times." Cheyenne *Daily Leader* (November 11, 1909).
8. Cheyenne *Daily Leader* (November 6, 1909); Rhodes, "The Rest That Came," 12.
9. Interview with Margaret Sutherland Cogdill, Ten Sleep, Wyoming (May 26, 1987); Cheyenne *Daily Leader* (November 7, 1909).
10. Cheyenne *Daily Leader* (November 7, 1909).
11. Arlene G. Robinson, "Reminiscences," available in the Miscellaneous Files on Ten Sleep Raids, Wyoming State Archives, Cheyenne; Rhodes, "The Rest That Came," 40-41; Gage, *Tensleep and No Rest,* 17-18.
12. Gage, *Tensleep and No Rest,* 149-153.
13. Rhodes, "The Rest That Came," 42.
14. *Ibid.,* 38.
15. Cheyenne *Daily Leader* (April 14, 1909).
16. Gage, *Tensleep and No Rest,* 156; Rhodes, "The Rest That Came," 41; Cheyenne *Daily Leader* (November 7, 1909).
17. Cheyenne *Daily Leader* (April 13, 1909).
18. *Ibid.* (April 9, 1909).
19. Gage, *Tensleep and No Rest,* 178; Cheyenne *Daily Leader* (November 6, 1909); Kurt, "Massacre at Big Horn Basin," 26.
20. Cheyenne *Daily Leader* (November 6, 1909); Kurt, "Massacre at Big Horn Basin," 26-28; Gage, *Tensleep and No Rest,* 211.
21. Kurt, "Massacre at Big Horn Basin," 28.
22. *Ibid.*
23. Cheyenne *Daily Leader* (April 8 and 11, 1909); Gage, *Tensleep and No Rest,* 180.
24. Cheyenne *Daily Leader* (April 9 and 21, 1909).
25. Kurt, "Massacre at Big Horn Basin," 29, 46.
26. *Ibid.*
27. *Ibid.,* 46.
28. Cheyenne *Daily Leader* (April 8, 20, and 21, 1909).
29. Rhodes, "The Rest That Came," 26.
30. *Ibid.,* 32.
31. *Ibid.,* 33; Cheyenne *Daily Leader* (May 11 and 22, 1909).
32. Rhodes, "The Rest That Came," 33-34.
33. *Ibid.,* 34.
34. Cheyenne *Daily Leader* (May 8 and 11, 1909); and Kurt, "Massacre at Big Horn Basin," 47.
35. Rhodes, "The Rest That Came," 35; Riverton *Republican* (May 22, 1909); Cheyenne *Daily Leader* (May 11, 1909).
36. Rhodes, "The Rest That Came," 36-37; Cheyenne *Daily Leader* (October 20, November 4, 6, and 10, 1909).

37. Rhodes, "The Rest That Came," 38; Cheyenne *Daily Leader* (October 24, 26, 27, and 28, November 5 and 6, 1909).
38. Cheyenne *Daily Leader* (November 9, 1909).
39. *Ibid.*
40. *Ibid.* (November 10 and 11, 1909).
41. *Ibid.* (November 12, 1909).
42. *Ibid.*
43. *Ibid.*
44. *Ibid.* (November 13, 1909).
45. *Ibid.*
46. *Ibid.* (November 14, 1909).
47. *Ibid.* (November 16, 1909).
48. *Ibid.* (November 14, 16, and 17, 1909); Rhodes, "The Rest That Came," 46; Gage, *Tensleep and No Rest,* 220.
49. Cheyenne *Daily Leader* (November 23, 1909); Rhodes, "The Rest That Came," 46.
50. Cheyenne *Daily Leader* (December 8, 1909); Rhodes, "The Rest That Came," 47; Gage, *Tensleep and No Rest,* 219.
51. Rhodes, "The Rest That Came," 46–48; Gage, *Tensleep and No Rest,* 219.
52. Cheyenne *Daily Leader* (November 10, 1909); Gage, *Tensleep and No Rest,* 220–222.
53. Cheyenne *Daily Leader* (November 12 and 13, 1909).

CHAPTER 10: FINAL TROUBLES

1. George W. Rollins, "The Struggle of the Cattleman, Sheepman and Settler for Control of Lands in Wyoming, 1867–1910" (diss.), 283; Edward N. Wentworth, *America's Sheep Trails,* 543.
2. Tombstone *Prospector* (February 9, 1916).
3. John Rolfe Burroughs, *Where the Old West Stayed Young,* 342–343.
4. *Ibid.*, 342; Ora Brooks Peake, *The Colorado Range Cattle Industry,* 90 fn.; William MacLeod Raine and Will C. Barnes, *Cattle,* 263–264.
5. Burroughs, *Where the Old West Stayed Young,* 345–346.
6. *Ibid.*, 346.
7. *Ibid.*, 347.
8. Peake, *The Colorado Range Cattle Industry,* 90.
9. Burroughs, *Where the Old West Stayed Young,* 347–350. For the poisoned corn incident, see Wentworth, *America's Sheep Trails,* 524.
10. Tombstone *Prospector* (December 9, 1912).
11. *Ibid.* (April 6, 1917).
12. *Ibid.* (February 16 and 18, 1918).
13. *Ibid.* (January 31, 1919).
14. *Ibid.* (March 6, 1919).
15. *Ibid.* (May 1, 1919).
16. *Ibid.* (June 21, 1919).
17. *Ibid.* (January 18, 1920).
18. *Ibid.* (March 31 and April 9, 1920).
19. *Ibid.* (June 21, 1920).

Notes

20. *Ibid.* (August 14, 1920).
21. *Ibid.* (February 21, 1921).
22. *Ibid.* (June 23 and October 27, 1921).
23. *Ibid.* (November 11, 1921).
24. Will Henry to the author (August 9, 1983).
25. Zane Grey, *To the Last Man*, foreword.
26. *Ibid.*, 7.
27. As a lifelong fan of western movies, I have accumulated a large research library on the subject. For three years I wrote a monthly feature for *True West*, "Reel Cowboys," dealing with western motion pictures. I have seen almost all of the movies mentioned in this chapter, many of them several times, as well as the television episodes, and I have extensive notes on scenes and dialogues depicting the cattleman-sheepherder conflict.
28. Will Henry to the author (August 9, 1983).

Bibliography

Documents

Case nos. 261–273, Criminal Docket #1. District Court Office, Crook County Courthouse, Sundance, Wyoming.
Congressional Record — Senate (December 15, 1970), 41589–41590.
Field Book No. 1, County of Big Horn, Property of County Surveyor Office. On file at the American Heritage Center, University of Wyoming, Sundance.
The State of Wyoming vs. Tom Horn. On file at the Wyoming State Historical Association, Cheyenne.

Manuscripts

Allison, Robert. "The Blevins Family: An Episode in the Pleasant Valley War," rewritten by Mrs. M. M. Lathrop, August 1936. Typescript on file at Arizona Heritage Center, Tucson.
Castle, Tom. "Hanging Tom Horn, Nov. 20, 1903." Typescript on file at Wyoming State Historical Society, Cheyenne.
Fish, Joseph. "Autobiography of Joseph Fish, 1840–1926, Revised and Enlarged by Himself From His Journal." Unpublished manuscript on file at Arizona Heritage Center, Tucson.
Hazelton, Drusilla. "The Tonto Basin's Early Settlers." Manuscript on file at Arizona Heritage Center, Tucson.
Horn, Tom. File of Wyoming State Archives, Cheyenne.
McClintock, James H. "Pleasant Valley War." Typescript in Arizona State Archives, Phoenix.
Melton, Henry. "Recollections of Tom Horn." Typescript on file at Wyoming State Historical Society, Cheyenne.
Owens, Commodore Perry. File, Arizona State Archives, Phoenix.
Pleasant Valley War. File, Arizona State Archives, Phoenix.
Rhodes, Marvin B. "The Rest That Came, A History of the Ten Sleep Raid." Typescript available in Miscellaneous Files on Ten Sleep Raids, Wyoming State Archives, Cheyenne.
Rollins, George W. "The Struggle of the Cattleman, Sheepman and Settler for Control of Lands in Wyoming, 1867–1910." Doctoral dissertation, University of Utah, Salt Lake City, 1951.
Ten Sleep Raid, File. Wyoming State Archives, Cheyenne.

Interviews

Bronh, Bob. Interviewed by the author in Ten Sleep, Wyoming (May 26, 1987).
Cogdill, Margaret Sutherland. Interviewed by the author in Ten Sleep, Wyoming (May 26, 1987).
Cogdill, Ronald. Interviewed by the author in Ten Sleep, Wyoming (May 26, 1987).
Farthing, Merrill. Interview on file at Wyoming State Archives, Cheyenne, n.d.
Henry, Will. Interviewed by the author by telephone (October 26, 1984).
Starr, Helen. Interviewed by the author in Ten Sleep, Wyoming (May 26, 1987).

Newspapers

Arizona Gazette (1887, 1892)
Arizona Republican (1909, 1940, 1967)
Arizona Silver Belt (1887, 1923)
Austin *Democratic Statesman* (1880)
Cheyenne *Daily Leader* (1890, 1895, 1902, 1909, 1917)
Cococino *Sun* (1887)
Craig *Courier* (1895, 1896)
Denver *Republican* (1897)
Evanston *News-Register* (1894)
Laramie *Daily Boomerang* (1887, 1901, 1904)
Phoenix *Gazette* (1974)
Prescott *Journal Miner* (1887)
Riverton *Republican* (1909)
Saint Johns *Herald* (1887)
Tombstone *Epitaph* (1887)
Tombstone *Prospector* (1889, 1912, 1915–1923)
Tucson *Daily Citizen* (1901–1909)

Books

Abbott, E. C. ("Teddy Blue"), and Helena Huntington Smith. *We Point Them North*. Norman: University of Oklahoma Press, 1971.
Arizona Business Director, 1905–1906. Denver, CO: The Gazetteer Publishing Company, 1905.
Atherton, Lewis. *The Cattle Kings*. Bloomington & London: Indiana University Press, 1967.
Austin, Mary. *The Flock*. Boston: Houghton Mifflin and Company, 1906.
Bailey, William A. *Bill Bailey Came Home*. Logan: Utah State University Press, 1973.
Barnes, Will C. *Apaches and Longhorns*. Los Angeles: The Ward Ritchie Press, 1941.
Bradbury, Margaret. *The Shepherd's Guidebook*. Emmaus, PA: Rodale Press, 1977.
Brogan, Phil. *East of the Cascades*. Portland, OR: Binford-Metropolitan, 1976.
Brooks, Bryant B. *Memoirs of Bryant B. Brooks*. Glendale, CA: The Arthur H. Clark Company, 1939.
Brosnan, Cornelius J. *History of the State of Idaho*. New York: Charles Scribner's Sons, 1918.
Brown, Mark H., and W. R. Felton. *Before Barbed Wire*. New York: Henry Holt and Company, 1956.

Bibliography

Brown, Robert Harold. *Wyoming, A Geography.* Boulder, CO: Westview Press, 1980.
Burroughs, John Rolfe. *Guardians of the Grasslands, The First Hundred Years of the Wyoming Stock Growers Association.* Cheyenne: Pioneer Printing & Stationery Co., 1971.
———. *Where the Old West Stayed Young.* New York: Bonanza Books, 1962.
Cady, John Henry. *Arizona's Yesterday.* Los Angeles: Privately printed, 1916.
Call, Hughie. *Golden Fleece.* Boston: Houghton Mifflin Company, 1942.
Carlson, Paul H. *Texas Woollybacks, The Range Sheep and Goat Industry.* College Station: Texas A&M University Press, 1982.
Clay, John. *My Life on the Range.* New York: Antiquarian Press, Ltd., 1961.
Cleaveland, Alice Morley. *No Life for a Lady.* Boston: Houghton Mifflin Co., 1941.
Comeaux, Malcolm L. *Arizona, A Geography.* Boulder, CO: Westview Press, 1981.
Cook, Dave. *The Way It Was.* Denver: The A. B. Hirschfield Press, Inc., 1980.
Coolidge, Dane. *Arizona Cowboys.* Tucson: University of Arizona Press, 1984.
———. *Fighting Men of the West.* New York: E. P. Dutton & Co., 1932.
Crawford, Thomas Edgar. *The West of the Texas Kid, 1881–1910.* Norman: University of Oklahoma Press, 1962.
Cunningham, Eugene. *Triggernometry, A Gallery of Gunfighters.* Caldwell, ID: The Caxton Printers, Ltd., 1952.
Dale, Edward Everett. *The Range Cattle Industry.* Norman: University of Oklahoma Press, 1960.
Dary, David. *Cowboy Culture, A Sage of Five Centuries.* New York: Alfred A. Knopf, 1981.
Dobie, J. Frank. *Cow People.* Boston: Little, Brown and Company, 1964.
Dobie, J. Frank, Mody C. Boatright, and Harry H. Ransom, eds. *In the Shadow of History.* Hatboro, PA: Folklore Associates, Inc., 1966.
Dodds, Gordon B. *Oregon, A Bicentennial History.* New York: W. W. Norton & Company, Inc., 1977.
Duke, Cordia Sloan, and Joe B. Frantz. *6,000 Miles of Fence, Life on the XIT Ranch of Texas.* Austin: University of Texas Press, 1961.
Elman, Robert. *Badmen of the West.* Secaucus, NJ: The Ridge Press, Inc., 1974.
Faulk, Odie B. *Arizona, A Short History.* Norman: University of Oklahoma Press, 1970.
Federal Writers' Project of Works Progress Administration for the State of Montana. *Montana, A State Guide Book.* New York: The Viking Press, 1939.
Forbis, William H. *The Cowboys.* New York: Time-Life Books, 1973.
Forrest, Earle R. *Arizona's Dark and Bloody Ground.* Tucson: University of Arizona Press, 1984.
Frink, Maurice. *Cow Country Cavalcade.* Denver, CO: The Old West Publishing Co., 1954.
Frome, Michael. *The Forest Service.* New York: Praeger Publishers, Inc., 1971.
Gage, Jack. *The Johnson County War.* N.p.: Flintrock Publishing Co., 1967.
———. *Tensleep and No Rest.* Casper, WY: Prairie Publishing Company, n.d.
Gammel, H. P. N., comp. *The Laws of Texas, 1822–1897.* Vols. 8 and 9. Austin: The Gammel Book Company, 1898.
Gay, Beatrice Grady. *Into the Setting Sun: A History of Coleman County.* N.p., n.d.
Gibbs, Rafe. *Beckoning the Bold: Story of the Dawning of Idaho.* Moscow: The University Press of Idaho, 1976.
Gilfillan, Archer B. *Sheep: Life on the South Dakota Range.* Minneapolis: University of Minnesota Press, 1956.
Grey, Zane. *To the Last Man.* New York: Pocket Book edition, 1976.

Grover, David H. *Diamondfield Jack: A Study in Frontier Justice*. Norman: University of Oklahoma Press, 1986.
Haley, J. Evetts. *Charles Goodnight: Cowman and Plainsman*. Norman: University of Oklahoma Press, 1949.
―――. *The XIT Ranch of Texas and the Early Days of the Llano Estacado*. Norman: University of Oklahoma Press, 1953.
Hamrick, Alma Ward. *The Call of San Saba: A History of San Saba County*. N.p., 1969.
Hendrickson, Gordon Olaf, ed. *Peopling the High Plains: Wyoming's European Heritage*. Cheyenne: Wyoming State Archives and Historical Department, 1977.
History of Coleman County and its People, A. Vol. 1. San Angelo, TX: Anchor Publishing Company, 1985.
Holt, R. D., ed. *Schleicher County, or, Eighty Years of Development in Southwest Texas*. Eldora, TX: The Eldorado Success, 1930.
Horan, James D. *The Authentic Wild West: The Gunfighters*. New York: Crown Publishers, Inc., 1976.
Horn, Tom. *Life of Tom Horn, Government Scout and Interpreter, Written by Himself*. Norman: University of Oklahoma Press, 1983.
Hough, Emerson. *The Story of the Cowboy*. New York: D. Appleton & Co., 1933.
Julian, Ralph. *Our Great West*. New York: N.p., 1893.
Kendall, George Wilkins. *Letters from a Texas Sheep Ranch, 1860–1867*. Urbana, IL: University of Illinois Press, 1959.
Kennedy, Michael S., ed. *Cowboys and Cattlemen*. New York: Hastings House, Publishers, 1964.
Krakel, Dean. *The Saga of Tom Horn*. Laramie, WY: Powder River Publishers, 1954.
Kupper, Winifred. *The Golden Hoof: The Story of the Sheep of the Southwest*. New York: Alfred A. Knopf, 1945.
Larson, T. A. *A History of Wyoming*. Lincoln: University of Nebraska Press, 1978.
―――. *Wyoming: A Bicentennial History*. New York: W. W. Norton and Company, 1977.
LeFors, Joe. *Wyoming Peace Officer: An Autobiography*. Laramie: Laramie Printing Company, 1953.
Lehmann, V. W. *Forgotten Legions: Sheep in the Rio Grande Plain of Texas*. El Paso: Texas Western Press, 1969.
Lockwood, Frank C. *Pioneer Days in Arizona*. New York: The Macmillan Company, 1932.
Malone, Michael P. and Richard P. Roeder. *Montana: A History of Two Centuries*. Seattle: University of Washington Press, 1976.
McCarty, John L. *Maverick Town: The Story of Old Tascosa*. Norman: University of Oklahoma Press, 1946.
McClintock, James Harvey. *Arizona*. Vol. 2. Chicago: The S. J. Clarke Publishing Co., 1916.
McGregor, Alexander Campbell. *Counting Sheep, From Open Range to Agribusiness on the Columbia Plateau*. Seattle and London: University of Washington Press, n.d.
Mercer, A. S. *The Banditti of the Plains*. Norman: University of Oklahoma Press, 1954.
Milek, Dorothy. *Hot Springs: A Wyoming County History*. N.p., n.d.
Monaghan, Jay, ed. *The Book of the American West*. New York: Simon and Schuster, 1963.
Morris, Edmund. *The Rise of Theodore Roosevelt*. New York: Coward, McCann & Geoghegan, Inc., 1979.

Myers, John Myers, comp. *The Westerners, A Roundup of Pioneer Reminiscences*. Englewood Cliffs, NJ: Prentice-Hall, Inc., 1969.
Osgood, Ernest Staples. *The Day of the Cattleman*. Minneapolis: The University of Minnesota Press, 1929.
Paine, Lauren. *Tom Horn: Man of the West*. Barre, MA: Barre Publishing Company, 1963.
Paul, Virginia. *This was Cattle Ranching, Yesterday and Today*. New York: Bonanza Books, 1973.
———. *This was Sheep Ranching, Yesterday and Today*. Seattle, WA: Superior Publishing Company, 1976.
Peake, Ora Brooks. *The Colorado Range Cattle Industry*. Glendale, CA: The Arthur H. Clarke Company, 1937.
Peterson, Charles S. *Utah, A Bicentennial History*. New York: W. W. Norton & Company, Inc., 1977.
Potter, Colonel Jack. *Cattle Trails of the Old West*. Clayton, NM: Laura R. Krehbiel, 1935.
Preece, Harold. *Lone Star Man: Ira Aten, Last of the Old Texas Rangers*. New York: Hastings House Publishers, 1960.
Raine, William MacLeod. *Famous Sheriffs and Western Outlaws*. Garden City, NY: Doubleday, Doran & Company, Inc., 1929.
———, and Will C. Barnes. *Cattle*. Garden City, NY: Doubleday, Doran & Company, Inc., 1930.
Rathjen, Frederick W. *The Texas Panhandle Frontier*. Austin: University of Texas Press, 1973.
Redford, Robert. *The Outlaw Trail*. New York: Grossett & Dunlap, 1976.
Robertson, Pauline Durrett, and R. L. Robertson. *Panhandle Pilgrimage*. Canyon, TX: Staked Plains Press, Inc., 1976.
Savage, Pat. *One Last Frontier*. New York: Exposition Press, 1964.
Shirley, Glenn. *Shotgun for Hire*. Norman: University of Oklahoma Press, 1970.
Smith, Helena Huntington. *The War on the Powder River*. University of Nebraska Press: 1966.
Steen, Harold K. *The U.S. Forest Service: A History*. Seattle: University of Washington Press, 1976.
Sullivan, Dulcie. *The LS Brand*. Austin: University of Texas Press, 1968.
Tanner, Ogden. *The Ranchers*. Alexandria, VA: Time-Life Books, 1977.
Thrapp, Dan. *Al Sieber*. Norman: University of Oklahoma Press, 1964.
Tinker, George H. *A Land of Sunshine: Flagstaff and Its Surroundings*. Flagstaff, AZ: Arizona Champion Print, 1887.
Toole, K. Ross. *Twentieth-Century Montana, A State of Extremes*. Norman: University of Oklahoma Press, 1972.
Towne, Charles W., and Edward N. Wentworth. *Cattle and Men*. Norman: University of Oklahoma Press, 1955.
———, and ———. *Shepherd's Empire*. Norman: University of Oklahoma Press, 1946.
Trimble, Marshall. *Arizona: A Panoramic History of a Frontier State*. Garden City, NY: Doubleday & Company, Inc., 1977.
Vaughan, Thomas, ed. *High and Mighty: Select Sketches about the Deschutes Country*. The Oregon Historical Society, 1981.
Vestal, Stanley. *Short Grass Country*. New York: Duell, Sloan & Pearce, 1941.
Walgamoth, C. S. *Reminiscences of Early Days*. 2 vols. Twin Falls, ID: Privately published, 1927.

Wasden, David J. *From Beaver to Oil.* Cheyenne, WY: Pioneer Printing & Stationery Co., n.d.
Wentworth, Edward N. *America's Sheep Trails.* Ames: Iowa State College Press, 1948.
Whitlock, V. H. (Ol' Waddy). *Cowboy Life on the Llano Estacado.* Norman: University of Oklahoma Press, 1970.
Williams, Clayton W. *Texas' Last Frontier: Fort Stockton and the Trans-Pecos, 1861–1895.* College Station: Texas A&M University Press, 1982.
Woody, Clara T., and Milton W. Schwartz. *Globe, Arizona: Early Times in a Little World of Copper and Cattle.* Tucson: Arizona Historical Society, 1977.
Writers' Program of the Works Progress Administration. *Wyoming: A Guide to Its History, Highways, and People.* New York: Oxford University Press, 1941.
Yeats, E. L., and Hooper Shelton. *History of Nolan County, Texas.* Sweetwater, TX: Shelton Press, 1975.

Articles

Arnot, John. "My Recollections of Tascosa Before and After the Coming of the Law." *The Panhandle-Plains Historical Review* (1933): 58–79.
Baker, Ray Stannard. "The Tragedy of the Range." *The Century Magazine* (August 1902).
Barnes, Will C. "The Pleasant Valley War of 1887." *Arizona Historical Review* (October 1931 and January 1932):5–34 and 23–45.
Beeler, Sylvia. "County Profile, Romance of Early Day Carbon County Sheep Industry." *The Snake River Press* (December 1, 1977):3.
Best, J. C. "More on Tom Horn." *Real West Yearbook* (Fall 1984):40–43.
Brewster, Lyman. "December 1900: The Quiet Slaughter." *Montana, The Magazine of Western History* (January 1974):82–85.
Briggs, Harold E. "The Early Development of Sheep Ranching in the Northwest." *Agricultural History* (July 1937):161–180.
Brown, Mabel. "Lawman Joe LeFors Sends Tom Horn to Gallows." *Quarterly of the National Association for Outlaw and Lawman History* (Winter 1983–1984):6–9.
Carlson, Alver War. "New Mexico's Sheep Industry, 1850–1900: Its Role in the History of the Territory." *New Mexico Historical Review* (January 1909):25–49.
Connor, L. G. "A Brief History of the Sheep Industry in the United States." American Historical Association, *Annual Report for 1918.*
Crawshaw, S. J. "The Irish Highway." *Empire Magazine* (November 24, 1974):12–13, 15.
Douglass, William A. "The Vanishing Basque Sheepherder." *The American West* (July/August 1980):30–31, ff.
Fenley, Florence. "Sheep Camps and Old-Time Mexican Herders." *Sheep and Goat Raiser* (August 1945):8, 10–11.
Ford, Lee M. "Bob Ford, Sun River Cowman." *Montana, The Magazine of Western History* (Winter 1959):30–43.
Gard, Wayne. "The Fence-Cutters." *Southwestern Historical Quarterly* (July 1947):1–15.
Gregory, Leslie E. "Arizona's Haunted Walls of Silence." *Arizona Highways* (October 1947):4–7, 26–29.
Harrell. "Arthur G. Anderson, Pioneer Sheep Breeder of Texas." *Southwestern Sheep and Goat Raiser.* (N.d.)
Haskett, Bert. "History of the Sheep Industry in Arizona." *Arizona Historical Review* (July 1936):3–50.

Bibliography

Havens, T. R. "The Passing of the Frontier in Brown County." *West Texas Historical Association Year Book* (June 1932):43–50.

———. "Sheepmen-Cattlemen Antagonism on the Texas Frontier." *West Texas Historical Association Year Book* (1942):10–23.

Hinkle, James F. "A New Mexico Cowboy on the Pecos." *Frontier Times* (May 1938):352–361.

Holliday, J. S. "The Lonely Sheepherder." *The American West* (Spring 1964):36–45.

Holt, R. D. "The Introduction of Barbed Wire Into Texas and the Fence Cutting War." *West Texas Historical Association Year Book* (June 1930):65–79.

———. "The Saga of Barbed Wire in Tom Green County." *West Texas Historical Association Year Book* (1928):32–49.

———. "Sheep Raising in Texas in 1881–1882." *West Texas Sheep and Goat Raiser* (December 1956):18–20, 40–41.

———. "Woes of the Texas Pioneer Sheepman." *Southwestern Sheep and Goat Raiser* (December 1940):60–63.

Jeffers, Jo. "Commodore Perry Owens." *Arizona Highways* (October 1960):2–7.

Jones, J. M. "History of the Range Sheep Industry in Texas." *Southwestern Sheep and Goat Raiser* (March 1, 1936):8–9, 32, 34.

Kittredge, William, and Stephen M. Krauzer. "Marshal Joe LeFors vs. Killer Tom Horn." *American West* (November/December 1985):36–45.

Krakel, Dean. "Was Tom Horn Two Men?" *True West* (January/February 1970).

Kupper, Winifred. "Folk Characters of the Sheep Industry." *In the Shadow of History*. Texas Folklore Society (No. 15):85–118.

Kurt, Charles. "Massacre at Big Horn Basin." *Official Detective Stories* (December 1941):26–29, 46–47.

Lamar, Howard R. "Edmund G. Ross as Governor of New Mexico Territory: A Reappraisal." *New Mexico Historical Review* (July 1961):177–209.

Love, Clara. "History of the Cattle Industry in the Southwest." *Southwestern Historical Quarterly* (July 1916):1–18.

Lux, Mabel. "Honyockers of Harlem, Scissorbills of Zurich." *Montana, The Magazine of Western History* (Autumn 1963):2–14.

Malone, Michael P., and Richard B. Roeder. "1876 in Field and Pasture: Agriculture." *Montana, The Magazine of Western History* (Spring 1975):28–35.

McAdams, Charles. "Sheep Camp Murders." *Frontier Times* (June–July 1970):6–9, 54–56.

McKinney, Joe T. "Reminiscences." *Arizona Historical Review* (April 1932):33–54; (July 1932):141–145; (October 1932):198–204.

Michelson, Charles. "War for the Range." *Munsey's Magazine* (December 1902):380–382.

Moyer, Curt. "The Frank A. Hubbell Company, Sheep and Cattle." *New Mexico Historical Review* (January 1979):64–72.

Nickell, Dennis Trimble. "Who Were Tom Horn's Victims?" *Yesterday in Wyoming* (n.d.):23–38.

Parish, William J., ed. "Sheep Husbandry in New Mexico, 1902–1903." *New Mexico Historical Review* (July 1962):201–213; (October 1962):260–309; (January 1963):56–77.

Raine, William MacLeod. "The War for the Range." *Frank Leslie's Popular Monthly* (September 1903):432–442.

Rasch, Philip J. "Two Diamonds Bid: Two Diamonds Down." *Quarterly of the National Association for Outlaw and Lawman History* (Autumn 1984):8–9.

Reeve, Frank D., ed. "The Sheep Industry in Arizona, 1903." *New Mexico Historical Review* (July and October, 1963):244–252 and 323–342.

―――, ed. "The Sheep Industry in Arizona, 1905–1906." *New Mexico Historical Review* (January 1964):40–69.

―――, ed. "The Sheep Industry in Arizona, 1906." *New Mexico Historical Review* (April 1964):111–156.

Romero, Jose Ynocencio. "Spanish Sheepmen on the Canadian at Old Tascosa." Edited by Ernest R. Archambeau. *Panhandle-Plains Historical Review* (1946):45–72.

Saban, Vera D. "Joe LeFors, Lawman on the Run." *Frontier Times* (October 1984):42–46.

Saban, Vera, and Earl L. Saban. "Bay State Marked an Era." *Annals of Wyoming* (Fall 1982):67–71.

Schlup, Leonard. "A Taft Republican: Sen. Francis E. Warren and National Politics." *Annals of Wyoming* (Fall 1982):62–66.

Schultz, Jessie Donaldson. "Adventuresome, Amazing Apikuni." *Montana, The Magazine of Western History* (October 1960):2–18.

Scobee, Barry. "Highland Country Once Strictly Cattle, Now Vastly Changed." *Sheep and Goat Raisers' Magazine* (November 1941):11, 13.

Snow, E. P. "Sheepmen and Cattlemen." *Outlook* (April 4, 1903):839–840.

Thomson, Rebecca W. "The Federal District Court in Wyoming, 1890–1982." *Annals of Wyoming* (Spring 1982):10–25.

"Tramp Sheepman of the Pecos, The." *Frontier Times* (July 1927):1–3.

Walter. "Economic History and Settlement of Converse County, Wyoming." *Annals of Wyoming*.

Whipple, Charles T. "Commodore P. Owens Was a Tough Sheriff in Apache, Arizona." *Quarterly of the National Association for Outlaw and Lawman History* (Autumn 1983):1, 8–11.

Wyeth, N. C. "A Sheep-herder of the South-west." *Scribner's Magazine* (January 1909):17–21.

Photo Section

Sacks of wool being hauled to market in Texas.
—Courtesy Texas State Archives, Austin

Mexican and Anglo sheepherders with their dogs. Sheepherders of Mexican extraction frequently were targeted because of frontier racial prejudices.
—Courtesy Texas State Archives, Austin

Lambs were vulnerable to coyotes, raiders, and other predators.
—Courtesy Texas State Archives, Austin

Sheep dogs often were killed when raiders attacked flocks they were tending.
—Courtesy Texas State Archives, Austin

Texas cattleman Charles Goodnight sometimes forced sheepherders to vacate range he intended to use.

—Courtesy Panhandle Plains Historical Museum, Canyon, Texas

Grave of Wiley Berry, brutally murdered in an Arisona sheep camp in 1903.
—Photo by the author

Grave of seventeen-year-old Juan Vigil, murdered alongside Wiley Berry.
—Author's collection

In the second decade of the twentieth century, Arizona cattlemen still reacted violently on occasion to sheep and sheepherders.
—Author's collection

Commodore Perry Owens, the flamboyant and deadly sheriff of Apache County.
—Courtesy Arizona Historical Society, Tucson

The Blevins house in Holbrook where Commodore Perry Owens gunned down four men. The building still stands.
—Courtesy Arizona Historical Society, Tucson

William Mulvenon, sheriff of Yavapai County, who led the fight at Perkins' store on September 21, 1887.
—Courtesy Arizona Historical Society, Tucson

Loopholes are still visible at the old Perkins' store, where John Graham and Charley Blevins were killed.
—Photo by the author

John Graham was slain at Perkins' store within sight of the Graham ranch house.
—Courtesy Arizona Historical Society, Tucson

Tom Graham, leader of the Graham faction. Murdered from ambush in 1892, he was the last man killed in the Pleasant Valley War.
—Courtesy Arizona Historical Society, Tucson

The road where Tom Graham was shot from ambush.
—Courtesy Arizona Historical Society, Tucson

Tom Graham's grave at the old cemetery in Phoenix.
—Courtesy Arizona Historical Society, Tucson

The Young Cemetery in Pleasant Valley, which originated as a boot hill graveyard on the Graham ranch. Combatants buried here include William and John Graham, Charles Blevins, Henry Middleton, and Al Ross.
—Photo by the author

The grave of William Graham, who was killed on August 17, 1887, and who was the first man buried in what became Young Cemetery.
—Photo by the author

Ed Tewksbury, leader of the Tewksbury faction.
—Courtesy Arizona Historical Society, Tucson

John Tewksbury, killed within sight of the family cabin on September 2, 1887.
—Courtesy Arizona Historical Society, Tucson

Paul Bloomer standing in front of the cabin built by the Tewksburys on the east side of Cherry Creek in Pleasant Valley.
—Courtesy Arizona Historical Society, Tucson

The Tewksbury cabin and outbuilding. A drove of half-wild hogs rooted at the bodies of John Tewksbury and Bill Jacobs, gunned down during the attack of September 2, 1887.
—Courtesy Arizona Historical Society, Tucson

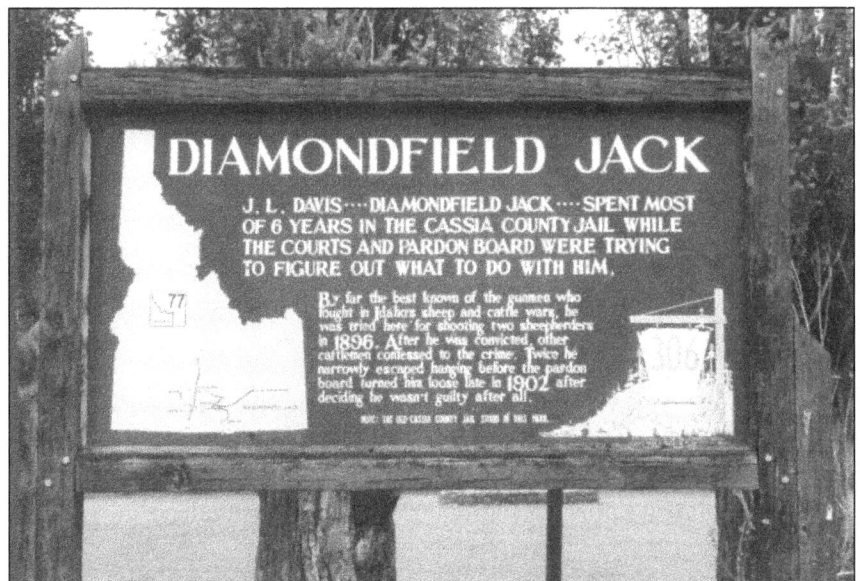

This sign designates the site of the Cassia County Jail, located across the street from the courthouse. The gallows for Diamondfield Jack was built beside the jail.
—Photo by the author

Originally built as a hotel, this two-story building in Albion served as a courthouse during the Diamondfield Jack trial. Today it is a grocery store.
—Photo by the author

In 1897 Idaho authorities extradited Diamondfield Jack Davis from Yuma Territorial Prison.
—Courtesy Arizona Historical Society, Tucson

Left: *Sheep near the Wyoming-Utah line in Brown's Park.*
—Photo by the author

Right: *In 1896 an army of cattlemen rode to rid Brown's Park of sheep.*
—Photo by the author

Left: *Sheep and cattle today share the lush grasslands of the Green River country.*
—Photo by the author

Right: *Forty miles north of Lusk, raiders burned a sheep camp and destroyed 500 animals. Today sheep and cattle graze contentedly side by side in the same area.*
—Photo by the author

Sheepmen have always displayed wry humor in the face of adversity.
—Photo by the author

A Two Bar sheep wagon, after Ora Haley began to stock his range with sheep.
—Courtesy Wyoming State Archives, Cheyenne

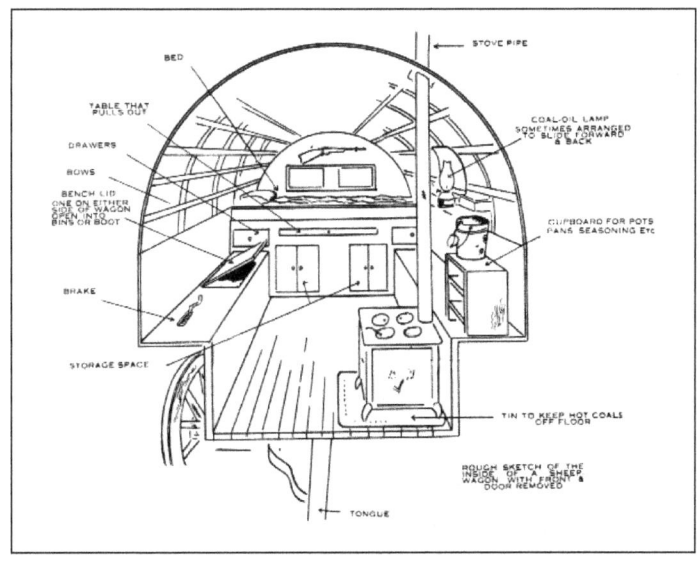

The wagon home of a sheepherder.
—Courtesy American Heritage Center,
University of Wyoming, Laramie

The Morrison cabin, built in 1884 at the foot of Copper Mountain, Wyoming. Luther Morrison came west on the Oregon Trail in 1853. His wife Lucy and their three daughters lived in a tent for more than two years until this cabin was finished.
—Photo by the author

The courthouse at Sundance was the scene of a major legal effort against sheep ranch raiders.
—Courtesy Wyoming State Archives, Cheyenne

3,000 sheep crosssing the Platte River in 1903—a sight that still could enrage Wyoming cattlemen.

—Courtesy Wyoming State Archives, Museums and Historical Department, Cheyenne

The Cheyenne Club, organized in 1880 as a social center for cattlemen. A glass-enclosed observatory is visible at the middle of the roof.

The dining room of the Cheyenne Club could be reserved by members for two dollars per evening.
—Both photos courtesy Wyoming State Archives, Museums and Historical Department, Cheyenne

The Enge-Allemaud units camped on opposite sides of Spring Creek near the public road on the evening of April 2, 1909.

—Photo by the author

The charred remains of wagons burned at the Maxwell–Stevens sheep camp near Tie Siding.
—Courtesy American Heritage Center, University of Wyoming

Sheep clubbed to death near Tie Siding in 1904.
—Courtesy American Heritage Center, University of Wyoming

Maxwell-Stevens employees skinning sheep killed in the Tie Siding raid.
—Courtesy American Heritage Center, University of Wyoming

Governor Bryant B. Brooks, Wyoming rancher and political leader.
—Courtesy Wyoming State Archives, Cheyenne

Ranch headquarters of Bryant B. Brooks, one of many Wyoming cattlemen who turned to sheep.
—Courtesy Wyoming State Archives, Cheyenne

On the morning after the murders, the town of Ten Sleep was electrified by news of the heinous crime.

—Courtesy Wyoming State Archives, Cheyenne

Burial site of the Ten Sleep murder victims.

—Photo by the author

Herb Brink long had nursed a passionate hatred of sheep and sheepmen.
—Author's collection

Milt Alexander killed the wounded Joe Allemand with a blow from a shovel.
—Author's collection

When his mask fluttered in the wind, Ed Eaton was recognized by Bounce Helmer.
—Author's collection

Imprisoned for his part in the Ten Sleep murders, George Saban was made a trusty—then fled Wyoming for Latin America.
—Author's collection

Tommy Dixon served three years in prison for his part in the Ten Sleep raid.
—Author's collection

Tom Horn in the cell block doorway. While in jail he lost so much weight that his hangman miscalculated the necessary length of the rope.
—Courtesy Wyoming State Archives, Cheyenne

During his long incarceration Horn braided horsehair lariats and bridles as gifts for his friends.
—Courtesy Wyoming State Archives, Cheyenne

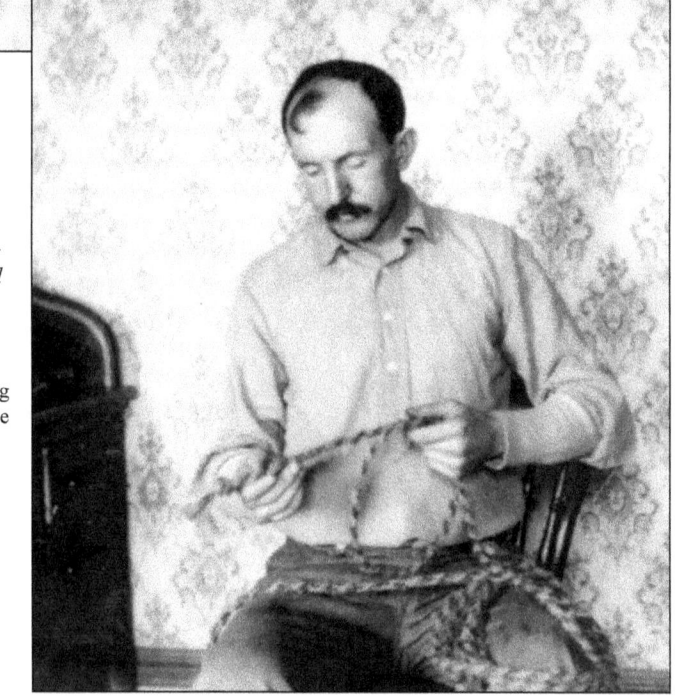

Schoolmarm Glendoline Kimmel, another admirer of Tom Horn.
—Courtesy American Heritage Center, University of Wyoming, Laramie

John C. Coble, at left, the employer and friend of Tom Horn.
—Courtesy Wyoming State Archives, Cheyenne

Murder site of Willie Nickell. The assassin hid behind the rocks (1) as Willie approached the gate (2). Mortally wounded, Willie collapsed a short distance away.
—Courtesy American Heritage Center, University of Wyoming

Trial testimony indicated that Tom Horn boasted about killing Willie Nickell while drinking in this Denver saloon.
—Courtesy American Heritage Center, University of Wyoming

Freddie Nickell and an older sister. Young Freddie found his brother's body the day after the killing.
—Courtesy American Heritage Center, University of Wyoming

As a young deputy sheriff, Les Snow overheard Tom Horn's "confession" to Joe Lefors, and testified at length during the famous trial.
—Courtesy Wyoming State Archives, Cheyenne

Joe LeFors won fame by extracting a controversial confession from Tom Horn. Later the noted detective was hired by sheep interests to obtain convictions in the 1908 raids near Sundance and in the 1909 Ten Sleep murders.
—Courtesy Wyoming State Archives, Cheyenne

The courthouse and jail where Tom Horn was incarcerated, tried, and hanged. The courtroom was on the second floor, the jail at the rear.
—Courtesy Wyoming State Archives, Museums and Historical Department

Tom Horn's jury.
—Courtesy Wyoming State Archives, Cheyenne

Cheyenne was a bustling western metropolis when it hosted the trial and execution of the notorious Tom Horn.
—Courtesy Wyoming State Archives, Cheyenne

In Montana *Australian sheepman Errol Flynn brings his flock into cattle country.*
—Author's collection

Glenn Ford starred as The Sheepman, *taking on the entire community in order to introduce his sheep.*
—Author's collection

Index

A
Adams, C. F., 23
  John D., 92
  Ramon, 5–6
Adams County (Washington), 73
Aldrich, O. A., 114
Alexander, Milt, 131, 135, 137, 140, 142, 145, 146, 147
Allemand, Jacques, 139
  Joseph, 131, 132–138, 144, 146
  Mrs., 144, 148
Allen, Henry W., 159
Alston, Felix, 138–139, 140–141, 143, 147
Anderson, Arthur G., 31
Angus, Red, 91
Apocada, Miguel, 55
Appaloosa, The, 160
Apperson, John, 106
Arden Ranch, 25
Arizona Cattle Growers' Association, 155, 157, 158, 159
Arizona Cowboys, 63
Arizona, incidents in, 1, 2, 15–16, 43–65, 149, 155–159
Arizona Pioneers' Historical Society, 65
Arizona Sheep Breeders and Wool Growers Association, 43
Arizona Strip, 159
Arizona Wool Growers' Association, 157, 158
Atchee, Colorado, 42
Autry, Gene, 161
Averill, Jim, 90–91

B
Badlands, Wyoming, 130, 133
Baltaesleque, Gabriel, 156–157
Bank of Arizona, 59

Banta, A. F., 53
Barber, Amos, 92
Barnes, Will C., 13, 44–45, 47, 48, 49, 50, 52, 53, 54, 56
Barry, Phil, 76
Basehart, Richard, 161
Baugh, Stanley, 128
Bear Creek (Montana), 71–72
Beckstead, ———, 93
Benevides, Carlos, 25
  Santos, 25
Bent County (Colorado), 34
Berger, Charley, 119
Berry, Frank, 151–152
  Thomas, 151–152
  Wiley, 61–63
  William W., 61, 63
Berry ranch, 127, 128
Bertrand, Peter, 20
"Big Die-Up," 7
Big Dry Lake, Arizona, 48
Big Horn Basin (Wyoming), 96
Big Horn County (Wyoming), 130
Big Horn County Wool Growers' Association, 139
Big Jake, 160
Big Red Park, 40
Big Spring, Texas, 29
Birchfield, Walter, 60
Birney, Montana, 71
Bishop, John, 69
  W. H., 46
Blaine, George, 46
Blake, ———, 93
  J. W., 126, 127
Blevins, Andy (*see* Cooper, Andy)
  Charley, 55, 57
  Eva, 51

187

Hamp, 48–49, 56, 57
John, 51, 52, 53, 54, 57, 59
Mart, 47–48, 57
Mary, 51, 54
Sam Houston, 51, 53, 54, 57
Boal, William, 71
Boar's Nest, 80, 83
Bonanza, 161
Booth, Jeremiah, 34
John, 62–63
Zack, 62–63
Borah, William E., 82
Bower, James E., 84–85, 86
Box Elder Ranch, 151
Boyer, Herbert, 156
Brady, Texas, 23
Bragg cattle outfit, 119
Brando, Marlon, 160
Brandt, Ed, 140
Brewster, George W., 71–72
Brimhall, ———, 153, 154
Brink, Herbert, 118, 130, 131, 135, 136–137, 140, 141, 142, 144, 145, 146, 147, 148
Brookins, R. W., 155
Brooks, Bryant B., 8, 10
Brown, Carl, 35
Sam, 52
Brown County (Texas), 23–25
Brown Ranch, 80, 83
Brown's Park Cattle Association, 38
Brown's Park, Colorado, 38–39, 103
Bryan, William Jennings, 83
Buck, Edward A., 123
buffalo, slaughter of, 69
Bureau of Public Lands, 154
Burke, Milo, 146
T. E., 110, 113
Burnet County (Texas), 27
Burning Hills, The, 160
Butterfield, Sam, 97

C

CA Bar cattle ranch, 67
Caddel, J. H. "Shorty," 71
Cady, John, 44
Cafferal, Pierre "Pete," 131, 133, 135, 136, 137, 139, 143, 148
California Park, Colorado, 37–38
Callahan, John, 148
Callan, Jim, 11

Campbell, John, 151
Canadian River Valley, 19–20
Candlish, James, 8
Carey, Joseph M., 92
Carlisle, ———, 67–68
Carpenter, Ferry, 153–155
Carrington, Bob, 49, 57
Carroll, Frank, 123
Carter, C. Dana, 138, 142
Cartwright, C. M., 39
Caruthers, John, 30, 31
Cassia County (Idaho), 78
Cassia County Wool Growers, 82
Cassidy, Butch, 103, 114
casualty, totals, 1–2, 15–16, 163
Cato, O. C., 72
cattle: drives of, 6, 70; in forest reserves, 12–15, 152–155; grazing habits of, 9; rustling of, 90, 103, 108, 109, 111; statistics on numbers of, 89
cattle raisers: association of, 73–74, 76, 90, 96, 157, 158–159; fraternal order of, 127
cattle ranching: economic factors of, 6–7, 88
Central Oregon Wool Growers' Association, 75
Champion, Nate, 91
Channeled Scablands (Washington), 73
Chaurros, 10
Cheyenne Club, 101, 115
Cheyenne, Wyoming, 111, 118
Chilson, John, 62
Chiricahua Cattle Company, 60–61
Chivington, L. H. "Doc," 150–151
Civil War, 6
Clark, Edward T., 110
Cleveland, Grover, 10, 12
Joseph Earl, 125
Coble, John, 101, 104, 106, 108, 115
Cococino County (Arizona), 157
Cococino National Forest, 156
Cody, Buffalo Bill, 71
Cole, Farney, 140, 141
Coleman County (Texas), 21, 25, 31
Collier, John T., 34
Colorado City, Texas, 23
Colorado, incidents in, 2, 15–16, 33–42, 149, 150–155

Colorado National Guard, 153
Coltharp, ———, 153, 154
Columbia Plateau (Washington), 73
Colvin, ———, 21
Congress, Arizona, 82
Conn, Creed, 77
Converse Cattle Company, 117
Converse County (Wyoming), 92
Cook, Alfred, 123
Coolidge, Dane, 46, 63–64, 160
Cooper, Andy, 47–48, 49, 50, 51, 52–54, 57
Coronado, 43
Cortinas, Juan Nepomuceno, 17
Cosgriff brothers, 40, 99
Cosgriff vs. Miller, 99
cowboys, described, 2–4
Cow People, 11
Cox, Phil, 73
Crabb, M. E., 158–159
Crook County (Wyoming), 74, 75, 125, 127
Crook County Sheepshooters Association, 76
Crosby, George, 72
Croxton, Fred W., 157
Cummings, Daniel, 80–85
 Ed, 58
Cusack, Ed, 138, 140, 143, 147

D
Daggs, P. P., 65
Daggs brothers, 43, 47, 50, 65
Dagmans, Bob, 158
Darnell, John, 152
Dart, "Nigger Isom," 103
Davis, Jackson Lee (Diamondfield Jack), 79–87
Dayley, E. R., 79
Dead Boy Point, 63
Delaney, Frank, 151–152
DeLong, ———, 43
Diamondfield Triangle Gold Mining Company, 87
Diamond Tooth Lil, 87
Dickey, Hugh, 126
Dingley Tariff of 1897, 10, 90
Dix, Richard, 160
Dixon, Thomas, 145, 146
 Tommy, 131, 135–136, 140, 142, 147–148

Dobie, J. Frank, 11
Door Key Ranch, 26
Doty, Christopher Columbus, 21–22
Duncan, Jim, 118
Dunn, Oliver, 80
Durbin brothers, 89
Dyer, Leigh, 18

E
Eastwood, Clint, 161
Eaton, Ed, 131, 135, 137, 139, 140, 141, 142, 145, 147, 148
Eberle, Louis, 150
Edwards, George, 35
 Griff, 35, 38–39
 Jack, 35, 36–38, 39
Emge, Joe, 96, 131–136, 138, 144
Engbrson, Cyrus, 123
Enterline, E. E., 141
Ervay, Jacob, 93
Escallier, Joseph, 73
Evans, Dale, 161

F
Fall, Albert B., 155
Farris, Charles, 131, 135, 140, 142, 143, 144, 146–147
Fawcett, E. K., 24
Feild, Albert, 28
 Andy, 27–28
 Marcus A., 27
fence-cutting wars, 1, 24–26, 32
Fenton, Jack, 119
Ferris, George, 8
Fiscus, Walt, 134
Fish, Joseph, 43
Fisher, Clay, 159
Fisher County (Texas), 31
Flagstaff, Arizona, 43, 158
Flake, W. J., 52
Flynn, Errol, 162
Ford, Glenn, 162–163
forest reserves, 12–15, 42, 77, 126, 152–155
Forrest, Earle, 56, 58
Forrester, Willard, 59
Forshey, John, 93–94, 95
Fort Apache, Arizona, 44
Fort Bridger, Wyoming, 94
Fort D.A. Russell, Wyoming, 91, 114
Fort Davis, Texas, 31
Fort Stockton, Texas, 29–30

Four Mile Creek (Colorado), 38
Foxley, J. H., 79
Franc, Otto, 95–96
Fremont County (Wyoming), 125
Frontier Days, 108

G

Gantz, Louis A., 124–125
Garfield County (Colorado), 35
Garland Mercantile, 125
Garrison, Bill, 140, 141–142
   John C., 142
Garside, Aaron, 97
Gates, Steve, 6
Geddes Sheep Company, 39
Geronimo, 100
Gibson, Thomas H., 123
   William, 144
Gilbertson Ranch, 71
Gillespie, Bob, 49, 57
Gilliland, John, 46–47, 57
Gisela, Arizona, 61, 63
Gladden, Amanda, 51
   Beatrice, 51
Gleason, Fred, 78–79, 80, 82, 83, 84
Globe, Arizona, 63
Goodman, Frank, 38–39
Goodnight, Charles, 2, 18
Goodrich, Billy, 140, 141–142, 143, 144, 146–147
   Jake, 133, 137
Graham, Anne, 58
   Bill, 46, 47, 48, 49, 50, 57
   John, 46, 47, 48, 49, 50, 55, 57
   Tom, 46, 47, 48, 49, 50, 56–57, 58
Gray, Jeff, 85, 86
grazing fees, 14
grazing lease program, 73
Green, Billy, 21
   Lorne, 161
Green River Valley (Wyoming), 96, 97
Greet, Frank, 135
   Fred, 135, 138
Greet brothers, 137, 138
Grey, Zane, 159–160
Grube, ———, 75
Gunnison National Forest, 151
"gunnysacker," 27
Gutherie Company, 127–128

H

Haley, Ora, 40, 104, 125
Hall, Barney, 71
Hamilton County (Texas), 21, 24
Hamrock, Pat, 153
Hanging Woman Creek (Montana), 70
Hanna, Charles, 23
Harrell, Andrew, 78–79
Hart, John K., 40
Hash Knife cattle ranch, 44, 47, 48
Havens, W. E., 29
Hawley, James, 82–87
Hayden, Carl, 64
Hayden Stockgrowers' Association, 153
Haydon, George, 150
Hayes, Gabby, 161
Heaven With a Gun, 162
Helmer, Bounce, 131, 133, 134–135, 136, 137, 139, 141, 143, 148
Henderson, Fred, 121
Hennessey, Patrick, 120
Henry, Joe, 141–142
   Will, 115, 159, 162
Henry's Fork Valley (Wyoming), 93–95
Herefords, 78
Hernandez, Alberto, 156
Herndon, John C., 55
Herr, Hubert, 114
Hewitt, ———, 73
Hinkle, James F., 67
Hitchcock, Ethan A., 13
Hoctor, Frank, 156
Holbrook, Arizona, 51
Holden, William, 160
Homestead Act, 90
Horn, Tom, 38, 118: in army, 103; arrest of, 109–110; autobiography of, 114–115; background, 100; described, 101–102, 103; escape of, 113–114, 119–120; execution of, 115, 162; jobs of, 100–101; trial of, 110–113, 162
Horseshoe Ranch, 117
Horton, Tom, 70
Houck, Jim, 50, 56
Houck's Tank, 56
Hough, Emerson, 3
Howard, George E., 93
How the West Was Won, 160
Huerfano County (Colorado), 33

Index 191

Hulett, Mrs., 128
Hunter, Davis, 80–81
　Tab, 160
Hurt, Joe, 8
Huson, W. O., 58

I

I, Tom Horn, 115
Idaho, incidents in, 2, 15–16, 77–87
Idaho State Penitentiary, 86
Idaho Supreme Court, 78, 84
Idaho Wool Growers Association, 82
Imlay, J. W., 155
Ireland, John, 25
Iron Mountain Cattle Company, 101
Iron Mountain Station, 106
"Isley's Stranger," 159
Izee Sheep Shooters, 74

J

Jackson Hole, Wyoming, 96
Jacobs, Bill, 50, 57
Jacques, Ricardo, 67
James, Frank, 147
Jensen, Henry, 119
Jensen, Utah, 152
Johnson, Albert, 149
　Snellen, 151–152
　Westley, 122, 123, 124
　William A., 158
Johnson County (Wyoming), 91, 116
Johnson County War of 1892, 135
Johnston, J. C., 18
　James, 147
Jones, ———, 92
　Allie, 75
　William, 92

K

Kanab Creek, 157–158
Kane County (Utah), 157–158
KC Ranch, 91
Keeley, Winfield D., 151
Kendall, George W., 17
Kendrick, Eula, 71
　John B., 70–72
Kennedy, T. Blake, 110
Kent County (Texas), 31
Keyes, Albert, 131, 135, 140, 142, 143, 144, 146–147
　Billy, 144
　Harry, 123, 124
　William, 122, 123

Kibbey, Joseph H., 64
Kilgore, M. H., 26–27
Kimberly, William, 93
Kimmel, Glendoline, 105
Kirby, Wyoming, 121
"Knights of the Knippers," 24
Knox, Roscoe, 76
Kochler, Herman, 29
K Ranch, 152
Kreutzer, William E., 151
Kuykendall, John, 108
KYT Ranch, 101

L

Lacey, J. W., 110, 113
Lacy, Booker, 71
Lake County (Oregon), 76
Lamb, Porter, 135, 137, 138, 140
L'Amour, Louis, 160
Lampasas *Dispatch*, 23
Landis, Charlie, 70
Langhoff outfit, 101
Langston, J. H., 24
Laramie County (Wyoming), 97, 107, 125
Laramie, Wyoming, 118
Las Animas County (Colorado), 34
Laufler, Jacob, 57
Lazier, Jules "Joe," 131, 133, 134, 135, 136, 138, 148
Lee, Dave, 63
　W. M. D., 19–20
Lee-Scott Cattle Company, 19
LeFors, Joe, 107–113, 115–116, 128, 140, 141, 143
legal action, 45, 67–68, 77–78, 89, 98–99, 128–129, 145, 149, 157–159
legislation, 22–23, 25–26, 67, 73, 77–78, 95, 98–99, 157–159
Lehmi Valley (Idaho), 77
Leonard, Dean, 151
LE Ranch, 19
Lewis, William, 101
Lincoln County (New Mexico), 68
Llano County (Texas), 20
Lonetree, Wyoming, 92
Long, Thomas, 125
longhorns, 69, 70
LS Ranch, 19–20

Lunis, Victor, 39–40
Lynn, Jess D., 124

M

McCall, George, 24
McClellan, George B., 88, 96, 146
McCloud, "Driftwood Jim," 114, 119–120
McCormick, Dave, 18
McCrea, Joel, 162
McDonald, Bill, 115
MacDougall, George, 158
McGregor, Archie, 73
  John, 73
McKay, ———, 123
McKean, Andrew, 128
  Isaiah, 128
  Samuel, 128
McKinney, Frank, 71
McKune, Guy, 75
MacLaine, Shirley, 162–163
McQueen, Steve, 162
Mahoney, G. W., 25
  William, 106
Majors, Billy, 78–79
Man Killers, The, 160
Mann, ———, 132
  William, 151
Maricopa County (Arizona), 64
Martin, George, 128
  Price, 97–99
Matador Land and Cattle Company, 18
Matson, R. N., 110
Maxwell, William, 117, 121–122
Mead, George, 147
  H. L., 145
Meadows, John, 51
Meigh, Robert, 126–127
Melton, Anne, 56
Meredith, John, 135, 137, 138
Mesa County (Colorado), 42
Metcalfe, C. B., 25
Metz, Percy, 138, 141, 143–144, 146
  William S., 141, 145
Middlestacks ranch, 80
Middleton, Harry, 54, 57
Miller, Gus, 105, 107
  I. C., 99
  James, 105, 107, 115
  Killin' Jim, 28–29
  Victor, 105, 107

Minick, Ben, 118–119, 130
  William, 118–119
Moffatt County (Colorado), 152, 153
Mogollon Rim, 45
Mogollon River, 45
Mondell, Frank W., 13
Montana, 161–162
Montana, Don Pedro, 60
Montana, incidents in, 2, 15–16, 68–72, 161–162
Montana Stockgrowers Association, 72
Moore, ———, 73
  Curtis, 89
  H. Waldo, 110
  Jeff, 26
  Lucy, 89
Mormon Church, 82
Mormons, 5
Morris, Logan, 157
Morrison, Lincoln A., 121, 130
  Lucy (*see* Moore, Lucy)
Morrow County Wool Growers Association, 74
Morton, Al, 138
Mosberger, Dan, 128
Muddy Trail, 41–42
Mulholland, Jefferson, 128
Mulvenon, William, 49, 55–56
Munson, Bill, 71

N

National Live Stock Association, 13, 72
National Wool Growers Association, 3, 14, 98, 139
Natrona County (Wyoming), 93
Navajo Indians, 43
Nelson, Earl, 59
Newman, J. D., 156
New Mexico, incidents in, 2, 15–16, 67–68, 149, 150
Newton, George A., 57
Nicholson, Samuel D., 155
Nickell, Fred, 106
  Kels, 101, 104–108, 114
  Mrs. Kels, 107–108
  Willie, 100, 105–106, 108, 109, 111, 115, 116, 162
Nolan County (Texas), 20
Northern Pacific Railroad, 73
Nostrum, Ezra, 118
Nowood River Valley, 130

Index

O
Oates, Warren, 161
Ochoa, ———, 43
Oh-Be-Joyful-Creek (Colorado), 151
Ohnhaus, Charles, 109, 111, 112, 115
O'Neal, Ryan, 160
O'Neill, Buckey, 59, 100
open-range ranching, 6–7
Oregon, incidents in, 2, 15–16, 73–77
Owens, Commodore Perry, 51–54, 55–56, 59
OW Ranch, 70, 71

P
Packard, W. H., 145
Padilla, Jose, 60
Paine, John, 48–49, 57
Palo Duro Canyon, 18
Panchito, 18
Park County (Wyoming), 95
Parker, ———, 75
Parmalee, C. H., 143, 145, 146
Payne, Dad, 143
Payson, Arizona, 50, 55, 62
Pearce, ———, 96
Pecos County (Texas), 29
Penrose, Charles B., 103
Perea, Jesus Ma, 153
Perkins, Harvey, 81
Perky, Kirtland I., 83, 84
Philbrick, ———, 70
Philly, Horace, 57
Phipps, Lawrence C., 155
Pickard, Dave, 96
Pickens, Slim, 163
Pinchot, Gifford, 13–14
Pinkerton Detective Agency, 101
Piper Sheep Company, 157
Platte Valley Sheep Company, 97–98
Pleasant Valley, Arizona, 45
Pleasant Valley War, 1, 2, 45–65, 159–160
Plinton, ———, 24
Pomeroy, Roney, 95
Porter, ———, 77
Potter, Albert, 13–14, 52
Powell, Fred, 101
Powers, O. W., 82
Prairie Cattle Company, 153
Price, James E., 152
Proctor, Richard, 119–120

Puckett, Will, 82–83, 85–86
Pueblo County (Colorado), 33
Pyeatt, Ben, 62

Q
Quarter Circle U Ranch, 71
Quayle, Charles, 157

R
Rafael, Juan, 61–63
   Vigil, 61, 63
raids, typical aspects of, 10–12
Raine, William MacLeod, 39, 118
Ramrod, 162
Ramsay brothers, 20
Randolph, John, 3
Rash, Matt, 38–39, 103
Rawhide, 161
Rawlins, Wyoming, 41, 147
Ray, Nick, 91
Red Bank Cattle Company, 88, 96
Reed, Frank, 54
Regulators, 91–92
Reilly, ———, 24
Reison, Edouard, 127, 128
   Fritz, 127
Reynolds, Albert, 19
   Dick, 69
   Glen, 100
   Robert M., 150
Rhodes, John, 58
Richards, DeForest, 97
   William, 46
   William A., 96, 103
Richmond, ———, 118
Rio Blanco County (Colorado), 154
Roberts, Jim, 48–49, 50, 54, 55, 56, 59
   Mose, 51, 53, 54, 57
   Pernell, 161
Robinson, A. D., 33–34
   George, 158
Rodney King Company, 127–128
Rogers, C. R., 62–63
   Ed, 48
   John C., 82
   Roy, 161
Rolland, Eugene "Curley," 150
Roll on Texas Moon, 161
Romero, B., 157
   Casimero, 18–19
   Joe M., 157

Roosevelt, Theodore, 126
Roper, John, 60
Rose, Al, 55, 56, 57
Ross, E. C., 67
Rough Gulch, Colorado, 152
Routt County (Colorado), 35, 37, 39–40
Routt National Forest, 152
Russell, Charlie, 3

S

Saban, George, 131, 135–136, 140, 142, 143, 144, 145, 146, 147
Sais, Arcadio, 68
Salmon Falls Creek, 80
San Carlos Indian Reservation, 55
Sanchez, Nestor, 60
Sandoval, Candy, 40
San Luis Valley, 34
San Saba County (Texas), 20–21
Saratoga, Wyoming, 92
Saturday Evening Post, 87
Saunders, ———, 125
Savery Creek Trail, 41–42
Saxon, John, 160
Sayles, John, 118
scab, 5, 23, 95
Schleicher County (Texas), 22
Scott, Jim, 56, 57
  Lucien, 19
  Randolph, 160
  Richard H., 113
Scurry County (Texas), 31
Seger, A. J., 39
Selway, Robert R., 70–72
Sevens Ranch, 36, 39
77 Ranch, 117
Shafer, Sheriff, 107
Shaw, ———, 96
sheep dogs, 9
sheepherders: associations of, 63, 74, 75–76, 95, 125–129, 157, 158–159; described, 4–5, 63–64
sheep: in forest reserves, 13–15; grazing habits of, 9, 65; husbandry, 10, 35, 126; quarantine of, 22, 95; slang terms for, 5; statistics on numbers of, 67, 69, 70, 89, 90; techniques for herding, 9–10
Sheepman, The, 162
Sheep Queen of Idaho (*see* Yearian, Emma)
"Sheep Shooters" associations, 12
sheep ranching: economic advantages of, 7–8, 10, 126, 162; railroad effect on, 43
sheep wagons, 8, 9
Shell Creek (Wyoming), 124
Shepherd of the Hills, The, 160
Sheridan, Wyoming, 70
Shields, Dan B., 157–158
Shoe, Matt, 128
Shoe Sole Ranch, 78
Shoshone Indian Reservation, 126
Shoup, Oliver, 153
Siddoway, R. K., 3
Sieber, Al, 100
Sigsby, Bob, 49
Simpson, William L., 141
Sizer, James Harl, 41–42
Slater Park, Colorado, 37–38
Sloane, Everett, 161
Smalley, Edward J., 109, 113, 114, 120
Smith, Alexis, 162
  Fred, 76
  Walter, 147
Snake River Stock Growers' Association, 37
Snow, Les, 109, 111, 113, 116, 120
Snyder, Walt, 71
Southern Pacific Railroad, 23
Sparks, Charley, 38, 39
  John, 78–79, 84, 86
Sparks-Harrell corporation, 79, 80, 82, 84, 86
Spaugh, A. A., 117–118
Springtime in the Rockies, 161
Spry, William, 154, 155
Squires, Orin, 128
Stanford, D. A., 43–44
Stanley, E. B., 159
Starkweather, Horace, 25
Steunenberg, C. B., 84
Stevens, Bart, 24
  Henry L., 122, 123
Stinson, Jim, 46
Stoll, Walter, 109, 110, 111, 112–113
Stonewall County (Texas), 31
Story, R. T., 81–82, 83
Stott, Jim, 56, 57
Sublette County (Wyoming), 149

Index

Summers, William, 94
Sunbeam, Colorado, 153
Sun River Valley, Montana, 69
Sutherland, George, 135
Swan Land and Cattle Company, 101, 102, 104, 118
Sweetwater County (Wyoming), 93, 95
Sweetwater, Wyoming, 90

T
Tainter FL Ranch, 70
Tankersley, R. F., 21
TA Ranch, 91
Taylor, Thomas, 94–95
Taylor County (Texas), 24
Temple, Shirley, 160
Ten Sleep murders, 2, 130–148
Ten Sleep, Wyoming, 130
Terrell County (Texas), 30
Tewksbury, Ed, 45, 46–47, 48, 49–50, 55, 56–59, 65
    James, 45, 46, 47, 48–50, 55, 56
    John, 45, 46, 47, 50, 57
    John D., 45–46
    Lydia Crigler Shutes, 46
    Mrs. John, 50
Tewksburys, 49–50, 54, 65
Texas, incidents in, 1–2, 15–16, 20–32
Texas Legionnaires, 161
Texas Rangers, 17–18
Texas Wool, 21, 22, 23
Thex, Charles, 71
Thomson, A. B., 74
Thoren, Emil, 118, 119
Three Circle Ranch, 72
Tie Siding raid, 121–124
Tippett brothers, 31
To the Last Man, 160
Tolman, Bill, 79–80
Tom Green County (Texas), 25, 27
Tom Horn, 162
Tongue River Valley, Montana, 70
Tonopah, Nevada, 87
Tonto Basin, 45, 59, 61
Trujillo, Pedro, 34
    Teofilo, 34
Tucker, Tom, 48, 49, 57
Tully, ———, 43
Turner, Virgil, 92

Tweedy, Joseph, 21
Two Bar Ranch, 36, 40, 41, 125

U
U.S. Forest Service, 155
Uinta County (Wyoming), 95
Underwood, Joe, 54, 55, 57
Union Pacific Railroad, 41, 42, 91, 94, 96, 99, 108
United States Forest Service, 13–15, 152
United Verde Copper Company, 59
Utah, incidents in, 72, 151, 152–155, 157–158

V
Van Houten, J. P., 39
vaqueros, 6
Voss ranch, 142

W
Walnut Development Company, 155
Wamsutter, Wyoming, 41
Warren, Francis E., 72, 92, 97, 98, 125
Warren Live Stock Company, 98
Washakie County (Wyoming), 130
Washington, incidents in, 2, 15–16, 73
Waters, Ira, 142
Watson, Ella "Cattle Kate," 90–91
Wattron, Frank, 51, 52, 53
Watts, Clyde, 110
Wayne, John, 160
Weaver, Mrs., 122
Webb, Harry, 118
Wells, Nevada, 80
Wheeler County (Oregon), 75
Whiskey Park, 40
White Mountain Indian Reservation, 61
White River National Forest, 152–155
Whitlock, V. H., 4
Wild Bunch, 103, 114
Wild Rovers, 160
Williams, Lieutenant, 143
    Mrs., 29
Williams River Cattle and Horse Growers' Association, 149
Wilson, Billy, 56, 57
    Charles, 149
    J. M., 97, 126
    John C., 80–85
    Joseph, 80
    Loren, 80
    Tug, 71

William, 68
Wisner, ———, 126
Wolcott, Frank, 91
Wood, Natalie, 160
Woods, Billy, 60
Woolley, George, 150
wool: market, 10, 64, 66; mills, 43; tariff, 10
Worland, Charlie, 133
Worland, Wyoming, 133
Wyman, Jap, 153–154
Wyoming, incidents in, 2, 15–16, 72, 88–99, 117–129, 149–150; *also see* Horn, Tom; *also see* Ten Sleep murders
Wyoming National Guard, 115, 143, 147
Wyoming State Legislature, 95
Wyoming Stock Growers Association, 13, 88, 90, 91, 103, 125, 140, 149–150
Wyoming Supreme Court, 98, 99, 114
Wyoming Wool Growers Association, 126, 128, 139

Y

Yale, Mrs., 156
Yavapai County (Arizona), 59
Yearian, Emma, 77–78
Young, Billy, 29
    S. W., 57, 58
Yuma Territorial Penitentiary, 54, 82

Z

Zimmerschied, Henry, 128
Zulick, C. Meyer, 55

www.ingramcontent.com/pod-product-compliance
Lightning Source LLC
Chambersburg PA
CBHW050550160426
43199CB00015B/2611